Praise for *Jump-Starting Boys*

"For parents who want to be sensitive to the struggles in their boys' lives, here are wise words from two parents who have been through these trials and lived to tell the tale. *Jump-Starting Boys* is loaded with hints from the expert but it r   om the experience   ponsive to their nee...'

—Michael Sullivan,
author of *Connecting Boys With Books 2:*
Closing the Reading Gap

"In an age when the culture of childhood is defined by digital screens, consumerist messaging, and cynically violent and sexualized media, *Jump-Starting Boys* provides sage advice on what parents can do to help kids—particularly boys—grow into responsible, happy, and well-rounded individuals. Encourage reading, help with homework, and limit screen time—these simple measures have proven effective time and again, as Pam Withers and Cynthia Gill show. A must read for parents, teachers, and anyone else concerned about children."

—Joel Bakan,
author of *Childhood Under Siege:*
How Big Business Targets Your Children

"Pam's books have wide appeal to boys and girls, to avid and reluctant readers, to teens and to younger children who are looking for a challenging high-interest book."

—*The Bookmark*, newsletter of
the British Columbia Teacher-Librarians' Association

JUMP-STARTING
BOYS

JUMP-STARTING
BOYS

HELP YOUR RELUCTANT
LEARNER FIND SUCCESS
IN SCHOOL AND LIFE

PAM WITHERS
AND
CYNTHIA GILL, MA, LMFT

FOREWORD BY DR. JOHN DUFFY

370.15

Copyright © 2013 by Pam Withers and Cynthia Gill.

All rights reserved. Except for brief passages quoted in newspaper, magazine, radio, or television reviews, no part of this book may be reproduced in any form or by any means, electronic or mechanical, including photocopying or recording, or by information storage or retrieval system, without permission in writing from the publisher.

Published in the United States by Viva Editions, an imprint of Cleis Press, Inc., 2246 Sixth Street, Berkeley, California 94710.

Printed in the United States.
Cover design: Scott Idleman/Blink
Cover photograph: Dorling Kindersley/Getty Images
Text design: Frank Wiedemann
First Edition.
10 9 8 7 6 5 4 3 2 1

Trade paper ISBN: 978-1-936740-39-0
E-book ISBN: 978-1-936740-49-9

Library of Congress Cataloging-in-Publication Data

Withers, Pam.
Jump-starting boys : help your reluctant learner find success in school and life / Pam Withers and Cynthia Gill, MA, LMFT
    pages cm
Includes bibliographical references and index.
ISBN 978-1-936740-39-0 (pbk. : alk. paper)
1. Academic achievement. 2. Underachievers. 3. Home and school. 4. Boys--Psychology. 5. Parenting. I. Gill, Cynthia. II. Title.
LB1062.6.W57 2013
370.15'4--dc23
                              2013009246

3 2126 00130 509 8

9/13

Dedicated to our father, Richard S. Miller,
and our late mother, Anita Miller,
who both instilled a lifelong passion for reading
in their children.

un·der·a·chiev·er: a student who performs less well in school than would be expected on the basis of abilities indicated by intelligence and aptitude tests.

Jump-Starting Boys: Help Your Reluctant Learner Find Success in School and Life offers positive, practical solutions to parents of preteen and teen boys who are underperforming in school and in life. With this upbeat guide, parents can stop despairing and start working with their child to help him be the best he can be.

TABLE OF CONTENTS

IF YOU HAVE A SON WHO IS HAVING PROBLEMS at home and school, don't panic. Pam Withers and Cynthia Gill have bottled so much wonderful reassurance, advice, and practical wisdom into this informative gem of a book that will help turn your struggling child's life around. I keep a copy of *Jump-Starting Boys* on my shelf and I highly recommend it to every mom and dad who is raising a son.

Young adolescents grow tremendously; their bodies undergo so many changes so quickly that it's easy to forget their brains are growing and changing at the same breakneck pace. Remember what it was like to be a teenager, addled with hormones and bursting with the desire to make your way in the world, all while having to deal with algebra homework and annoying parents? It's easy to forget how stressful that is!

Many of my patients are teenage boys who can't remain focused in the classroom or don't care about school at all. One of the most common reasons for their problems are endless distractions—TV, video games, texting, mindless time-sinks on the Internet—and their parents need help with these twenty-first century issues. Is it any wonder, then, that many teen and tween boys lag behind their peers?

In my book *The Available Parent*, I implore parents to check in on their kids when they're not in school. Don't smother your kids (and spoil their fun) by being overbearing—just check in a couple times a day to let them know you're interested in what they do during their spare time. I promise you won't regret it, and it could reveal habits or activities that are holding your children back.

My point—along with Pam and Cynthia's—is that I think all teenagers have dormant passions that can only be uncovered through acknowledgment and listening. Your teen may be afraid to speak of his interests for various reasons, but if you stay curious, the outlines of his passions will evolve and change shape as they come into focus.

The story of how Pam and Cynthia came to research and write *Jump-Starting Boys* never fails to amaze me. Pam is an author whose young adult books became popular among teen boys. She discovered that they preferred her novels because the stories were full of action and matched their maturation levels. This inspired Pam to rise to the challenge of encouraging boys to read and succeed. Pam spoke to her sister, educator Cynthia Gill, about the phenomenon of underachieving boys, and together they researched and interviewed experts about what it takes for boys to get excited about reading.

Jump-Starting Boys is their solution. This book is filled with more than two-hundred methods parents can use to work with their sons to discover their learning styles, ignite their passion for reading, and ultimately succeed in school and in life.

I've worked with hundreds of teen and tween boys over my career as a clinical psychologist. I can absolutely confirm that helping your child cultivate a love for reading and lifelong learning is one of the best things you can do for him as a parent. Following the advice that Pam and Cynthia provide in *Jump-Starting Boys* will give you the tools you need to help your child grow into a competent, confident person.

—Dr. John Duffy,
author of *The Available Parent:*
Radical Optimism for Raising Teens and Tweens

INTRODUCTION

"Boys are falling victim to an epidemic of...having the ability to read and no compulsion whatsoever to do so."
—MICHAEL SULLIVAN, *CONNECTING BOYS WITH BOOKS 2*[1]

EVERYONE KNOWS BOYS ARE FALLING BEHIND girls in education. And that has lots of people, especially educators and politicians, busy pointing fingers and engaging in loud discussions.

Largely left out of this discussion are parents of boys, who are perhaps more aware than anyone that their bright, eager sons hit an invisible wall somewhere near fourth grade, after which they go from engaged to unengaged, discouraged, and disaffected. By their teens, too many seem determined to be slackers in school regardless of parental pleas, incentives, or discipline.

There are lots of books on underachieving boys, but most address educators and come complete with intimidating graphs, case studies, academic-speak, and lists of remedies on which parents are powerless to act.

What about the average guilt-ridden, frustrated mother or father of an underachieving boy? Someone who wants to know in plain language what's behind this trend and what they can do about it? What about mentors who crave positive support, not political shrillness?

Most existing books on "the boy problem" make parents feel even more helpless than the school system and their job demands have made them feel already. In *Jump-Starting Boys*, we have endeavored to empower parents and mentors, and to give them a sense of being able to reclaim the duty and rewards of helping their children.

Toward this end, we have heartwarming true stories and take-action checklists. Our aim has been to reassure and support, to turn fear and guilt into can-do confidence.

Who are we? Sisters who have raised boys, and sisters who have worked four careers between us: teacher, family therapist, journalist, and author. Pam is the award-winning author of young adult books particularly popular with boys (including *Peak Survival, Skater Stuntboys,* and *First Descent*). Cynthia, a former teacher who now counsels troubled families, speaks regularly at parents' groups and women's gatherings.

We firmly believe that reading confidence is a keystone to educational success, which in turn increases one's chances of a more stable, satisfying life. We hope you'll find insight in *Jump-Starting Boys.*

PAM WITHERS AND CYNTHIA GILL ARE SISTERS.

PAM WITHERS

Pam Withers is a former business journalist and bestselling, award-winning author of more than a dozen adventure books particularly popular with teen boys. They include *First Descent, Peak Survival, Skater Stuntboys,* and *Vertical Limits.* She is also coauthor with John Izzo of the highly acclaimed *Values Shift: The New Work Ethic and What It Means for Business* (Prentice Hall Canada, 2000).

Pam travels North America extensively, speaking at schools, librarians' and writers' conferences. The second of six siblings, she spent her growing-up years trying to measure up to her smarter, better-looking older sister, Cynthia. (She has just about outgrown that.) Pam and her husband, a university professor, live in Vancouver, Canada, where they recently completed raising a high-energy son who spent his adolescence as the official teen editor of Pam's teen adventure novels. Her website is www.pamwithers.com.

CYNTHIA GILL, MA, LMFT

During her thirty-year career as a high school teacher, Cynthia Gill worked on innovative curricula development and served as an academic dean, while winning acclaim for her work in the classroom. She completed her master's degree in Adlerian psychotherapy and counseling in 2006, and has since worked with families, adolescents, and children as a licensed marriage and family therapist. Her website is www.cynthiagill.info.

Cynthia has taught as an adjunct faculty member at Globe University and enjoys public speaking, particularly on parent education. She has led numerous groups of students on educational and service trips to Russia, Germany, and Latin America. A former homeschooling mom, Cynthia also served as a consultant to homeschooling families with an accrediting organization. She and her husband live in Minneapolis and like to bicycle and travel. They have three grown sons, two daughters-in-law, and five grandchildren. As the eldest child, Cynthia admits to being bossier than Pam.

CHAPTER ONE

WHO'S UNDERACHIEVING NOW? YES, BOYS. WHO SAYS AND WHY?

"Almost everywhere in the industrialized world, in places where boys and girls have equal access to education, the underperformance of boys is not just an uncomfortable fact but a real and pressing problem."

—PEG TYRE, *THE TROUBLE WITH BOYS*[2]

RIGHT UP TO THE AGE OF NINE, EDDIE WAS A fireball of enthusiasm for reading, sports, and outdoor activities. He was a bright student, stable and happy, and not one to worry his parents—especially his mother, a bookstore employee and reading enthusiast. All that was true until he hit two walls at once: puberty, and the split-up of his parents. He withdrew into himself, and his grades began a downward spiral. It wasn't that he'd lost the ability to thrive in school; he'd simply lost interest and motivation. He lived with his mother and saw his father much less than before. The more his mother fretted about his grades, the more sullen and resentful he became. Her lectures about the importance of good grades for getting into college and launching a career fell on deaf ears. His father just shrugged; he himself hadn't finished college and had a decent-paying job, after all.

Eventually, former friends in the "brainy" clique avoided him, or he avoided them. He fell in with a new, less ambitious crowd that, in his mother's opinion, was a bad influence. He still read, but less. He preferred computer time or running around with friends. His mother became increasingly distressed that a boy she knew to be highly intelligent would turn in barely passing grades. She breathed a sigh of relief when he managed—barely—to graduate from high school, but by then, the economy presented a dim job market, and the jobs that existed didn't interest Eddie. Like many boys of his generation, he'd been raised to believe a job should be special, fun, and rewarding. So he quit jobs and training programs that weren't, working only now and then in construction.

The weeks of unemployment grew to years, and his self-confidence fell as he saw girls in whom he was interested favor boys who earned more money. He became increasingly self-destructive, despite attempted interventions on the part of both parents. Once or twice he applied for a program of study, only to find himself rejected for his low grades in high school. At the age of twenty-one he was living at his mother's house on her expense, sleeping in till noon, playing video games much of every afternoon, and going out to party at night. Their relationship deteriorated, but she feared if she kicked him out while he was unemployed, he'd spiral further downward.

Finally, on a counselor's advice, she ordered him to get a job, do volunteer work, or move out. The volunteer work he reluctantly took involved coaching young soccer players. Connecting with the program's male director as a much-needed mentor for himself, he received praise for his skill at working with kids, and found that getting out of the house each day revived his motivation to look further ahead. He eventually enrolled and was accepted in a community college.

"It used to be girls who underachieved in school. Now it's boys," his mother told us.

She's right but that's only half the story. For decades, boys have typically underachieved in elementary and high school, then thrived once they entered the workplace. Why? Check as many of the following as you think apply:

- ❏ the old-boys network of job referrals and workplace favoritism,
- ❏ a disconnect between school grades and skills that the workplace values,
- ❏ the widespread availability of high-paying jobs that don't require higher education,
- ❏ a late (some would say belated) spurt of maturity and responsibility,
- ❏ a revived sense of self-esteem once they escape a school system that beat them down, or which they felt favored girls.

However many you checked, here's the stark truth: The first three are going down the drain as the global economy makes the workplace more competitive, as we shift from an industrial to a service economy and as women break ever more glass ceilings. As our sons emerge from (or drop out of) high school, they're looking at a whole different job landscape than their fathers did. And the longer and more tightly a boy has wrapped himself in an underachiever's cloak, the less certain that the "late spurt of maturity" and "revived sense of self-esteem" will rescue him.

That being said, boys aren't in crisis. *They are the underdogs only when it comes to reading and writing.* If they find their grades slipping relative to girls, it's not because they're less intelligent than girls, but because they're less motivated. For a variety of reasons—some new to this generation, as we'll explore—they don't believe school (reading and writing in particular) is relevant to their long-term future. A generation ago, they may have had a point. The trouble is, boys are slipping in reading ability at a time when reading ability has skyrocketed in importance for long-term success in life. Comfort with reading is essential for graduating from high school or college, and today's college degree is equivalent to last generation's high school degree in the job market.[3] Parents are unaware of this, or they feel powerless to do anything about it. Getting your kid to read is the school's job, right? Disaffection for reading and writing means poor grades, which means fewer and fewer males are being accepted for higher education. There's now an approximately fifty-seven/forty-three percent split for university acceptance in women's favor, and the gap is growing.[4]

In the past, men could often obtain high-paying jobs without higher education; they could still be the breadwinners. That was thanks largely to manufacturing, construction, and sales jobs. Unfortunately, the first two have taken a nosedive and sales jobs require ever more educational qualifications. But those trends are too new to have seeped into the consciousness of boys—or of many of the men who influence their lives. So the new circumstances have yet to make a dent in the attitude so pervasive among boys today.

Are young men ready to start playing second fiddle to the women in their lives? (For that matter, are women ready to accept it?) When their lack of education eventually catches up with the new workplace requirements, will they shrug their shoulders about earning less, working at lower-status jobs, suffering more periods of unemployment and underemployment? Will they happily opt for being stay-at-home fathers?

A few will. The rest will do what resentful, underemployed

or unemployed men have done for centuries: turn to addictive substances, crime, and abuse of those they resent. Ignoring the growing reading gap does nothing to benefit females, as illustrated by our sidebar, "Why Tackling Boys' Issues Helps Girls Too," on page 9.

As we look for solutions, we can benefit from the wisdom of a little-known but highly influential pioneer in the field of child rearing, Alfred Adler. He was a medical doctor whose concern for children led him to examine how family members affect each other. His work laid the foundation for a growing field of "family systems theory," and here's what he had to say about boys who suffer a slide in achievement: "A misbehaving child is a discouraged child."[5]

Adler and his disciple Rudolf Dreikurs (author of *Children: The Challenge*) have said every human has three needs—security, belonging, and significance—and that we're all on a quest to overcome a sense of inferiority. Children's portion of this journey is a natural stage; after all, they are surrounded by more capable adults. Adler, who coined the term "inferiority complex," believed that as children attempt to replace a sense of inferiority with one of superiority, they often do so in less-than-useful ways. Who do they learn these ways from? From us, their parents, many of whom haven't completed the journey out of inferiority ourselves.

Here are some not-so-useful ways we try to pursue a sense of belonging and significance: control tactics, "one-upmanship," perfectionism, and becoming a people-pleaser. Others engage in victim mentality ("poor me"), give up, or try to prove that they're the "best at being bad," especially if they have a sibling who is "the best at being good."

So what do we as parents of underachieving boys do with this information? We rethink how important it is to encourage and motivate them, and we depart from traditional ideas of how to do so. Chapters Four and Ten cover new and more effective parenting styles, which are also well explained by Jane Nelsen in her *Positive Discipline* books.

In a nutshell, effective parenting recognizes the child's heart and emotional needs, rather than focusing only on behavior. Children's needs for belonging and significance are vital, and they're not addressed when parents say "Mind!" or "Be good!"

The good news is that a growing number of parents, parent educators, and schools are adopting this approach. For now, let the notion of more positive parenting be a glimmer of hope in the dark room of despair that every parent of discouraged sons feels.

SEVEN REASONS WHY BOYS ARE UNDERACHIEVING

Physical. Or, more accurately, denial that there's a physical factor. In the age-old debate of nature versus nurture, it has become politically incorrect to acknowledge nature at all. In short, we've gone overboard in denying the physical differences between boys and girls and how this influences behavior, despite a growing body of studies replacing conjecture with facts.

Reading/writing gap. In our commendable effort to right the historical wrongs of how girls have been treated and educated, we've blindsided ourselves to the *one solitary respect* in which boys are disadvantaged: reading and writing. And we've let that slip dangerously even as other trends (including the shift from industrial to service jobs) have aligned to make it of skyrocketing importance. The following cannot be emphasized enough: Boys are not the new underdogs; they are not suddenly suffering in all respects—only in reading and writing. *But more than at any point in the past, reading and writing have become the linchpin of success in life.* Boys, not to mention many parents, don't know this. And some parents, teachers, and librarians have been loath to address that increasing gap on the false assumption that focusing on it will necessarily mean a backward slide for girls just as girls have secured some hard-won progress. Yet, on the contrary, a backward slide for boys has ominous potential for females who, in the end, must share their world with males.

Home structure. An increasing number of boys are growing up in households with limited or no access to positive and involved male role models. While there are ways to minimize the potential negative impact of this, many parents are unaware of the implications and of some solutions, which we cover in upcoming chapters.

School structure. The overwhelming majority of teachers and school librarians are female, and we're also seeing an increase in female principals, education board members, legislators, and other education policymakers. Perhaps it is only natural, then, that classroom approaches, school policies, and sometimes the laws affecting education have shifted to formats that (often unwittingly) favor girls. Some eighty-five percent of children's authors as well as most editors are also female, which means that the vast majority of people writing *and* editing *and* selecting books for school libraries are female. Parents are typically unaware of this, or feel they can do nothing about it. We believe awareness is important, and outline what parents can do. Of course, many of these biases are subtle and unintended. Female staff, like mothers in general, are well intentioned, but their hidden biases are no longer sufficiently countered by males at home and at school.

Fear-based backlash. Because males are overrepresented among criminals and those who do females physical harm, individuals and sometimes organizations treat normal young boys' tastes in reading and writing (war heroes, etc.) as unacceptable. This can be counterproductive to persuading them to read and write.

Morals. Due to laws, education policies, societal changes, and multiculturalism, the onus for disciplining school-age children and giving them moral guidance has shifted from schools to the home. However, children spend more waking hours in school than at home, and parents are often unwilling or unable to provide the moral lessons that might help stem the bullying and violence that take place at school. This typically works against education, especially for boys.

Parenting styles. For a generation or two, parents have been bombarded with the message that above all, they must build self-esteem in their children. Dutifully, they offer encouraging words as often as possible, repeatedly telling their beloved offspring that they *can be something special.* The result, say a growing number of experts, is children who grow up knowing deep down that many episodes of praise were unearned, which breeds insecurity rather than self-esteem. And the focus on self-esteem robs them of something more important for both work and personal life: empathy. So, more children feel *entitled* to special treatment, special jobs, a special life. Is it unreasonable that this sense of entitlement, combined with the factors outlined above, might feed into boys' rejection of school if school is a struggle for them?

Add to that, parents' desire to keep their children safe, which can lead to overprotection and reduces kids' opportunities to gain self-confidence and independence. Then there is the fact that some parents allow a child's schedule to get so packed, structured, and parent-monitored that again, certain characteristics best nurtured by independent free time are stunted.

WHY TACKLING BOYS' ISSUES HELPS GIRLS TOO

"A rising tide lifts all boats."

—JOHN F. KENNEDY

1) This is the first generation of young men likely to achieve *less* education than their fathers and to find themselves on a lower rung of the socioeconomic ladder.[6]

2) Men now account for only four of every ten undergrads.[7][8]

3) The more educated a woman is, the more reluctant she is to "marry down" in terms of education and lifetime earning potential.[9]

4) Where there is a large educational gap between partners, divorce is more likely, and the struggles of children who go through divorce are well documented.[10]

5) College-educated people of both genders are more likely to get married and are much more likely to stay married.[11]

6) The decline in marriage rates has been greatest among men with less education.

7) Those without a college education find it harder to stay employed in a rapidly changing work environment.[12]

8) Roughly three-quarters of the job losses inflicted by the 2008 U.S. recession fell on men.[13]
9) Marital conflict usually occurs when a man works less than his wife, or becomes unemployed.[14]
10) One in three married, working women today outearns her husband—up from one in ten in the 1970s.[15]
11) Men who are economically dependent on their female partners are more likely to cheat on them. Women dependent on male partners are less likely to cheat.[16]
12) Two-thirds of all divorces are legally initiated by women.[17]
13) The poorer the household, the more likely parents are to send a girl rather than a boy on to college. This abrupt change from previous times reflects the parents' desire to apply limited resources to the child who does best in school.[18]

And finally, highlighting the ominous long-term effects of an imbalance: Children of unemployed fathers seem particularly vulnerable to psychological problems, are more likely to repeat a grade in school and to earn less as adults.

On a more positive note, "When boys' test scores go up, so do girls' scores," says therapist and educator Michael Gurian in *The Purpose of Boys*.[19] When adolescent boys find education to be purposeful and relevant, they are less defiant and more willing to learn, which frees girls up from having to deal with hours and days of behavioral problems around them.

In upcoming chapters, we expand on the reasons boys are underachieving, and we offer solutions. We offer the stories of former underachieving boys we've interviewed. We also offer insights provided by literacy consultants, psychologists, teachers, librarians, and parents. If there's an underachieving boy in your life, rest assured that you are not alone, and there are ways to turn your son around.

SEVEN WAYS
TO HELP TURN YOUR SON AROUND

Yes, today's kids are heavily influenced by school, peers, and the media, but parents can and should reassert control to ensure they prosper in work and in life. Here are some tips for concerned parents.

1) This generation's college degree is the equivalent of last generation's high school degree. So talk with your son about how the world has changed since you were young—how decent grades are much more important, and how studies show that the more he reads, the better grades he'll get. If a male relative or friend conducts the chat with him, even better for the role-model factor.

2) Determine your son's learning style (see Chapter Four) and adapt homework support sessions and teaching moments to it.

3) Limit children's total media time to no more than one to two hours of quality programming per day, as recommended by the American Academy of Pediatrics. (See Chapter Seven's sidebar, "Screen Limits," on page 136.)

4) Engage in short family debates on a regular basis to sharpen his confidence with reasoning and words, and comment on his delivery more than content.

5) Shift from a focus on building his self-esteem, independence, and individualism to one of modeling and promoting perseverance, humility, and community service. Jean M. Twenge, associate professor of psychology and author of *Generation*

Me, writes that self-esteem without basis encourages laziness rather than hard work, and the ability to persevere and keep going is a much better predictor of life outcomes than self-esteem.[20] Her book, *The Narcissism Epidemic,* includes a self-test for determining one's degree of egocentrism, and suggestions for lessening it.

6) Guard against overprotecting and over-scheduling your son, since many characteristics that lead to achievement are best nurtured by independent free time. Further, resist engaging in a sense of competition with other parents, which encourages him to compare himself with fellow classmates, often leading to lowered empathy and a lifetime habit of stress, frustration, and over-scheduling.

7) Expand your tolerance for toilet humor and fighting scenes in books he selects, and don't pressure him to abandon picture books or graphic novels (a classy version of comic books) before he chooses to. Literacy experts say these books can develop a child's critical thinking skills in particular ways, and the vocabulary is often more challenging than in a chapter book.[21]

BOOK CLUB MAESTRO

Few people have put as much time and effort into figuring out what makes a book club successful as Christianne Hayward, who has been running them for sixteen years. As a single mother of two boys (one a keener reader than the other), she decided to apply her Ph.D. in education toward inspiring a love of reading in children of all ages. She started her first parent-and-youth book club at the local community center as a way to ensure that her sons had a literary group to socialize with. This book club was so well received that she added a new book club each year, culminating in seventeen parent-and-youth book clubs ranging from preschool to grade twelve. Today, her Lyceum of Literature and Art in Vancouver, Canada, provides a unique, cozy, and specialized learning environment that brings forth the best of afterschool reading and writing experiences for hundreds of children per week. Her book clubs are a family affair where parents read the books, attend the groups, and participate in the discussion along with their children.

Hayward serves as a consultant to educators and book club leaders around North America. What she finds most gratifying, however, is running into families of her grown students who say, "You made such a difference. Even though my child attended your club for only a year, he became a reader for life." The Lyceum's website is www.christiannehayward.com.

Q: What are some of the key ways you engage the boys in your clubs, as opposed to the girls?

A: First, you need a lot of humor. Boys respond well to a bit of lighthearted ribbing. Second, I serve food and hot chocolate, hot apple cider, or herbal teas; humans gather more willingly if food is involved. (At home, we all settle in with a comfort drink in a comfortable space to read.) Third, I put up lots of books with male protagonists and subjects to which boys can relate easily. A democratic voting system for selecting the books to be read, buys a certain ownership and involvement from all participants. Fourth, I use kinesthetic ways of learning: crosswords that test whether they've taken in details of the book we've just read, art projects connected to the book's scenes, and breaks that feature food mentioned in the book. Finally, I let them move around. In a photo of a kindergarten story-time at the Lyceum, you can see the girls sitting straight and staring at the book, and the boys lounging on the pillows. But if you look closely, you can also see how incredibly engaged those boys are.

As for the older boys, I tell them that the best way to understand that strange group of people called "girls" is to read some books with a female protagonist. It's amazing how they internalize that. Once I ran into a boy in second-year university who'd been in one of my book clubs years before. "You were so right about that!" he enthused.

Q: Some of the boys in your clubs come with their mothers, and some with their fathers. How important is the gender role-model factor?

A: For the boys to see a male involved in a book club is huge, but it doesn't have to be *their* father. We often get uncles, older brothers, and grandfathers and everyone benefits from their presence. Boys who come with their mothers forge better communication with them than boys who don't; book clubs allow the mothers to talk to their sons about difficult topics through a literary character. Dads who attend our clubs raise the bar for everyone, because they tend to be avid notetakers and they hate not doing well on the crosswords.

Most importantly, the youth see men reading *and* discussing reading, or what I call "socializing around reading." Women do this more naturally, while men tend to socialize around sports or games instead. Since coaches don't usually read books between periods, and guys don't typically discuss books after a game, you have to find a way to expose them to this modeling, by making an effort at home or enrolling them in a book club.

Q: Roughly what percentage of boys are reluctant readers?

A: In my experience, it can be as high as forty percent. The divide begins in about fourth grade, and has to do with under-acknowledged brain differences, a lack of books that interest boys (especially after sixth grade if they're not into fantasy), not seeing men socialize around reading, and a more auditory-driven education system. Boys often respond better to kinesthetic and visual learning: Pictionary, graphic books, charades, dramatizations, debates, crosswords, exercise balls for sitting, and art. At-home reading and book clubs can cater to these needs more easily than traditional classrooms. The optimal point at which you can make a big difference is in grades four, five, and six, by choosing books that are fun and engaging, by pumping up the number of graphic books you let him read, and by modeling and sharing your passion for reading at home.

Q: Some parents steer their kids away from picture books and graphic novels before the child wishes to give them up, on the assumption that these are unsophisticated forms of reading holding him back. What's your advice?

A: Don't get too stuck on this. Our youth have to be more visually literate than we were, able to deconstruct symbols in images and make meaning. Even PowerPoint presentations at CEO meetings today have more animation, logos, and visual symbols. When parents read a graphic novel, it seems choppy to them, but today's children know how to bridge between cells in much the same way you do between lines of a poem. Graphic books engage a different type of literacy. This doesn't replace textual literacy but is just as important.

If you keep throwing books at your boy that are too difficult, you'll lose him. One of my sons didn't read for enjoyment until age ten; it was a graphic novel that finally hooked him. He'd always been able to decode competently, and had been read to, but reading for enjoyment took longer to kick in. Get them graphic books, auditory tapes, interactive books online, whatever it takes. Keep them in the game until their maturity catches up with them.

Q: What's your best advice to parents who want their child to be a keen reader?

A: Let him be involved in choosing what he reads, and continue reading to him even after he can read by himself. Where you apply your greatest influence in *what* your son reads is through the books you read *to* him. Start reading to him long before seventh or eighth grade; otherwise he might be less open to reading aloud experiences. Choose themes that interest him, books that have the hook within the first chapter. Read several chapters ahead yourself before sitting down with him, so you won't stumble over names and if you start to lose his attention, you can synthesize what's happening and take him forward to an exciting bit, closing on a cliffhanger if at all possible. This way, he'll plead and beg you to read more, but don't give in. Make him come to the book hungry the next day. Also, read to your kids when you're fresh. For me as a single mother, being fresh meant early in the morning instead of at bedtime, and always in the same space with our comfort drinks in hand.

There are three kinds of reading: independent reading (he reads by himself, preferably books he has chosen; no more than one error per page), guided reading (he reads a page, you read a page; no more than four errors per page), and reading aloud (you do all the reading). There's typically a two-year reading-level gap between expressive and receptive language development, meaning there is a dramatic spread between what he can read on his own and what he can understand orally. By reading aloud, you're building the scaffolding that will make him a stronger reader, helping him understand patterns, reinforcing his ability to predict plotlines, helping him understand causal relationships, and exposing him to the cadence of oral language.

Q: Why is it important to learn to enjoy reading?

A: Reading is an investment in yourself, an education in itself. It nurtures curiosity and a thirst for learning more; it can be very addictive once you have a good experience with it. Literacy is incredibly important for accessing information, engaging personal growth, and nurturing breadth of knowledge. It supports emotional intelligence, which you need in order to excel at the top levels of industry. Emotional intelligence helps you relate to someone different than you at work. It helps you articulate your thoughts, which can boost your ability to speak in front of a group. Broad reading exposes you to other perspectives, which is very precious in a diverse society.

WHO'S THE BOSS?

Too many parents lack the security or skills to lead their children. They allow children to call the shots, especially in the battle of determining how much screen time they will have. Who is in charge here? Dr. Thomas Phelan, author of *1-2-3 Magic: Effective Discipline for Children 2-12* and a national authority on parenting, says parents make two mistakes: too much emotion and too many words. When you or the child are angry, limit your words to ten at the most! Lectures are simply wasted energy, flood the kids' brains, fuel their anger, and drive you further from the solution.

Moms struggling with sons especially need to curtail wordy feedback: Educator and clinical counselor Barry MacDonald in *Boy Smarts* says that he is never discouraged by a non-response because he understands boys' silence as processing time. "Productive conversations with boys come in fits and starts. Boys need space to digest what's been said."[22]

When Cynthia's clients come to her with parenting struggles, she finds they are usually making one of the following mistakes: too many words, too much emotion, too little confidence, too much hovering, too much military-like barking-out of orders, or too little underlying relationship, which must be built up over time. Children trigger the issues we experienced while growing up, but we can learn to override those default settings.

Parents and mentors who want to pass values on to kids need to do it in an "up-close and personal manner," as author Josh McDowell says. These adults must enter the youngster's world and be aware of what is happening in their lives.[23]

HAPPY ENDING

"I read some as a boy, mostly the Hardy Boys novels. But as I got a wee bit older, I wasn't interested in reading anymore. I was more into running outside and playing. My sister embraced reading, but I was more fidgety and restless.

"My family didn't watch much television and my parents certainly read a lot. There were always books around, and I remember my dad reading spy novels. But I figured I read enough at school, which was a challenge for me. I had a hard time concentrating. I didn't have a learning disability; I was just averse to school. I did have one teacher who was a role model to me. He took me under his wing in grade four or five and paid me the extra attention I needed. That probably wouldn't have worked if he hadn't been a male.

"When I was nine or ten years old, I got interested in hockey, and my mom and dad bought me books on hockey. I started reading short stories and rule books and that is how I got back into reading for a while. But I dropped off again until I became a Big Brother (mentor) in my thirties.

"I'd just gone through a nasty divorce, and after I'd moved out and started living on my own again, I decided I had an opportunity to make some changes and give back to my community. When I met my 'Little Brother,' he had just turned nine. The first time we went for a walk, I asked him what kind of things he enjoyed. It turned out reading was one of his interests, and so we talked about reading as a conversation icebreaker. He talked about the books he was reading, so I started picking up books and reading as well. That way I could talk about the books I was reading. And given that I was going through so much personal change, I found I needed that chance to get lost in a book. Meanwhile, I found that being a Big Brother removed all of the ugliness from my divorce experience.

"Sometime not long after I'd become a Big Brother, I

was at my parents' home, but not downstairs visiting with them. My younger brother came up, saw me engrossed in a book, and returned downstairs to tell my parents, 'Something's wrong with Kieran.' My mom and dad came upstairs, concerned; they hadn't seen me engrossed in books for so long. I was thirty-eight. They didn't know that these days, I always have a book with me as I travel for work. Nowadays I try to encourage reading, including with my nephew. I see a lot of me in him. I buy him books when I can, and we have a book exchange program.

"If I'd read more during my school days, I'd have applied myself there better. What I believe is that boys take longer than girls to read, and you can't put too much pressure on them. Get them comfortable and make it fun."

—KIERAN, AGE FORTY-TWO

CHAPTER TWO

THE LITERACY LINK: WHY READING AND WRITING SKILLS ARE KEY

"There are teenagers who have fallen behind academically, don't see a way to catch up, and stop trying. They often adapt to a lesser lifestyle, one far below their potential, and far less satisfying."

—WALTER DEAN MYERS[24]

NO MATTER HOW MUCH PARENTS READ TO A SON before he enters school, when he lands in kindergarten he almost instantly realizes that: a) most girls are ahead of him when it comes to language and reading skills, b) reading time means sitting still when he may not feel like sitting still, and c) the teacher gets crabby if he doesn't sit still or appear to enjoy reading.

What to do? What anyone would do on finding themselves outclassed and unwilling to lose face: He'll wonder briefly if he's stupid, he'll decide instead that reading simply isn't his strong point, he'll squirm even more during reading time, he'll try out some "attitude," and eventually, he'll decide it's not really all that important. If most of his fellow males seem to have come to the same conclusion, and he realizes that both his teacher and the parent who does most of the reading at home are female (not to mention that most children's books are *by* females), he feels positively reinforced. While most boys do eventually learn to read competently, that's not the point. The minimal effort he starts putting in and the negative association reading now holds, can start him down a slippery slope.

Not all boys travel this path, of course. A percentage that we'll call "elites" embrace reading, schooling, and academic achievement continuously from an early age. (Thirty-two percent of elementary and high school boys are A students, compared with forty-six percent of girls.)[25] More than likely, the "elites" have been read to since toddlerhood, have strong male role models, have no disabilities to hold them back, and enjoy a high level of self-esteem (perhaps also tutors) to carry them through any periods of lagging behind girls on language skills. We'll reflect in Chapter Six on "elites" and how their families may have helped steer them into that category, but for now, note that if your son isn't one of them, you're part of the majority, at least until you act on insights from this book and create a keener reader.

When we use the word "literacy" we mean more than an ability to read; we mean comfort with reading. Assured reading is the keystone of education, a secret code to a locked door that swings open—or not—to a successful life. If boys set out with *relative* disadvantages not widely recognized, and these are compounded by other unrecognized barriers along the way, it is not boys' reading skills that are at risk. At stake is the early-formed attitude toward learning, classrooms and teachers in general, and the student's overall academic self-confidence.

Here are the facts: The more kids read, the better the grades they get. The better their grades, the better they do on exams and the more academic self-confidence they develop. Good grades and self-confidence clearly take them further in life in terms of higher education, careers, and a stable social life. And good grades and self-confidence help protect them from the low self-esteem and unemployment that often leads to a cycle of bullying, substance abuse, crime, and relationship difficulties.

The journal *Child Development* found that poor reading among boys leads to antisocial behavior, while the *Journal of Abnormal Child Psychology* has identified a strong link between persistent reading problems and depression in boys ages seven to ten. Meanwhile, rates of suicide and depression among boys are rising, and numerous studies link low literacy with dropping out of high school and criminal activities.[26][27] (See "Slippery Slope of Facts and Stats," on page 35.)

We're not saying that a lack of confidence with reading leads to a life of crime, but statistics do reflect strong and disturbing links; they spotlight a path that most parents do not want their sons to travel. We're here to support parents in their efforts to nudge their boys along a healthier route. We're also here to remind caring parents that the hand that rocks the cradle is powerful indeed. Ensuring that your son is comfortable with reading is not a matter to entrust entirely to schools.

"As a parent, you are essential in making sure that books and the sheer joy of reading are part of your child's experience," says Paul Kropp, educator and author of *How to Make Your Child a Reader for Life*.[28] "No one can encourage reading nearly as well as you can. No other skill will ever be quite as important."[29] Kropp has also said that even where school programs manage to turn a reluctant reader around, it's often temporary without parents keeping up the pressure and providing encouragement and perhaps a tutor.[30]

James McCann came from a family of nonreaders. He recalls his mother reading one or two books per year. There was no father in the picture, although he hung out with his grandfather a lot.

Not reading—watching television. "The TV was always on. We were a family that bonded and got along because we liked the same TV shows."

His mother made a few stabs at encouraging him to read, but since she didn't read much herself, it didn't work. "She wanted me to be a reader; she just didn't know how to make me become one," James muses. He got decent grades even though, reflecting back now, he knows he could have done better had he been more comfortable with reading. He loved comic books, but never read novels, not even when they were assigned in high school classes. "High school novel-reading assignments kicked off a big competition with my friend as to who could write a better essay given that I read only a summary of the novel. Oddly, I always won."

Around that time, one of his male friends gave him a novel for his birthday. "I was very mad at him. I couldn't believe that he would give me a novel. It sat on my shelf for months, and then I finally read it." That particular book served as a bridge to a new world: the world of reading. Soon James was reading stacks of books, and even started writing secretly: fantasy stories he showed no one, not even his mother. He was placed in an advanced English class and his grades went up; his school grades overall improved. He went on to college, where he eventually studied writing and launched a career as a bookseller, then as a novelist for teenage boys. These days, he's a busy advocate for boys' literacy, and for parents letting boys read anything they want, just to keep them reading until they feel inspired to read more substantial works (www.jamesmccann.info).

Although James wishes his mother had pushed books more in his childhood, he appreciates that she never belittled or forbade his comic book habit. He's also proud of the fact that he eventually turned her on to reading.

Most happy, skilled readers were raised by parents who expected and encouraged them to read; James is an exception to that rule. His schooldays attitude is all too typical of boys, who take to reading later and with less gusto than girls unless provided with special encouragement. Boys often depend on more help in reading just to be on par with females.[31]

Below we've summarized three stages where boys feel their inadequacy compared with girls, and when they may rebel against reading.[32] Unfortunately, rebelling against reading can only lead to rebelling against schoolwork in general, as all subjects require a comfort level with reading. In fact, it turns out there's a direct connection between the amount of time kids read for pleasure, and how well they do in math and science.[33]

The Kindergarten Slump

This is when children learn letter sounds, the basis for language. They need listening skills to make this transition—something gained at home through conversation and storytelling. Children who get caught in the kindergarten reading slump may have hearing problems not yet diagnosed (see Chapter Four), or may be from a family where little meaningful conversation takes place between children and adults, or where there is limited English conversation. They may also come from a chaotic or abusive home. In fact, a disturbing twenty percent of four- and five-year-olds do not have the language background for kindergarten success.[34] One study indicates that too much screen time as a baby or toddler may be a factor: When the television is on (even if no one is watching it), there is a sharp reduction in conversation—or words the child hears from adults—which can lead to delayed language development at a critical time of childhood. That's one reason the American Academy of Pediatrics' Committee on Public Education recommends against screen time for children under two years of age, urging more interactive play instead.[35]

Boys may be at special risk because parents are more likely to read, tell stories to, and visit the library with daughters than sons.[36] Why? Perhaps they haven't heard experts emphasize that when boys fidget while being read to, it's best to let them do so or play while you keep on reading, as long as they're listening.

So, how to identify preschoolers at risk of being part of the first reading slump? Advice from Kropp, a former reading teacher: Just before entering school, can they hear the difference between "b" and "t" and between "m" and "n"? If so, they're good to go. If not, they may need testing or just special attention and encouragement.[37] Relatively few boys get caught in the kindergarten slump, but for those who do, getting turned around grows harder as they age.

The Fourth-Grade Slump

This is the big one, where a quarter to a third of all children but especially boys, start to struggle.[38] "Reading scores begin dropping precipitously for boys in the third, and especially in the fourth, grades," according to the Guys Read Pilot Program at the Fairbanks North Star Borough Library in Alaska.[39]

Here's a roundup of theories as to why:

Because they can now read on their own, parents stop reading to them—even though doing so continues to help accelerate their reading.

With less adult supervision, kids gravitate to activities other than reading.

The vocabulary and thinking skills at this level of reading accelerate so quickly that some (especially those whose families don't have conversations that make such words and ideas familiar) get frustrated and turned off. (See "What Is the Fourth-Grade Reading Slump?" on page 31.)

Again, undiagnosed reading disabilities.

Unfortunately, the consequences of not nipping this in the bud are serious. A boy who loses interest before grade four is all too likely to remain disenchanted with school right through high school.[40] In fact, typically, fourth graders who duck out on reading end up entering high school with a sixth-grade reading capacity— never mind that some of the textbooks they'll be assigned there require college-level reading skills.[41]

The High School Slump

It's often pegged at ninth grade, but can begin brewing in seventh or eighth grade. This is when many teens abandon reading for pleasure. Increasing numbers drop all except "required" reading. Some fifty-five percent, like James in our earlier story, will do the absolute minimum they can get away with. Twenty-five percent pretty much stop reading altogether. Between middle school and the end of high school, then, the number who read for pleasure freefalls from almost two-thirds to less than a quarter of the student population.[42]

Why? Most books seem irrelevant to these kids because they don't deal with a teen's world. It's not true of the growing number of books that specially cater to this crowd, as we emphasize in Chapter Eight. But unfortunately, many highly educated parents and even some teachers snub or forbid these.

Also, puberty entails great changes in brain chemistry. Spikes in the male hormone testosterone cause males to seek their self-esteem through competition and aggression. How does the traditional classroom meet that need? More than likely by squelching it, punishing those who act out, or, at best, trying to divert it to non-reading activities. None of that helps boys' literacy.

Certainly, parents give teens more freedom to do what they like at this age, and let up on pushing them to read. Without strong direction, kids are more inclined to fill their free time with television, other screen time, and social life. Plus, as we discuss in Chapters Five, Six, and Seven, boys in particular lack male role models—at home, at school, and in the media—who champion reading. And worst of all, in many circles, boys decide that reading is no longer "cool," which reinforces their tendency to abandon it or to hide the fact they're reading from their peers. The result? Boys increasingly consider themselves nonreaders.[43]

"My main worry is about boys who are alienated from school itself, who find the reading and writing in schools unrelated to anything that matters to them," says Thomas Newkirk, an English professor and author of *Misreading Masculinity*. "Such boys—and I was one of them—partition their lives into 'schoolwork' and 'things that really matter.'"[44]

The kicker is that reading and the academic achievement it helps build are more important now than ever. As we've emphasized, the traditional safety net for boys who don't thrive academically—construction, finance, and industrial jobs—is rapidly eroding. Fathers and mothers who shrug their shoulders over a son not keen to read, saying, "Well, your dad doesn't like to read either, and look how well he has done," are whistling past the graveyard. It is far better to embrace that these are different times and to ensure that a male role model (father, uncle, tutor) encourages your son to read. If the chosen male role model objects or feels uncomfortable, remind him that this act may be the single most important way he can contribute to a boy's success in life.

So What Is a Reluctant Reader?

From these slumps emerge what are variously called "slow," "struggling," or "reluctant" readers. And the majority of these are boys.[45] But beware: There is no widespread agreement on what a reluctant reader is. In fact, one sunny optimist, Donalyn Miller, a sixth-grade teacher who wrote *The Book Whisperer*, says, "Lord help the students with [those] labels." She prefers:

developing readers: those not reading at grade level, whether due to inadequate reading experiences or learning disabilities,

dormant readers: unmotivated, uninterested, "good enough" readers who don't engage with reading due to a lack of support and role models,

underground readers: gifted or beyond the average student's level, individuals simply uninterested in what school requires them to read.

Sticking for now with the term "reluctant reader," we'd like to add that some of these boys have fallen so far behind (one to two grade levels) that reading now elicits fear and embarrassment. Perhaps they started out with the disadvantage of speaking English as a second language (ESL). There are also "closet readers" who prefer to read at home so they're not seen as a reader in school. And there are kids who slide into and out of all these descriptions.

"These categories shift and change and vary with socioeconomics and ESL factors," says David Ward, an assistant professor in literacy at Lewis and Clark College in Portland, Oregon, and a children's author. "We've seen a terrible crash in wages to middle class and below, and loss of jobs. That impacts the children, home literacy, how many books a family can buy, even affordability for getting to the library."

Ward says that in conversations with parents across North

America, the word he hears most is "unmotivated." Yet when he delves deeper, he finds that half the parents using that term have a child with a physical challenge, diagnosed or not. The other half could benefit from putting stricter limits on their child's television, video game, and other media time, he notes (more on that in Chapter Seven).

Screen time is often just a symptom of a larger problem, however: parental busy-ness, or a lack of one-on-one interaction between child and adult. In their formative years, children desperately need the one thing that busy parents often cannot or will not give them: time. It's a theme well addressed in David Elkind's *The Hurried Child*.

Regardless of why a boy gets labeled a reluctant reader, determined parents can help turn him around. If we had to boil all the advice into a sentence, it would be: Get him reading one-on-one with someone—with you, a reading buddy, a reading specialist, whomever—and pull out all the stops to make reading a bigger part of his life.

Again, there's a direct link between how much time he spends reading for pleasure and his future achievement in life. Or, as Henry David Thoreau wrote, "How many a man has dated a new era in his life from the reading of a book!"

WHAT IS THE FOURTH-GRADE READING SLUMP?

Your kid loved reading books until he hit fourth grade. Now it's a royal pain getting him to pick up a book or magazine at all. He says reading is boring. He says school is too hard. If that rings true, join the club.

Forty percent of kids between the ages of five and eight read every day, but by fourth grade, that drops to twenty-nine percent.[46] It's called the "fourth-grade slump," a term coined by Jeanne S. Chall, a Harvard Graduate School of Education psychologist, writer, and literacy researcher for more than fifty years.

There are many reasons why a child might start resisting reading around the age of nine (actually, anywhere from the end of second to the middle of fifth grade), but here's the simplest explanation: That's when schools expect children to go from "learning to read" to "reading to learn." Suddenly, it's not good enough to simply sound out words. The child has to make sense of the context in ever more difficult textbooks. Whether or not he has the motivation, maturity, or physical capacity (including brain development) to do that, teachers will now throw more and more sophisticated reading materials at him, along with expectations that he'll do plenty of reading outside of school hours.

In other words, children struggling with reading prior to fourth grade will be left in the dust unless they receive help, understanding, and encouragement, especially at home. They'll have increasing trouble keeping up. They'll get ever more frustrated. They'll read less and less. And eventually they'll decide reading isn't important and develop attitude about everything connected with reading.

How to counteract that? It may be as simple as parents reading up on the topic of reluctant readers or arranging a reading buddy for him. Or it may involve testing for anything from eye to hearing problems.

The point is that failure to intervene at an early stage means a less-than-keen reader will suffer academically, which impacts his self-confidence (even if he hides it well) and potentially puts him at a disadvantage for life.

Somewhere around fourth grade, too, smart reluctant readers learn to "fake read," which means neither parents nor teachers may catch on that there's a problem. (If you've ever read a foreign-language phrase aloud without actually knowing what the words mean, you get the idea.)

Cris Tovani, author of *I Read It, But I Don't Get It: Comprehension Strategies for Adolescent Readers*, has two terms for fakers: "resistive readers" (they can but choose not to read) and "word callers" (they can read aloud by sounding out words; they just haven't learned to "get" what they're reading yet). Fake readers survive by listening to the teacher, copying the work of others, and laying low when someone wants them to read. They cope temporarily, sometimes even right through high school, but it drags down their academic self-confidence and eventually catches up with them.

Tovani's book can be a helpful resource for dedicated parents who want to identify and turn around a fake reader of any age. Other options are literacy coaches and reading specialists (twenty percent of U.S. schools have the former and sixty percent the latter) and more effort on the part of parents to role model reading and designate family reading time.[47] Nip it in the bud and gift him with a tool he needs for life.

WHY READ?
QUOTABLE QUOTES FROM EXPERTS

"Adolescents entering the adult world in the twenty-first century will read and write more than at any other time in history. They will need advanced levels of literacy to perform their jobs, run their households, act as citizens, and conduct their personal lives."

—INTERNATIONAL READING ASSOCIATION, 1999

"What today's children don't get is the time to be on their own, to be inventive or contemplative, to use their imaginations and to be creative. They need a break. Reading can become a way of having quiet time to escape from the pressures of reality and let the forces of their imagination roam."

—RON JOBE AND MARY DAYTON-SAKARI[48]

"[Teens] may encounter characters who are like them, who face challenges similar to their own. Reading about these characters can often help teens sort out their own worlds."

—CATHY FLEISCHER[49]

"A [troubled student once] thanked me for providing books and 'a place I could be when I couldn't be in the world.'"

— MARILYN REYNOLDS[50]

QUOTABLE QUOTES FROM ORDINARY BOYS AND MEN WE INTERVIEWED

"By not reading, I didn't really apply myself that well in school. If I'd picked up on reading, I'd have done a lot better in school. Now, it opens my eyes to authors, experiences, conversations. It's an avenue to meeting different people."

—KIERAN

"I grew up a nonreader but today I understand the value of reading and appreciate it. I wanted to become part of the reading world because it takes you to different places, stimulates the brain."

—CHRIS

"Reading gives my imagination power. I learn a lot about myself."

—JASON

"Imagination does more for me than movies."

—BRIAN

"What do I get from books? I'm able to share the narrator's experience or perspective. It shows me I'm not the only one who thinks a certain way. It can open your eyes to people's experiences and lives. It showed me that people have similar thoughts to mine. It has influenced places I choose to travel, and my love of travel. It has also affected my politics. It affects the choices I make in life."

—SHANNON

"When characters in a book feel like friends and do cool stuff, you get hooked. That's why series books are so great."

—MATT

SLIPPERY SLOPE OF FACTS AND STATS

Boys read less than girls do.

Parents read to boys for shorter periods of time than they read to girls.[51]

Teen girls read almost twice as much as boys on a per-hour basis.[52]

Some thirty-seven percent of male college freshmen, and only twenty-three percent of female college freshmen, say they spend *no* time reading for pleasure.[53]

More boys than girls struggle with reading and writing.

The average eleventh-grade American boy writes at the same level as the average eighth-grade girl.[54]

Boys start school with a considerable verbal and psychosocial developmental lag (up to eighteen months), behind girls. They often do not catch up until into their late teens—if then.[55]

The majority of reluctant readers are boys.[56]

While seventy percent of children learn to read with no special support, most of the rest—those with problems—are male, non-white, and economically deprived.[57]

Boys get most of the D's and F's in school grades.[58]

Adolescent males are significantly more likely than adolescent females to be left back a grade.[59]

Boys have a harder time finding books on their own.[60]

Adolescent girls outscore adolescent boys in reading and writing—the gender gap being equivalent to a year and a half of school. In other words, the average high school freshman girl is reading as well as the average high school junior boy.[61]

Boys are four times more likely than girls to be in learning disability programs.[62]

The gender gap in literacy is worldwide. Even in Finland, which boasts the top-ranked students in literacy, girls scored much higher than boys.[63]

Adolescent males drop out of high school at four times the rate of adolescent females (this includes females who drop out to have babies).[64]

Boys have more attitude and are less active in the school community.

Males are more likely to view schooling in general (and specifically literacy) as artificial, even unmanly.[65]

Ninety percent of adolescent discipline problems in schools involve males, as do most expulsions and suspensions.[66]

Boys are the primary victims of violence in schools, and comprise the majority of dead, injured, mentally ill, and substance-abusing adolescents.[67]

The majority of salutatorians and valedictorians now are female. Adolescent females also dominate school clubs, yearbooks, and student government.[68]

Boys are four times more likely to be referred to a school psychologist.[69]

There's a direct link between comfort with reading and attitude.

"Once they begin to fall behind, they act out because they are bored or disengaged, and a really difficult downward spiral results."[70]

"Poor reading among boys leads to antisocial behavior."[71]

Low literacy is related to crime, poverty, and unemployment.[72]

There's a direct link between comfort with reading and academic achievement.

The most important predictor of academic success is the amount of time children spend reading books; it is even more important than economic or social status.[73]

"The act of reading or being read to develops the mind and increases intelligence."[74]

"Kids who stop reading start to fall behind their classmates. They lose ground in vocabulary, in comprehension, in advanced thinking skills, even in the ability to write."[75]

"The achievement gap between boys and girls is driven primarily by performance differences in literacy."[76]

Teaching boys science, math, or social studies poses problems if they have difficulty reading the textbook and won't admit it.[77]

There's a direct link between academic achievement and life achievement.

With the decline of high-paying work in traditional male occupations, such as manufacturing, and the increase of high-paying work in occupations requiring informational processing skills, men without a college education have been left behind.[78]

A college degree is linked to higher earnings, increased civic participation, marriage and family stability, lower rates of incarceration, and national economic competitiveness in a global environment.[79]

"A college degree today is as necessary to success as a high school diploma was a few decades ago."[80]

Those with a bachelor's degree earn upwards of forty percent more than high school graduates, a gap slowly but steadily widening.[81]

Eighty percent of high school dropouts are male.[82] Eighty

percent of convicted felons are high school dropouts.[83]

Sixty-eight percent of the people incarcerated in federal penitentiaries have limited literacy skills.[84]

Sixty-three percent of Canadian social assistance recipients have not completed secondary school.[85]

Boys' enrollment in institutes of higher education is decreasing.

In the U.S., women earn sixty-two percent of all associates' degrees, fifty-seven percent of all bachelors' degrees, and sixty percent of all masters' degrees.[86]

Boys finish their education less frequently (high school graduation rate of only sixty-five percent),[87] they finish high school with lower average grades (girls average 3.10 GPA, boys average 2.90 GPA),[88] and fewer go to college. Since 1981, more women than men have been enrolling in college.[89]

Between the years 1990 and 2009, the male undergraduate enrollment dropped from forty-five percent to forty-three percent in the U.S.[90]

"Something is not working for boys, but there is little to no direct research on gender and literacy, and not much in the way of support for boys' literacy," Jon Scieszka declares on his Guys Read website (www.guysread.com).

We like to think that's changing, but not fast enough, and certainly insufficiently in terms of information parents receive.

HAPPY ENDING

Cynthia worked with a troubled family named the "Joneses," who always seemed to be at odds with their six sons' schools and teachers. The parents complained about the teachers in front of their boys at home, which of course encouraged their sons to do the same, and to resist doing what the teachers encouraged them to do. Nor did the boys feel a need to take responsibility for their homework, which gave them a negative attitude toward reading. Mr. Jones believed that academic success was not important. He just wanted the kids to "get their chores done," and when they got old enough, "to get an honest job."

When the boys were with her, Cynthia related some stories to them about children overcoming adversity. She summarized the stories from books like *Snow Treasure* (about how kids saved Norway's gold in World War II) and *Seven Alone* (about how seven orphans made it to Oregon after suffering hardships like crossing the mountains in winter). Some of the boys bought into her encouragement and began to take more interest in reading. Two of them used reading as an escape from their family's difficult circumstances. Those two ended up succeeding in school, and became the most well adjusted in this struggling family.

CHAPTER THREE

MATH, SCIENCE, AND UNDER-ACHIEVEMENT: MAKING THE DIFFERENCE

Only thirty-five percent of eighth graders are "proficient" in math, while only thirty-two percent of eighth graders are "proficient" in science.[91]

"I sit staring at my math test, my pencil newly sharpened but dangling limply over the page. I studied, but what was the point? I hear the math problems shouting at me that I'm stupid and useless. I want to jump up from my desk and run away. Or turn invisible. Math and me, we hate each other."

—ANONYMOUS

MATH PHOBIA IS RIGHT UP THERE WITH SNAKES, public speaking, and heights.[92] And then there's science, which gives some kids the same sense of failure. Never mind that in today's world, ever more influenced by science and technology, mastering both topics is of growing importance for success in school and in life.

The good news is that on average, boys are slightly better at math and science than girls, and interest in these subjects can actually convert them to becoming better readers in general. But when it comes to science grades, we're in trouble, says Gerald Wheeler, interim executive director of the National Science Teachers Association. (See sidebar, "Youth and Science," on pages 55-56.) "We're flat and definitely not in line with satisfying what we need for a workforce in the next ten to fifteen years."

"And if our kids don't improve in math," adds Linda M. Gojak, president of the National Council of Teachers of Mathematics, "North America is going to continue to ship jobs overseas."

The two issues for parents are what students need in order to get into college, and what they need to successfully enter the workforce. Researchers say that college readiness requires competence at writing, research, language, grammar, math ("especially anything higher than Algebra II"), and science ("particularly physics"). The workforce wants the same, except "with less emphasis on advanced mathematics and science," according to a 2008 report funded by the Bill and Melinda Gates Foundation.[93]

"But hey," we hear your kid inserting at this point, "I'm going to be an artist/writer/musician/whatever. So I won't really need math and science." This is where you might be tempted to reply, "You're right, son, and I never got good grades at that stuff either, so I understand. Just try to pass, okay?"

Hold on! Don't say it! First, reflect on the fact that "rapid changes in the world—including technological advancement, scientific innovation, increased globalization, shifting workforce demands and pressures of economic competitiveness—are redefining the broad skill sets that students need to be adequately prepared to participate in and contribute to today's society."[94] In other words, your son is growing up in a different world than you did, and if you care about his future success, rest assured that you can—and must—empower him without any strong math and science background on your part. Math and science are essential today for business (making market predictions, preparing budgets, estimating for a construction project), medical careers, sales positions, technical jobs, and far, far more.[95] Your future writer, artist, or musician will someday find himself negotiating contracts or trying to get the best deal on a computer, loft, or violin, never mind feeling forced to take on a second job or change careers to something that (surprise!) requires math or science.

And then there's everyday life. Math and science are essential for understanding the evening news, sounding intelligent during job interviews, impressing colleagues over lunch, and casting an informed vote. Need more examples? Below is a list we've compiled from Marilyn Burns's *Math: Facing an American Phobia* and an interview with an accomplished scientist.[96]

Math: budgeting household expenses, tipping in restaurants, doing home-woodworking projects, deciding how much wallpaper or paint or carpet to buy, keeping score when playing games, cooking, calculating gas mileage, figuring discounts while shopping, converting money when traveling abroad, making change, dividing a check at a restaurant.[97]

As Burns notes, "When you're in the grocery store with only a twenty-dollar bill, overestimate on things you put in the basket or you will be embarrassed at the checkout... Too much fertilizer and you can burn your lawn."

The Gates report found that math is a major stumbling block to employment; whether people want to be nurses or police, large numbers end up in less interesting work after failing math exams.[98]

Science: In the wake of the 2004 Indian Ocean earthquake, a child in Thailand saved her family members' lives. How? By knowing that when the ocean sucked water from their local beach on a massive scale, it was a sign that a tsunami wave was about to hit, and therefore time to run for higher ground rather than toward the receding water to collect stranded fish, as many villagers did.

Many years earlier, in the United States, a young boy witnessed a live electrical wire fall on his father, causing the man to lose consciousness. The boy knew to lift the wire off with a wooden pole (which does not conduct electricity) rather than with his hands, which otherwise might have killed the boy and prevented him from saving his father.

While it may be rare that a child's memory of something learned in science class ends up saving a life, basic science knowledge is important for several reasons. First, it teaches kids to "read with skepticism," all-important in today's bombardment-of-information age. The "scientific method" also introduces the concept of forming a hypothesis and gathering facts rather than accepting information at face value; it thus helps individuals distinguish between a belief system and one based on provable facts, which makes for more thoughtful voters and a stronger democracy.

Second, being able to comment intelligently on the day's news (be it an earthquake, eclipse, sports-doping scandal, oil spill, global warming, or promising medical cure) impresses and informs colleagues and potential bosses.

Finally, there are the day-to-day applications: knowing what to use for cleaning, painting, or gluing different things; why putting water in a brake fluid container will cause trouble; and when mixing household cleaning agents might be dangerous. Why eating too fast causes abdominal gas, how more nutritious eating can prevent or resolve health issues; how to save fuel or energy in the family home or car; why placing a lid on a pan makes the food cook faster; and how to entertain a younger sibling with a safe science experiment that makes things fizz or go pop. What about knowing the difference between identical and nonidentical twins, renewable versus nonrenewable energy and geological time scales?

Bottom line: math and science literacy is as important as reading and writing literacy, and parents can make all the difference in turning their kids on or off these subjects. Not by becoming their child's teacher, but by saying and doing the right thing when their child seems discouraged.

As mentioned in this chapter's opening quote, only thirty-five percent of eighth graders are proficient in math (down from forty percent of fourth graders), while only thirty two percent of eighth graders are proficient in science. Boys and girls rate fairly evenly in math, while boys still hold an advantage in science.[99]

The math shortcomings in particular bode poorly considering that seventy-five percent of all jobs require proficiency in simple algebra and geometry.[100] How many students think they've got that? Sixty-two percent. But how many employers think they've got that? Eight percent.[101] And, as Wheeler confirmed earlier, students are coming up short on science as well.

These are big gaps to close, and the schools aren't doing it well, partly because few teachers are confident with teaching math or science.[102] (Most signed on for only the first two Rs in "reading, writing, and 'rithmetic.") And partly because math and science curriculum is proving slow to respond to what research is saying: kids do best when they learn the skills in context rather than as dry memorization feats. "Involve them in activities, explorations, and experiments," says Burns, who adds that kids don't respond well to the approach, "Yours is not to question why; just invert and multiply."[103]

Of course, parents who were no great shakes at math or science can only blanch at the idea that they're in charge of making up for weak teachers or school curriculum. Relax! There is much you can do simply by being a caring parent. Here are our best tips. (See sidebar, "More Tips for Helping Your Math- or Science-Challenged Child," on page 51.)

Don't pass on a negative math or science attitude to your children. Burns suggests saying things like, "Let's look at that together." "I'm not sure I remember that, but if we can't figure it out, we'll ask for help." "Tell me what you learned about this so far." "Boy, you're learning things I never learned. Let's work on it together."[104]

Let your children see you doing math or science, be that figuring out change at the store, mumbling aloud about why you need to check which solution to clean your paintbrush with, or figuring out how to calculate which bus to catch for a flight. ("Plane leaves at three, gotta be there by one, it takes the bus twenty minutes to get there but it might not come for fifteen minutes...")

Involve your child by letting him figure out how much admission the movie theater will charge for all the family or leading him in a discussion on why plants need sunlight to grow (photosynthesis) or how to measure wood for a treehouse. (Try "fun science" or "fun math" on the Internet.)

Tell him that effort is what counts. "Honey, just prove to me that you can improve. That's way more important than whether you're doing better than others in your class."

Don't give undue praise, and praise the task rather than the child: "Good job" or "I knew you could do it" rather than "You're so smart." In general, lots of little praise is more effective than big praise.

When Pam's son Jeremy was eight, she bought him some math and science workbooks to increase his confidence in those subjects. Together, they calculated which pages in those workbooks represented one-quarter, one-half, and three-quarters of the way through, then negotiated rewards that Pam wrote down beside those page numbers. (Ice cream at one-quarter the way through, dinner-out at the finish.) When Pam's mother was visiting shortly thereafter, she arose early one Saturday morning to find her young grandson sitting on the living room sofa working math problems.

"You prefer that to cartoons on television?" she asked, astonished.

"Yup," Jeremy responded, hardly pausing in his quest to make it to the reward page.

"He's a very smart boy," she later commented to Jeremy's Aunt Cynthia, not aware that it was really all about food.

There's a great book for math-haters written by actress and mathematician Danica McKellar, called *Math Doesn't Suck: How to Survive Middle School Math without Losing Your Mind or Breaking a Nail.* Although it is written specifically for girls (hey Danica, we need one for boys too!), here are a few unisex pointers we think you can offer your son, some of which transfer easily to science, too:

To those who think math is scary: "Get in touch with your competitive, aggressive side! Refuse to be beaten."[105]

To those who get confused and lost during class: "Don't be shy. Be bold and read ahead in your textbook."

To those who think the material seems clear, only to find it marked as incorrect: "Read the directions closely, stop racing through your homework, and don't skip steps."

To those who find their memory packs up when a test is in front of them: "Do the easy problems first."[106]

To those who just can't get into math: "Open your math book and look at the first problem you have to do. Read it to yourself in your head, and interject all sorts of enthusiastic words into it. Seriously, I know this is wacky and totally uncool, but no one can hear what goes on in your head. (Thank goodness, right?) For example, if the problem is 1/4 plus 3/4 = ?, think to yourself, 'Ah, 1/4! I love 1/4! What a great fraction! And I can't wait to add it to 3/4. Yay! Let's see, how should I do this? Well, since the denominators are the same, I can just add across the top. Great! So the answer is

4/4. But wait! That doesn't look reduced; I have to reduce it first. I mean, I get to reduce it, because I love reducing fractions almost as much as I love adding them together! Yippee!'"[107]

And finally, "Working on math sharpens your brain, actually making you smarter in all areas. Intelligence is real, it's lasting, and no one can take it away from you. Ever."[108]

[From *Math Doesn't Suck* by Danica McKellar, copyright ©2007 by Danica McKellar. Used by permission of Hudson Street Press, an imprint of Penguin Group (USA) Inc.]

Again, making math and science seem relevant is the trick. One teen boy who hated math insisted he would never need it because he intended to sell cars for a living. But in his Consumer Math class, where he learned how to calculate everything from the best discounts on the vehicle to the highest rates of interest on his savings account, he thrived. "That's the first math course I ever aced," he boasted to his parents. "That's math for real life."

TACKLING CHRONIC UNDERACHIEVEMENT

When boys perform beneath their capabilities, parents typically try encouragement, lectures, rewards, threats, teacher meetings, private tutors, and maybe even testing for issues like ADHD. Some go so far as to let their child fail, hoping that will teach him a lesson. When none of these works and the problem stretches to a year or more, chances are he's one of the fifteen percent of under-achievers known as chronic underachievers.[109]

If so, it's important to back off and dig deeper to understand the roots of the issue. Further attempts to help can actually make things worse. Chronic underachievement may stem from depression, anxiety, rebellion against authority (which applies to boys more than to girls),[110] a high level of self-doubt, or even a desire to not stick out among classmates.

Also, many kids (especially those with over-involved or under-involved parents) become masters at manipulating their parents, either because they've never learned how to do things for themselves or because they're seeking approval or a more emotional relationship from an aloof parent.[111] [112] In this case, showing anger or frustration rewards their subconscious need for attention and dependency. Or perhaps they're so busy trying to live up to parental ambitions that they don't get around to forming self-motivation. Regardless, this variety of chronic underachiever becomes expert at transferring responsibility to others, and/or develops a debilitating dependency on others often masked by a charming and manipulative personality.[113]

Does he do homework only when you're hovering? Does he continually blame shortcomings on the teacher, the class, or other factors? ("It's not my fault." "The teacher doesn't like me." "The class is boring.") Does he lie? ("I did my homework at school." "She didn't tell us there was going to be a test.")

Here's advice from Michael D. Whitley, Ph.D., author of *Bright Minds, Poor Grades: Understanding and Motivating Your Underachieving Child*: "The lies say to parents, 'If you really want to know the truth about me, then you have to become so involved and entangled in my life that I will never have to be separated from you.'...If parents focus only on the facts their children lie about and never on the deeper psychology of lying, then parents simply feed the problem even more."[114]

With chronic underachievers, rewards and punishments don't

work because they don't teach self-motivation. Tutoring often exacerbates these kids' dependency. And making them suffer the consequences doesn't work because they only fall back on excuses. Instead, chronic underachievers must "learn to understand themselves, think out their own solutions to their problems, exercise self-discipline, and learn to feel positive feelings about schoolwork."[115] This may require professional counseling, or parents may be able to turn things around by working through the advice in Whitley's book or Jane Nelsen's *Positive Discipline* books. Most essential is that parents don't fall into the common traps of shaming, humiliating, or rescuing their kids. Learn how to really encourage them, as we emphasize in Chapter Ten.

Another resource is *Why Bright Kids Get Poor Grades and What You Can Do About It: A Six-Step Program for Parents and Teachers* by Dr. Sylvia Rimm, who says she reverses underachievement in roughly four out of five children in an average of six months.[116] Here's a sampling of Rimm's advice: "Under no circumstances should your children expect to have you or your spouse sitting next to them regularly at homework time…If your children are accustomed to reminders, nagging, sympathy, and assistance, they have learned to get you to focus your attention on their dependence…Tough to watch them struggle, but don't deprive them of this only way to develop self-confidence."[117]

MORE TIPS FOR HELPING YOUR MATH- OR SCIENCE-CHALLENGED CHILD

Stick a times-table or periodic table of the elements on the back of his notebook.

Offer games that teach with several of the five senses (seeing, hearing, smelling, tasting, touching), as in sharing pizza or cake to learn fractions, or sorting silverware together.

Tie learning to the real world, for instance, use money for math exercises, and relay the child as hero tsunami and electrical-wire stories above.

Encourage him to use colored pencils to break up information.[118]

To reduce his anxiety, help him cut a window or slot in a square of cardboard so he can work on a page with only a portion of the text being visible.[119]

Encourage him to reword the question and create word problems for himself.[120]

For kids who transpose numbers (as in confuse 16 with 61), play card-search games.[121]

Find family games that reinforce science and math learning, and play them with him: Monopoly, Scattergories, Scrabble, Yahtzee, crossword puzzles, cribbage, Kings in the Corner, poker, and other card games. (Yes, solo computer games work too, but family games provide the extra key ingredient—time with you.)

Quote sports statistics, and ask him to find information on his favorite sports.

Cook and bake; he will use fractions without feeling intimidated as he reads recipes. Have him double his favorite recipes, then praise him for his effort.

Use jingles: "Six and eight went on a date; they became forty-eight."

Play with him using money; have him make change.

Have him help you figure out the best deal at the grocery store. ("Is it cheaper to buy a four-pack of pudding for $.99 or a twelve-pack for $2.79?")

Learn to use programs like Touch Point Math, a multisensory program designed to engage kids of all abilities and learning styles (www.touchmath.com).

In a family meeting, ask kids to solve a math problem a variety of ways. Example: "How many different ways can we figure out the number of packages of hot dogs we'll need for the party?" Then honor each child's method of coming up with the answer. Require them each to solve it differently, and praise their effort. That way it is not just the answer but the process that will get the praise.

Drill your kids on the basic skills while they are young. "Parents who think that calculators negate the need to learn multiplication tables are wrong," says Bloomington, Minnesota, math teacher Nancy Johnson. "Kids who don't memorize them don't get the higher concepts. I've seen it again and again."

MEMORY, MATH, AND SCIENCE

Many an individual who thinks he has math or science phobia really suffers from weak short-term memory. If you suspect that may apply to your son, here are some strategies, culled from Steve Chinn's *The Trouble with Maths: A Practical Guide to Helping Learners with Numeracy Difficulties.*[122]

1. Don't give a lengthy string of instructions. Let him write them down, perhaps in his own words.
2. Repeat the question without showing irritation.
3. Ask how he's going to solve the problem, then feel free to suggest alternatives.
4. If it's a math problem, accept an estimate.
5. Make sure he has a worksheet on which to scribble notes.
6. Let him know that ducking out of the work is not an option.
7. Present him with facts you know he already knows, so that you're reinforcing the process ("See? You get it!") rather than testing him on the actual information.

Why be flexible with kids who aren't big in the memory department? Because you can't necessarily change the memory factor, but you can build the interest and self-confidence that will allow him to detour around it to success. Says Chinn, "I recently assessed an art graduate in her mid-thirties, highly successful in her special field, who had a working memory for three items only. This is not a problem that children grow out of."[123]

WORDS AND NUMBERS TO PONDER

When high school math is optional, fifty percent of students choose not to take it.[124]

Children start to give up on math at age seven, sometimes even younger.[125]

One study found that between ten and fifteen percent of those entering college are not ready for first-year math. (Worse, a quarter of students are unprepared for college-level writing.)[126]

About five percent of children have high anxiety over math.[127]

Those who conquer their fear of math early in life are "more likely to invest intelligently later on, increase their financial knowledge and worth, and establish a more secure retirement," while those with low math comfort are risk-averse in general.[128] In today's world, which do we need more of?

Globally, "one billion school-age children will grow up with very minimal reading, writing, and math. People should be marching in the streets with pitchforks about this."—Jose Ferreira, online education pioneer[129]

YOUTH AND SCIENCE[130]

Dr. Gerald Wheeler is the interim executive director of the National Science Teachers Association (www.nsta.org), the world's largest professional organization representing science educators of all grade levels. A fuller version of this interview (conducted by Pam) is at www.keenreaders.org.

Q: How would you sum up the state of science knowledge among youth in North America today?

A: We're definitely not in line with satisfying what we need for a workforce in the next ten to fifteen years.

Q: Your thoughts on how to improve that?

A: Parents don't need to have a strong background in science to help their children learn and appreciate science. Doing science with your child can be as simple as helping him or her measure the ingredients for a batch of chocolate chip cookies. Don't let science become a weak part of your child's education. Get involved.

Q: Do problems with reading and writing affect science learning?

A: It turns out that science is actually a gift in this case. Science and technology can get struggling readers engaged, and actually improve their math and literacy scores. It's a door opening to get them engaged in their schooling. If they really like the hands-on, real-world problems, as soon as they do these, they get immersed in mathematics and reading.

Q: Is online learning suited or unsuited to science education?

A: It works pretty well, but is a challenge because a lot of science is hands-on.

Q: What can parents do to help kindle or grow their children's interest in science?

A: I think it starts long before high school. It's about engaging them by answering questions and exploring things. Dinnertime is a great opportunity for your family to have discussions about science-based news stories (space shuttle missions, severe weather storms, etc.). Movies and TV shows that feature science-related themes are also good topics for discussions. Too many parents say, "Well, that's the job of the schools, and don't give our kids homework because it interrupts our quality time." Also, too many families come home and eat at different times or head off to their separate computers or televisions. They need to get engaged in what's happening in the schools, and find ways to be supportive of the teachers and the school program. For example, parents can participate in their child's school science program by locating scientists and others to be guest speakers, or can accompany their child on a field trip to a science-related place.

It's a struggle with the disenchanted child; he is really destroying his future if he doesn't get engaged. We have to make sure we get them engaged.

YOUTH AND MATH[131]

Linda M. Gojak is president of the National Council of Teachers of Mathematics. A fuller version of this interview (conducted by Pam) is at www.keenreaders.org.

Q: How would you sum up math knowledge among kids in North America today?

A: International studies show that we're not competitive with the top countries in the world, but you have to be really careful when you look at international comparisons, because we strive to educate all our students, while other countries that competitively do well are much more selective. For example in China, at the eighth-grade level kids are given a very high-stakes test and only a select number get to go on to high school; others go to vocational schools or don't go on to school at all.

Q: Is online learning particularly suited to math and science learning?

A: To me, both math and science education offer opportunities to communicate and discuss and reason with others. There's a lot of good material online that can help enhance their mathematics achievement, but it's really important for kids to have an opportunity to share their thinking in real time with one another, and online learning does not always give them that opportunity.

Q: What can parents do to help their children engage with math?

A: First, let kids know that mathematics is as important as reading and writing. It really is a critical factor in a child's future options. Second, talk to the teacher. If your child is struggling, work with the teacher to provide opportunities so your child can do better in math. Sometimes parents think that they're the teacher when their kid gets home. But math education looks different today than when parents were in school, so it's more important to communicate with the teacher than to become the at-home teacher.

Third, our children are very overbooked these days. They come home from school while both parents are working, or they come home and have to go to soccer or baseball or music practice. It's real important for parents to realize that they need to set up a place for kids to do homework—a quiet place, and a time when the television and maybe computer are turned off. That homework is an important part of reinforcing what the kids learned in school that day.

Q: Is math competency more important today than it was in previous generations?

A: Absolutely. Career options aside, in today's economy, society, and political environment, we need to know when we're reading or hearing legitimate information. We need to be able to look at the numbers and say, "This just doesn't make sense." There is a wonderful book called *How to Lie with Statistics*. If there are a lot of people lying with statistics, we're going to be a very misinformed population unless we develop that ability to reason and see through the lies.

ONLINE LEARNING

"I had a student as both a fifth- and sixth-grader, who had no confidence in himself in math. He has ADHD and could not focus long enough to get through a math problem that involved more than a quick answer he could do in his head. The first few months of fifth grade, he struggled. He hardly did any homework and would come late to school (math was the first lesson of the day). He broke many pencils as he erased and pushed too hard out of frustration. He was about two years behind in our curriculum.

"Then our class began doing online math with the Khan Academy, which provides free online videos on everything from arithmetic to physics, and allows viewers to earn badges and points as they work their way through them at www.khanacademy.org.

"Now he was able to get immediate feedback on his answers, and he began to want to do more, to receive the badges everyone else was getting. He loved the fact you could take hints or be shown the answer without having to look 'dumb' in front of the whole class. With coaching from me when he was stuck on a module, or even from other students he was comfortable talking to, he was one of the first to log on every day, the first now to ask me questions, and gained in confidence every day. Once he started taking his math education into his own hands, he wanted more.

"When he was ready to apply the knowledge to real-world projects, activities, and situations, he really shone. He was finally confident enough in his skills to work collaboratively with others. Before this, he would sit back and let others do the work. He took pride in his projects, in learning more and showing me his progress. When we met each week to discuss his goals and reflections, it amazed me how articulate he was in his own learning, successes, struggles, and goals."

—KELLY RAFFERTY,
TEACHER AT SANTA RITA SCHOOL,
LOS ALTOS, CALIFORNIA

HAPPY ENDING

Jack came to his geometry class with a negative attitude toward math. Worse, he had not had first-year algebra due to switching schools the previous year. His teacher, Jeff Ray (a veteran math teacher at Bethany Academy in Bloomington, Minnesota, and also an athletic director), recognized that Jack needed individual encouragement before the boy would open his mind to acquire the needed skills. So he spent the one-on-one time Jack required. By the end of the school year, Jack wasn't getting A's, but he was enjoying math.

"It took building rapport with him," explains Jeff. "Older siblings, parents, peer tutors can all help, but the number one factor is changing their mindset. In basketball, we don't tell a player that just because they can't score twenty-four points in a game they shouldn't play, do we? No, we tell them to go out there and do their best! It's the same with math."

LEARNING CENTERS

Resources abound for helping children who struggle in school. Some, like Sylvan, Huntington, and Mathnasium Learning Centers, provide excellent teachers who work one-on-one with students. The teachers test their young clients for deficits in their understanding, determine which skills are lacking, then address the child's knowledge gaps through direct teaching. Many students thrive with this traditional approach.

Daren was an eleven-year-old African-American boy who grew up near Pensacola, Florida, and dreamed of becoming a pilot someday. He marveled as he watched the Blue Angels performing, and told his mom that he wanted to go to the Naval Academy so he could fly planes like "those amazing guys."

His mom was delighted with Daren's aspirations, but knew that his struggle with math would hold him back from achieving his goal. Single and on a tight budget, she somehow managed to squeeze out enough for a tutor, who worked with Daren four days a week for months. It was to little avail. He would know the material one day and completely forget it the next.

Daren's grandfather, who had read about a program with a reputation for helping minorities succeed in school, put Daren's mother in touch with a Learning Rx Center, a nontraditional system that focuses on specific learning skills based on research by Oliver W. Hill Jr., Ph.D. These centers offer a "personal trainer" who creates an individualized training regimen that takes into account such skills as memory, logic, reasoning, and visual processing. The trainer develops rapport with the child then engages him in exercises to strengthen each skill set.

Daren's mom was hesitant but decided to give it a try. Within weeks, she observed Daren's confidence soar, and within months, he was making significant gains in math and science. He went on to graduate near the top of his class. Four years later, his mother and grandfather were thrilled to watch Daren receive top honors at the U.S. Naval Academy, where he was selected for the coveted Naval Flight School. Today he lands planes on aircraft carriers and may yet realize his goal of flying the Blue Angels. The family agrees that Daren's turning point was the learning program he attended in sixth grade.

CHAPTER FOUR

WHAT HOLDS SMART KIDS BACK? PHYSICAL ISSUES

"I never meant to be annoying, forgetful, delayed, overwhelmed and dumb-sounding and -looking. I never wanted to be made fun of or anger my teachers or keep an entire class late because I didn't understand the concept. But that's often what happened as a consequence of my learning disability."

—PULITZER PRIZE-WINNING POET

PHILIP SCHULTZ[132]

THERE ARE TONS OF ISSUES THAT CAN WORK against a boy embracing reading and schoolwork. The best and worst of the reasons are physical. "Worst" because learning and behavioral challenges can mark a child as different—a target for bullies. Plus, physical problems take time to diagnose, and typically continue to challenge even when understood and supported. But "best" because once identified and studied up on, they can shed a whole new light on things for both youth and parent.

Learning disabilities (LD) are a group of disorders that run in families and impact listening, speaking, reading, writing, reasoning, math and social skills. They are just one physical barrier to reading and school achievement. Others include hearing issues, concussions (which sports inflict more on boys than girls), and ADD/ADHD (Attention Deficit Disorder/Attention-Deficit

Hyperactivity Disorder). And then there are the differences between male and female brains.

Jump-Starting Boys: Help Your Reluctant Learner Find Success in School and Life deals mostly with the nonphysical issues: motivation, reading material choices, role modeling, and the need for more communication between parents and schools. But these are often inseparable from the growing-up experiences of boys who are perceived as slow or difficult simply because they lag behind and get more excitable than girls. Or those with undiagnosed physical issues.

Take Philip Schultz, for instance. He performed so poorly in school that he was held back in third grade. He didn't know he had dyslexia until he had his own children, one of whom was diagnosed with the same disability in today's more LD-responsive school environment. What he did know as a kid, was that he couldn't seem to concentrate, follow rules, or read and write like his classmates. When a fellow third-grader told him he was a dummy who couldn't learn anything, Philip pushed the boy's face against a concrete culvert in the playground. The principal ordered him expelled.

But his mother never gave up on him, reading him comic books every night as he repeated the sounds she made, pretending he was reading them himself. He also thrived on his father's and brothers' storytelling.

At school, he was a loner, eating by himself in the school cafeteria as other kids made fun of him. "I felt truly comfortable and safe only when I was alone, with no one asking anything of me that I couldn't do," he said. "I thought not being able to learn anything made everyone hate me." Eventually he ate lunch at a restaurant across the road instead, ordering the same thing every day because he couldn't read the menu.

In school, teachers seated him and other special-needs students at the back of the room and ignored them "as if we weren't worthy of being addressed." He desperately wanted to prove himself capable, but had no idea how. Like many smart kids with an LD, he got in trouble for his inability to back down from the bullies. "In some ways, being scared and fighting was better than being lonely and ignored."

He found himself looking up the same word numerous times, unable to commit its meaning to memory. Any effort to speak a foreign language shut his mind down instantly and without warning—as did a stress overload. He couldn't understand or apply grammatical rules or recognize spelling patterns. And then there was the temper born of the ever underlying frustration: "If I thought I was being asked to do something [someone] already knew I couldn't do, I would feel attacked and cornered."

In fifth grade, following the threat of another school expulsion, Philip experienced his tutor laughing at him when he said he wanted to be a writer. That night, tucked in bed listening to his mother beside him reading a comic book aloud, he found the motivation to interrupt her to read the words himself for the first time.

After that, he found he could read well enough to pass classes. He became the high school cartoonist and wrote poems and stories for a school publication. At fifteen, he fell in love with a particular book—*The Moviegoer* by Walker Percy—and worked harder than ever at compensating for his reading and writing difficulties.

His dyslexia remains a challenge today. He says he often reads a sentence two or three times before he fully understands it. He says he has to "restructure its syntax and sound out its syllables" before he can absorb its meaning. He has to use a lot of positive self-talk to remind himself that endlessly repeating sentences is necessary and that ultimately it will benefit him both as a person and as a writer. "This argument, and it is an argument, isn't always easy to buy into and sometimes I quit out of frustration and exhaustion."[133]

By the time he got to high school, Philip realized that getting by wasn't enough. He buckled down even more to achieve what fellow students seemed to master so easily, eventually making it into San Francisco State University. Since then, he has authored seven collections of poetry, including *Failure*, which won him a Pulitzer Prize. He then published *My Dyslexia*, the story of his struggles to achieve in life.

Then there's Andrew's story. The summer before his senior year in high school, Andrew Ackerman met with an educational psychologist to take tests that would evaluate his "learning style" before sitting for college admissions tests. He now regards that day as one of the most important of his life, because for the first time, he was diagnosed as having a "nonverbal learning disability." (In first grade, he'd been diagnosed with dyslexia.)

In short, because he's wired to process information in a more complicated manner than others, it takes a lot more effort to achieve goals, which constantly tires and frustrates him. Andrew's psychologist expressed surprise that Andrew had made it through school with above-average grades without any help for his real disability.

"Without realizing it, I had been relying on strong verbal skills, which accounted for whatever success I had achieved," Andrew reflected in an article he wrote for the website SmartKidswithLD. org. Having his nonverbal learning disability explained to him provided instant results. Suddenly, instead of rejecting special help as a sign of weakness, he asked for it the minute he couldn't understand something. He signed up for special education classes and set himself the goal of acquiring as many learning strategies as he could before going to college. He also chose a small college to ensure small classes where his strong point—verbal skills—could shine. "For me, there was nothing better than sitting around a table with a professor and six or seven other students." (Reprinted, with permission, from the Smart Kids with LD website at www.SmartKidswithLD.org; copyright by Smart Kids with Learning Disabilities®.)

What Are the Most Common Physical Issues that Affect Reading and Writing?

1. ADD/ADHD: Attention Deficit Disorder/Attention-Deficit Hyperactivity Disorder

Symptoms: inattention, hyperactivity, and impulsivity (*not* run-of-the-mill restlessness, but a consistent degree that interferes with school and home life). In other words, kids who dash about, touch or play with whatever is in sight, and talk incessantly. Impulsivity and hyperactivity show up first, and inattention later.

How common: Two to five percent of American children between the ages of six and sixteen are diagnosed with ADD or ADHD—eighty percent of them boys.[134]

Cause: More and more studies point to biological, not home or environment causes.

Note: Appears in life before age seven. Is not an LD, but is often confused with LD, and shares some of the same symptoms. Those with ADD/ADHD should be screened for LD as well, since up to thirty percent of people with ADHD also have a learning disability. Unlike LD, ADD/ADHD requires a medical diagnosis. About eighty percent of children who need medication for ADHD still need it as teens, and over fifty percent as adults. Medications don't cure ADHD; they only control the symptoms on the day they are taken.

Bonus facts: In their first two to five years of driving, youth with

ADHD have nearly four times as many auto accidents, are more likely to cause bodily injury in accidents, and have three times as many citations for speeding as young drivers without ADHD. Teens with ADHD who remain on their medication during their teen years have a lower likelihood of substance use or abuse than ADHD teens who do not take medications.

2. LD: Learning Disabilities

Symptoms: difficulty with reading, writing, spelling, listening, thinking, speaking, or doing math. Can also involve issues with memory, coordination, social skills, emotional maturity, organizational and time-management skills.

How common: Reading disabilities affect up to eight percent of elementary school children. Of students with specific (as opposed to more general) learning disabilities, seventy to eighty percent have deficits in reading.

Causes: heredity, problems during pregnancy or birth, accidents, malnutrition, toxic exposure.

Note: Can be diagnosed by the school system using a psycho-educational assessment, or by private psychologists or educational specialists. "Individuals with LD can learn to compensate for areas of weakness and with early, effective support, can be highly successful and productive members of society," states the National Center for Learning Disabilities (www.ncld.org).

Bonus fact: "Parents can help by encouraging their strengths, knowing their weaknesses, understanding the educational system, working with professionals, and learning about strategies for dealing with specific difficulties," says the Learning Disabilities Association of America (www.ldanatl.org).

Common Forms of LD

Dyslexia: a language-based disability in which the person has trouble with specific language skills, particularly reading. One in every five children suffers from some form of dyslexia.[135]

Dyscalculia: a mathematical disability in which a person has a difficult time solving arithmetic problems, decoding symbols and grasping math concepts, and may frequently reverse numbers.

Dysgraphia: a writing disability in which a person finds it hard to form letters, write within a defined space, and express ideas. Keyboarding can help overcome that difficulty.

Nonverbal learning disabilities: motor clumsiness, poor visual-spatial skills, problematic social relationships, difficulty with math, and poor organizational skills. But students with these often have verbal strengths (early speech, reading and writing skills, a large vocabulary, excellent rote-memory, eloquent self-expression, and more).

Auditory processing disorder: can't pay attention if there's noise in the background. The student's ears work properly, but the brain has trouble recognizing and interpreting sound, especially sounds that compose speech.[136]

Sensory integration dysfunction: heightens and confuses the sensory information a child takes in. Such students answer when being called, understand when spoken to one-on-one, but when background noise is present, or he is being spoken to as part of a group, he doesn't always get it.

Note: Most students with LD have serious deficiencies in the area of visual memory. Visual memory involves the ability to store and retrieve previously experienced visual sensations and perceptions. Various researchers have stated that as much as eighty percent of all learning takes place through the eye with visual memory existing as a crucial aspect of learning.[137]

3. **Hearing and vision** issues less serious than deafness or blindness.

For instance, one study indicated that ten percent of children ages eleven and under suffer from a mild hearing loss related to middle ear infection.[138] Parents can ask teachers to seat their son near the front, or better yet, ensure that he learns to ask that for himself.

4. **Brain Injury**[139]

Symptoms: compulsive and explosive behavior, sensory issues, memory loss, behavioral issues, violence, and alcohol intolerance. Can impair ability to control emotions. Sufferers may have trouble responding to subtle social cues and planning difficult tasks. Although young children with a brain injury usually recover their mental abilities quite rapidly, they can have serious problems later, including learning deficits even when the IQ returns to normal.

How common: Significantly underdiagnosed, it's the most frequent cause of disability and death among children and adolescents in the U.S.[140] A Scottish study found that forty-seven percent of people classified as having mild head injuries were disabled to some extent a year later.[141]

Potential causes: injury, stress, disease, poor nutrition.

Note: Males are nearly twice as likely as females to injure their brains, in part due to sports activities.[142] [143]

Bonus fact: Nutritional supplements may help deter violent and antisocial behavior. When vitamins and minerals were given to elementary school children with behavioral problems, it reduced incidences of antisocial behavior (www.fi.edu/learn/brain/head.html#top).

More serious conditions not within the scope of this book include deafness, blindness, autism, mental retardation, Tourette syndrome, oppositional defiant disorder, conduct disorder, anxiety, depression, and bipolar disorder.

Parenting by "Type of Intelligence"

Now that we've belted readers with an alphabet-soup list of acronyms for physical challenges that can affect learning, here's an entirely different take: As we touched on in Chapter One, pioneering psychotherapist Alfred Adler observed that children who misbehave are discouraged children. Adler also taught that individuals have unique interpretations of life that influence both how they perceive life and how they learn.[144] Not himself an Adlerian, but a believer in individual-centered education, developmental psychologist and professor Howard Gardner views people as having one or more *types of intelligences*—only some of which are valued in the traditional school system. Here are the eight intelligences Gardner describes:

Verbal-linguistic: a mastery of language. Children with this tend to read and write well, and many will become teachers, journalists, writers, lawyers, translators, storytellers, and comedians. Most schools value and test for this type of intelligence.

Musical-rhythmic: a mastery of pitch, tone, timbre, and rhythm. Our culture currently minimizes the importance of this intelligence, but those with it thrive on composing and performing.

Mathematical-logical: innate skill for detecting patterns, reasoning deductively, and thinking logically. Because they can follow the logic of textbooks, this set of students thrives in the traditional school system, and may go on to become mathematicians, physicists, philosophers, or scientists.

Visual-spatial: an uncanny ability to perceive the visual world accurately; these children love color and imagine the world differently from their schoolmates. That often gets them ostracized for nonconformity, and they typically struggle with standardized tests. But many will become painters, sculptors, designers, navigators, hunters, scientists, and architects.

Bodily-kinesthetic: special skill at manipulating objects and tools. They often can't sit still for long; they love keeping their hands busy. They frequently fail where the above skills aren't involved, but these are our society's athletes, dancers, inventors, mimes, carpenters, plumbers, and sculptors.

Interpersonal: talent for understanding, perceiving, and discriminating between peoples' moods, feelings, motives, and intelligences. Is it any surprise that this set of individuals provides our politicians, religious leaders, teachers, and therapists?

Intrapersonal: a remarkable ability to understand one's self. These folks thrive on self-directed projects and self-paced learning. They're highly contemplative, self-aware, imaginative, original, patient, disciplined, and motivated, with lots of self-respect.

Naturalist: fascinated by plants, animals, and other features of the earth. Sadly, these children often fail if not motivated or rewarded by such interests, but the persistent will become veterinarians, forest rangers, ecologists, farmers, animal trainers, and scientists.

Remember, no one is restricted to only one of the eight intelligences. And the point is, if schools and standardized tests focus on only two of the above, it leaves massive potential for others to feel like failures despite their innate talents. Parents can correct for this simply by expanding their own viewpoint accordingly, and positively reinforcing those talents less valued at school. A very readable book on this topic is *Pathways of Learning* by David Lazear. Some parents go so far as to homeschool or move their children to one of the many alternative schools that incorporate multiple intelligences into their philosophies.

Both research and anecdotal evidence indicate a tremendous success rate in charter and home schools that use an encouraging approach. Students labeled as failures in traditional schools thrive in environments where they are allowed to learn in their own way, often pursuing the arts in a non-competitive classroom. One educator even calls the traditional school a "worksheet wasteland," an indictment on the high rate of students who suffer from a hatred of school and fail.[145]

Learning Styles

Better known than the eight intelligences are the so-called three "learning styles": auditory, visual, and kinesthetic.

Auditory learners like it when parents read in a dramatic way, encourage them to talk more than write, and give directions aloud.

Visual learners understand best after being shown; they especially like diagrams, charts, pictures, films, to-do lists, and written directions.

Kinesthetic learners like to touch, feel, and experience. They thrive on skits, field trips, and hands-on learning.

Everyone starts out as a kinesthetic learner in kindergarten. Some gravitate to visual around second or third grade. In late elementary, some gravitate to auditory.[146] We use the word "gravitate" rather than "evolve" because no one style is better than another.

But here's the kicker: Auditory learners form forty percent of the school-age population, and they're mostly girls. Kinesthetic learners form twenty-five percent, and are mostly boys.[147] Parents and teachers (the latter are especially likely to be reading/writing oriented) often interact with students in their own preferred style, rather than the one best for the child,[148] but adults who become aware of this can make simple adjustments to help the child thrive.

Numerous websites offer do-it-yourself tests to help individuals figure out their best learning styles (yes, most people have more than one). One site, which prefers the term "learning preferences," even has a version for kids ages twelve to eighteen, and splits the "visual" category into "symbolic visual" and "visual text" (www.vark-learn.com).

Clearly, knowledge of learning preferences or styles offers parents and children themselves valuable insights for learning more easily and effectively, and preventing that downward spiral in self-confidence.

Schools that provide alternative teaching methods and nontraditional approaches to these learners often foster success. We recommend reading Thomas Armstrong's *The Myth of the ADD Child*. Stories abound of students labeled as failures in traditional schools, who happily begin to flourish in non-competitive, collaborative environments. Locating a program structured on Adlerian philosophy or multiple intelligence theory is indeed a boon for a child struggling with ADD/ADHD and/or LDs.

Brains and Hormones

If boys and girls are different, is that how they're born, or the way we raise them? We can't emphasize enough what a silly question this is, because the answer is obviously *some of each*. Experts will never agree on *exactly how much* is nature versus nurture, nor *exactly which types* of behaviors align with which.

And that's okay, because parents don't need to get into the murky debate over how differently wired brains and hormones can affect language and learning, to get the information they need to raise their sons well. They just need to stay open-minded to the fact that there are differences, both physical and cultural, and that their parenting style will have only limited influence against these. While a degree of skepticism is healthy, it is counterproductive to ignore all the science. If women are particularly wary of the nature-versus-nurture debate, that's understandable, given that they've been the ones most hurt in the past by misinformation and manipulations.

As Christina Hoff Sommers says in *The War Against Boys*, "It wasn't all that long ago that intelligent men were deploying the idea of innate differences to justify keeping women down socially, legally, and politically. The corrective to that shameful history is not more bad science and rancorous philosophy; it is good science and clear thinking about the rights of all individuals, however they may differ."[149]

In recent years, key developments in many areas of science (neuroscience, evolutionary psychology, genetics, and neuroendocrinology) confirm the many differences with which boys and girls are born; in other words, differences that scientists pretty much agree can be chalked up to nature, not nurture.

Here's the key one: **Girls' brains tend to mature earlier than boys'.** That's why girls develop faster than boys in many ways, but *especially as regards reading, speaking, and writing.* The gap shows up at around age three, and closes about the time boys hit seventeen.[150]

Most people accept this in the preschool years; it seems everyone knows about it and alters their expectations accordingly. But by kindergarten, parents and teachers are wary of treating kids differently, or allowing for different sets of expectations based on gender. Add to that the trend toward kindergartens focusing on academics over activities that kids initiate (which favors girls over boys), larger class sizes (leading to "crowd control" measures to which girls adapt more easily than boys), and the lack of male teachers in elementary schools (allowing for inadvertent biases, like a lack of tolerance for squirming boys).

Now add the next key factor: **Boys tend to be more impulsive and need to move around more than girls.** Not a problem as long as parents and teachers accept this. But as the number of male teachers (and principals) has decreased in elementary schools, class sizes have expanded and energy-absorbing activities like art, gym, drama, and recess have been cut back, boys' natural energy is often seen as unnatural. Hence, the skyrocketing number of boys referred to those who would prescribe drugs to calm them. Have parents and teachers begun to see boys as faulty girls?

As they progress through elementary grades, boys feel the ever-heavier weight of disapproval. What parent isn't distressed when phoned by the principal or given a negative report at a parent-teacher conference? Imagine being told your son is not reading well (compared with whom?), not reading the "right" things (determined largely by female teachers and female librarians), and not settling into writing exercises (which may be heavily skewed to what females like as we discuss in Chapter Nine).

Any tolerance adults have for boys' language lag in preschool disappears by the time boys reach puberty, likely a major contributing factor to boys developing a negative view of their own language skills and beginning to tune out. The exceptions, as we've pointed out before, are the "elites," typically blessed with strict time limits on screen time at home, ample literary encouragement from their families, positive reinforcement at home for what reading and writing they are doing, and positive male role models in their lives.

Basically, differences in brain structure, hormone levels, and speed of maturing work against boys when it comes to reading, writing, and impulse control.[151] But the existence of "elite boys" proves that those who get encouragement and support can thrive.

As Michael Sullivan puts it in *Connecting Boys with Books 2*, "The reading gap can be explained largely in terms of brain development lag, making it much less frightening, because boys' brains eventually catch up, presumably along with their ability to handle language. What then becomes the issue is how we treat children while this brain lag exists, because the development lag really disappears only during the last stages of high school, and by then we have little opportunity to make up for any ground lost."[152]

The trick for parents is to give boys a more physical learning environment (let them be antsy, handle materials, illustrate or act out stories), give them more frequent breaks, and do whatever it takes to keep them supported and motivated until the gender gap starts to close so they won't label themselves stupid or lazy and give up. In other words, patience is required when it comes to boys' reading and writing. And starting them on reading themselves before they're ready (age five or so) can backfire.[153]

SET HIGH STANDARDS

"One thing I've noticed over the years is that some parents are reluctant to set tough academic standards for their children with learning disabilities (LD). They fear that setting the bar high will cause their kids to become overwhelmed and filled with anxiety.

"In reality, that attitude does more harm than good. Their insecurity comes across as a lack of confidence in their child's ability to do well in school. Truthfully, many students with LD want to be challenged!

"Every day, students with LD are reminded that they learn differently. From the support they receive to the accommodations they're given, the message is loud and clear: 'You don't learn like everyone else, and because of that you need special treatment.'

"Parents have an opportunity to counter the message kids get at school. By maintaining high academic standards and holding their children accountable for their schoolwork, they telegraph their belief that their kids can achieve at levels equal to if not better than their peers.

"For students with LD, school is often not a safe zone. They may spend a large part of the day feeling out of place and discouraged. Home, on the other hand, is a safe haven. It's an environment where the pressure is off, and they're free to explore who they are and gain self-awareness along the way.

"Parents should take advantage of that comfort level and push their child academically, helping her to gain confidence and develop the determination to succeed. With consistent encouragement and accountability, students will internalize the belief that they can meet any academic challenge that comes their way.

"I learned that lesson early on, and it's one I've never forgotten. When I was in fifth grade, one unit of my history class was dedicated to the Colonial era. My father, a history major, helped me through this class, explaining topics I didn't understand. But as a student with LD, tests were hard for me! On the first test my grade was thirty-two percent. I was pretty disappointed and nervous about showing my father, even though I was sure he would tell me it was okay. Instead he responded with the most motivating words I have ever heard: 'I don't ever want to see a grade like that again.'

"Harsh, yes for a ten-year-old, but empowering! I knew exactly what he meant: He had confidence in me, knowing full well I could do better. On the next exam I studied with dotormination and got a 100 percent! I couldn't have been prouder to show him that grade!"

—SAMANTHA TURNER

(Reprinted, with permission, from the Smart Kids with LD website at www.SmartKidswithLD.org; copyright by Smart Kids with Learning Disabilities®.)

Counter opinion: "I disagree with recommending pushing one's child academically," says Philippa Slater, director of the Learning Disabilities Association of British Columbia. "Each child, according to their make-up, reacts differently to their LD. Some are far more resilient than others. Some are very fragile. Any pressure has to come with a great deal of homework support and informed sensitivity to how much harder these kids have to study. As LD expert Richard Lavoie says, 'They have to work twice as hard to get half as far.'" (www.ricklavoie.com)

EVER RESTLESS

"I was a bad kid because I tapped my foot. And then I started tapping both feet; next I began drumming my fingers.

"In reality, a handful of kids in every classroom in America does the same thing. Eventually the teacher says, 'What is your problem?' That happens to be one of the most damaging statements you can make to a child. The child naturally concludes he has a problem or is broken in some way.

"Ironically, science tells us otherwise. We now know that kids who tap their feet are not doing so because they're bad, or trying to be irritating, or because they're on their way to a life of crime. They're doing it because it accesses a physical motor memory that facilitates focusing. It's what that child needs to do in order to learn.

"When the teacher yells, 'Focus!' it stops the tapping—but it also stops the learning."

—JONATHAN MOONEY, COAUTHOR OF
LEARNING OUTSIDE THE LINES: TWO IVY
LEAGUE STUDENTS WITH LEARNING
DISABILITIES AND ADHD GIVE YOU THE TOOLS
FOR ACADEMIC SUCCESS AND EDUCATIONAL
REVOLUTION, **AND** *THE SHORT BUS: A JOURNEY*
BEYOND NORMAL.

(Reprinted, with permission, from the Smart Kids with LD website at www.SmartKidswithLD.org; copyright by Smart Kids with Learning Disabilities®.)

WORDS AND NUMBERS TO PONDER

More than six percent of school-age children are currently receiving special education services because of LD—at least seventy-three percent of them boys.[154]

When *research* is used to identify students with LD, half are boys, half are girls. But when general or special education teachers do the identifying, twice as many boys as girls are given that label. Could that be because most of the people referring them are teachers frustrated by (and not trained or supported to deal with) some of the characteristics of LD (acting out, disruptiveness, impulsivity, etc.)?[155] Doctors are too quick to assume boys have

ADHD and put them on drugs, says Joel Bakan in his persuasive book, *Childhood Under Siege*. In *Boy Smarts*, MacDonald recommends embracing boys' spirited nature rather than seeing them as "abnormal or defective."[156]

Sixty-seven percent of young students at risk for reading difficulties become average or above-average readers after receiving specialized instruction in the early grades.[157]

Albert Einstein couldn't read until he was nine. Walt Disney, General George Patton, U.S. Vice President Nelson Rockefeller, Whoopi Goldberg, Thomas Edison, and Charles Schwab had learning disabilities, yet were successful.

JAY'S STORY

Cynthia noticed something different about her third son, Jay, long before he reached kindergarten. During family reading time, he would restlessly color or fiddle with books while his older brothers listened attentively. She knew enough to allow him to be restless because she knew he was still listening, and how else would she get any books into him? But her instincts told her that his inability to sit still or focus was not typical boy stuff.

His first-grade teacher noticed the same issues and worked with Cynthia and her husband to get Jay diagnosed as having ADHD. They noticed Jay's reading increase and improve immediately after he started taking Ritalin. But it wasn't enough to restore what Cynthia refers to as his lack of a social antenna and his dwindling self-confidence.

By the time Jay was old enough to ride the bus to school, he was trying out impulsive, attention-getting behavior that worked against making friends, like insulting children five years older and then feeling mystified when they were mean back. And although he was very intelligent, his schoolwork and other activities suffered from his hyperactivity.

"He would get singled out for discipline in almost every activity, even drama and Sunday school," Cynthia recalls. "He began to see himself as a loser very young. Even though you can medicate them and help them read well, it doesn't always help self-esteem unless they get more help. Plus, teachers and authorities don't always know how to deal with ADHD kids. In retrospect, I think we put too much stock in Ritalin."

In grade three, Jay was nearly kicked out of school for ongoing attention-getting behavior like declaring he intended to commit suicide. His parents, unaware of an ADHD child's needs, reacted like many parents, using punitive methods such as labeling, shaming, and punishments. Jay's father had less tolerance for his youngest son's antics than Cynthia, and he and Jay had a difficult relationship for some of Jay's formative years. However, they have an amicable, even close relationship today—evidence of children's resilience and what a parent's perseverance can accomplish.

Here is how Jay, now age twenty-seven, recalls his childhood: "I was above the norm at reading and writing and I was in an advanced math class. But I was bad at doing my schoolwork. I was lazy and have a hard time keeping my mind on something I'm not interested in at that moment. I'm kind of scatterbrained. And getting myself to study for a test took more effort than normal; I was strong-willed in not wanting to do that." He recalls hiding his actual reading level from friends. "That's pretty classic with most boys. The more aggressive guys are often the more unintelligent."

Cynthia has some regrets about her own handling of Jay: "I was too easy on him. I tried to make up for his problems by being too coddling, yet in so doing, I ended up spoiling him. In my own confusion, I vacillated between being too easy and too harsh."

Despite the challenges, Jay tried hard to succeed at school until he hit ninth grade, when he all but gave up. His parents enrolled him in an alternative school at that point, which Jay acknowledges helped him for a while, even though he didn't feel entirely comfortable with his fellow classmates. "The majority of kids in there were kids others were scared of. People started to look at me more like I was a criminal than a dork, and at the time, I kind of liked that. At sixteen, you have to find a group of people you fit in with."

Before his senior year, Jay dropped out, experimented with drugs, and ran away from home. Even so, he knew he wanted that high school degree. When he entered a General Education Development program to achieve it through taking tests (typically a year's process), he blew administrators away by attending only two classes, then passing all five tests on the first try.

Today, Jay maintains a close relationship with both of his parents. He's training to be an actor, and proudly names reading as one of his hobbies. Looking back, he particularly appreciates that his parents had a house well stocked with books, and emphasized the importance of reading with their kids: "Unlike television and music, books build your own imagination. They help you create rather than just consume and watch. Reading is good, school is important; knowledge is power and the more knowledge you have, the happier you'll be."

HAPPY ENDING

In *Boy Smarts*, Barry MacDonald tells the story of a truck driver who, when told his son had ADD, thought it meant his son needed more attention. So he began picking his son up from school and letting him ride along on his end-of-day deliveries. He also included him on long-haul trips over school holidays. They spent their time together talking about their lives and interests, eventually becoming comfortable enough to bring up topics about issues previously avoided. After several months of this, the school informed the father that the ADD problem had completely disappeared.[158]

CHAPTER FIVE

DADS AND OTHER ALPHA MALES: THE ROLE MODEL FACTOR AT HOME

"Adolescent boys have to know that they're at the center of the lives of one or more men they respect If they know they're at the center, they'll be okay."

—TERRY TRUEMAN, AUTHOR AND THERAPIST[159]

A FEW YEARS AGO, PAM WAS TELLING SOME sixth-graders about an upcoming sports novel she was writing when a boy eagerly volunteered his dad to work with her as an expert on the topic.

"Perfect!" Pam said.

When the boy's bemused father confirmed that he did indeed have experience in the sport and would be willing to offer background, Pam mailed his son an autographed copy of one of her teen books to thank him.

"He couldn't put it down," the father told Pam at their next meeting.

"That's great!" she replied. "So now you know what to get him for Christmas—another book from that series!"

The father blanched. "Oh no, I'd never get him a book for

Christmas. He'd kill me."

Pam was too stunned to respond. Imagine! A middle-school boy was enthused about reading (fiction, even), and his father was convinced that he didn't need to support or encourage that. The dad believed that his son's interest in electronic gadgets and sports equipment should overrule a golden opportunity to send a message about the importance of reading. In later conversations, Pam learned that the dad, a successful businessman, had not been a strong reader himself as a child. So clearly, he was projecting his own childhood feelings about books onto his son—and at an age where children (especially boys) are in desperate need of strong role modeling from parents on the importance of reading.

It was great, of course, that this dad spent time with his son. But he seemed to be missing one piece of information: In today's information age, reading is key to academic achievement like never before. With each passing generation, it's harder and harder to achieve any type of success (including business) without more reading and education than one's parents had. As we've already said, today's college degree is equivalent to yesterday's high school degree. And children whose interest in reading wanes before high school are the ones most likely to be left behind.

Too many parents believe that teaching their kids to read is the school's job, and too many a dad leaves at-home reading to his wife. But a comfort with reading begins at home, and boys—especially in their preteens, the age where their reading may slump—are all too aware of male versus female role models.

Boys begin forming gender identity at around age three,[160] but their need to watch and emulate a male role model really ramps up with puberty.[161] Even boys successfully raised by single mothers hunger for elder male attention because it's hardwired into their brain, says Michael Gurian in *A Fine Young Man*.[162]

Yet parents tend to overlook the importance of dad reading to the kids. They don't realize that regardless of how often a mother reads to her son, it's how often a *male* reads to him (or silently near him) that helps determine how well he takes to reading. Dads who read only at work or in rooms away from their sons, dads who leave kids' bedtime reading up to moms, and dads who don't make an effort to read a variety of materials themselves (including fiction) within sight of their children, are missing out on an opportunity of a lifetime to set their sons on a track for success. They should also take their sons to libraries and bookstores, and remember to select a book for themselves while there—again to role model.

In one study, when asked who does most of the reading at home, students in various grades responded their mothers fifty-five percent of the time and their fathers about six percent of the time. (Thirty-seven percent said both.)[163]

A literacy expert recalls a mother approaching him to say, "I've read to my daughter and son an equal amount, and my daughter is a keen reader but my son is a reluctant reader. Why?"

The expert responded, "Does your husband read to your son?"

"Of course not! He's way too busy."

"Then that's your answer."

The mother was dumbfounded. It had never occurred to her how crucial gender role modeling was. Another young mother who heard that story promptly reassigned the weekly job of driving her preteen son to a local book club, to her husband. Luckily, her husband was open to that, and made the evening into a true guy's night out, with a stop for cinnamon buns along the way. Their son remains a keen reader and high academic achiever as he enters his mid-teens.

Home is where comfort lives: the place to which a happy boy

can come bursting through the door and relate exciting things that happened that day, and where an unhappy boy can feel a warmth and support that slowly revives him from a bad day at school. Ideally, home is where he can cuddle into a lap for reading time when he's young, and dabble in reading and writing beyond school assignments when he's older.

Of course, we live in a less than ideal world, with single and busy parents who sometimes find themselves wringing their hands over what they're doing wrong and how to do things better. On average, fathers spend less than five minutes a day interacting with children by the time those children are adolescents.[164] Divorced fathers spend an average of two to four days a month with their biological offspring.[165] And more than half the kids born today will spend at least some time in a home without a father by the time they graduate from high school.[166]

But no one said that all male role models had to be dads. Wise moms who steer their prepubescent sons to other positive male role models (grandparents, uncles, friends, mentors) can reap enormous benefits, as we'll discuss further in Chapter Seven.

In any case, whatever a home's profile, it can and should beat out the influence of school, peers, and media by a mile. Don't doubt for minute that parents remain children's strongest influence, far more so than we believe, especially when it comes to reading. As Kropp has said, "The great part of reading together at home is the one-to-one interaction. No school program can provide this, and no teacher can give a child a kiss for sounding out a tough word or reading aloud a page. And everything a child reads at home can be of interest to him, not just books selected by the curriculum."[167]

Here are further reminders of parents' importance:

Studies consistently link parental involvement to school success, even as kids enter high school. Students of parents who visit school regularly and encourage education at home have higher social skills and lower rates of problems such as depression.[168]

Parents of middle schoolers who set clear expectations, foster goals, help with studies, and put a high value on education—but do not do their children's homework for them—make a difference in their children's achievement.[169]

Studies show that fathers are far less involved than mothers in all types of school activities. Yet, "even when fathers have limited schooling, their involvement in children's schools and school lives is a powerful factor in children's academic achievement."[170] (See sidebar, "Volunteer Dads Become Top 'D.O.G.S.'," on page 121.)

These are all reasons why we've chosen to examine the male role-model factor in boys' reading, writing, and academic achievement. Besides, mothers and fathers typically parent differently. Dads tend to be more hands-off (offer less attention and guidance), are more tolerant of risk-taking, encourage more independence, apply a competitive approach ("Bet you can't be sitting down and starting your homework in three minutes flat!"), and have a way of putting a quick end to displays of emotion. Mothers are more inclined to be empathetic, encourage dependency, and place an emphasis on everyone getting along.

Also, parents *help* daughters more than sons with homework but *check* the homework of sons more than daughters. Before kindergarten, mothers read and interact verbally with sons less often than with daughters. Parents attend more school events for their daughters and are more likely to talk with school officials about their boys (presumably about their behavior). They also place greater restrictions on the socializing of their daughters.[171]

Mom's influence is strong in that mothers are usually more involved in day-to-day parenting, and there are more single-mother than single-father primary caregivers. More than twenty percent of U.S. children are raised with a mother but no father in the home, while only four percent are raised with a father but no mother. Zoom in on black communities, however, and those statistics tilt dramatically. More than half of all black children under the age of eighteen in the United States have just one parent[172] and nearly half of all black children under age fourteen in Canada.[173] That has prompted commentators, like Rev. Eugene Rivers (president of the National Ten Point Leadership Foundation, www.ntlf.org), to remark, "The violence now being witnessed in...poor black neighborhoods is ultimately the voice of political orphans being denied the firm discipline and direction of the black fathers."[174]

So, regardless of the makeup of a household, many kids miss out on the male parenting approach and its benefits. Benefits? Yes, according to Gurian, discouraging displays of emotion can lead to better control and stabilization of emotions in boys, faster maturity, and less impulsivity and violence, especially in puberty. He also notes that engaging in competition fits well with the way a boy's brain is wired, and leads to experiencing failure now and again, which promotes growth.

In short, few people understand boys as well as men, even if men's parenting approach is subconscious and often criticized by moms who haven't read or bought into Gurian-style theory. And however bonded a boy is to his mother, by puberty he's on the lookout for, and needs, male role models too.

Boys must feel their mother's love and acceptance, then they must separate from her pre-puberty. Then learn from their primary male mentor, American poet and social commentator Robert Bly has said.[175]

If a child's emotional life has matured under a balance of male and female influence, says Gurian, "the child has a good chance of growing up with the ability to be empathetic and reserved, able to lead and to follow, emotionally stable and yet capable of joy."

An imbalance—defined by the following five factors—can prompt emotional neglect or trauma:[176]

1) the lack of an emotionally nurturing father and/or primary male mentor,
2) the lack of emotionally nurturing secondary male mentors such as teachers, coaches, grandparents, and family friends, who build on the influence of the father or father substitute,
3) a lack of adequate female nurturing,
4) a lack of spiritual development (nature, religion, etc.),
5) over-immersion in a cultural system that limits the emotional life of masculinity (i.e., too much time with video games and other sources that offer limited stereotypes of males or discourage emotion).

Again, organizations like Big Brothers can help supply positive male role models (more on that in Chapter Seven). But, some might wonder why a boy needs both a primary and secondary male role model, neither of which needs to be a father. It may be because females thrive on fewer bonds, whereas boys need lots of relationships, preferably centered around activities and involving both elders and peers, to get the emotional stimulation they need.[177]

Boys also recover from the trauma of their parents divorcing more slowly than do girls. If it happens when he's a preteen or adolescent, the disruption of a natural process of separating from his mother and forming a stronger gender identity can have serious consequences: "He wants to bond ever more powerfully with her because of the father's absence, but is equally compelled to pull away from her," says Gurian. He notes that three-fourths of crime in the U.S., and even more of the violent crime, is committed by males raised by single or divorced mothers. These males have less structure and fewer relationships that promote "appropriate masculine emotional development," he says.[178]

But hey, these kinds of findings can be taken too far. As Gina Panettieri says in *The Single Mother's Guide to Raising Remarkable Boys,* "Many teachers automatically believe that a boy being raised by a single mother is more likely to be learning-disabled, to have discipline problems, to be hyperactive, and to have serious deep-seated emotional problems even if he doesn't."[179] We think those last words are worth repeating: *even if he doesn't.*

What we are trying to emphasize is that even though this book focuses on *academic* achievement, achievement in general involves not just literacy, but *emotional literacy.* Emotional literacy (covered more in Chapter Ten) starts with the ability and the guts to express feelings succinctly, such as, "I feel rejected." It takes strength of character to do so. It takes practice. And it takes positive reinforcement on the part of a role model, especially a male role model, for a boy to dare try it more than once. After learning how to identify and express their feelings, boys need to learn how to manage them, especially as they relate to others. Empathy is a main characteristic of emotional literacy. Daniel Goleman's well-known book *Emotional Intelligence* gives a more comprehensive look at this ability, so crucial in today's world.

Reading itself can contribute to emotional literacy, as we'll explore in Chapter Eight. But far more important is time spent with male role models—and mom's acceptance of that fact, and the way she encourages or arranges men to play a greater role in her sons' lives.

Another ingredient of achievement is self-esteem, and that too differs between boys and girls. Common knowledge has it that in our male-dominated society, boys have tons of confidence and girls don't Nope. Boys fake it better than girls, sometimes to their own detriment, and parents need to wise up to that.

So here's a parent's primer on self-esteem and boys. When it comes to expressing personal shortcomings, boys and girls are subject to entirely different codes. Boys are less likely to acknowledge any, and are less likely to seek help or advice. Girls, on the other hand, might exaggerate their weaknesses or their need for help. Also, grades and reading ability aren't high on a male's "pride" list; they play a smaller part of boys' self-esteem than for girls, especially as they get older.

In short, boys have just as much or more academic self-esteem as girls *even when they're performing less well* than girls. In other words, their self-esteem is often built on thin ice. Ice that cracks as they grow older: One study found that boys' pride in their schoolwork dropped from fifty-three to sixteen percent between elementary and high school.[180]

Boys often fear that openly showing enthusiasm for language arts can undermine their status as a male, says Newkirk in *Misreading Masculinity*.[181]

What's the best way to counteract that? A male role model coaching him otherwise (with stories from his own boyhood, definitely not with lectures). Like old Uncle Joe's story of how he got kicked when he was trying to milk the cow: "Instead of admitting it, I tried to pretend I was okay. But when Dad saw me limping, he figured it out and asked me if I was brave enough to admit what happened. With a joke, he teased me into telling the truth, which I'll never forget." Stories connect, lectures alienate. Stories work better.

Meanwhile, the fact that girls can maintain lower self-esteem despite higher performance may reflect their inclination to be more self-effacing. And boys' cynicism toward school may involve a sense of entitlement: an outdated belief that traditional male traits (aggressiveness, competitiveness, physical strength, gregariousness, an outgoing personality) will more than make up for any academic deficiencies.

"This script worked well in an industrial time," Newkirk emphasizes, but "the rules of the economic game, without their noticing it, have changed." Moms need to persuade male role models to drive that message home to their sons, perhaps using examples of family friends who've tried that formula, only to find themselves struggling or underachieving.[182] Meanwhile, remember that your son's sunny confidence may be no more than cockiness and bravado. Anger and insolence are other ways that teens try to hide sadness, loneliness, and fear about how they're faring.

There's also a difference between self-esteem and self-respect. Self-esteem is inner confidence. Self-respect is earned over time through achievement. It requires lessons learned through failure and pain—precisely the experiences mothers try to protect their sons from, and fathers unconsciously lead them toward, as discussed earlier. Finally, girls tend to focus more on self-esteem and boys more on self-respect.[183] We offer specific advice on how to communicate with boys to build their self-esteem and self-respect in Chapter Ten.

Unfortunately, too many parents think they can raise their child's self-esteem by constantly telling him he's special, and by giving him what he wants. But this can lead to insecurity (he knows he doesn't deserve that praise every time), an overinflated sense of self, or unrealistically high expectations, as Jean Twenge has detailed in *The Narcissism Epidemic*. It can also lead to children who are antisocial, who have difficulty with authority, and who have an unhealthy level of need for recognition and status (which can work against them as they try to build their careers).[184]

Some of Twenge's findings:

Only twelve percent of teens agreed with the statement "I am an important person" in the 1950s, but more than eighty percent of girls and seventy-seven percent of boys did by the late 1980s.[185]

More than two-thirds of high school students say they expect to be in the top twenty percent at future jobs.[186] Hmmm, now there's a math conundrum!

The number of high school students who said that "having lots of money was extremely important" increased sixty-six percent between 1976 and 2006.[187]

College students taking a self-quiz showed a thirty percent increase in self-absorption between 1979 and 1985, and that appears to be accelerating.[188]

What's driving this? Parents who give children too much power, such as by asking them what they want to eat/buy/play-with, or when they want to go to sleep. Instead, give them a few limited choices, pre-chosen to convey important lessons and values.

Children with too much power interrupt you, demand that you buy them certain things, and refuse to do their chores. Dr. Kevin Leman in his humorous book *Have a New Kid by Friday*, says, "Are you running a home or a hotel?"[189] Too many kids have their parents trained to nag them, remind them, even do things for them. What are these parents teaching them? Laziness and learned helplessness, not qualities that set them up to succeed. Here's how to handle such a child:

Son: "Mom, everyone at school but me has Brand Z shoes. I need some, now!"

Mom: "Hmmm, those are expensive. Do you want to earn the money for them by doing extra chores, or do you want to wait until your birthday?"

Son: "No way! Why should I? Just buy them for me!"

Mom: "That wasn't one of the options I offered. Earn money for them or birthday?"

In the short term, children want their parents to give in, but it can make these same kids difficult to handle when they're older—and can produce children who have difficulty adjusting to real-world demands.

Parents who have trouble setting limits and who put an overemphasis on good feelings tend to overindulge their kids. Parents who want to be their child's friend have trouble enforcing household rules. The solution is introducing more limits (including on screen time), enforcing curfews, assigning chores, and establishing more structured family time (dinners together, reading sessions, board-games time). (More on this in Chapter Ten.)

"Praising children when they do good work or behave well is fine...[but stop] heaping on praise for the littlest achievement and even, sometimes, for poor performance...Treating children as 'special' leads to young adults who are self-absorbed but fragile in the face of hard work and negative feedback. They feel entitled to high-status occupations but quickly become discouraged when they aren't highly successful right away."[190]

Being a role model is a big job. Ensuring that boys get quality time with quality males is an even larger task. But it represents the most important investment we can make. Our boys' future is surely worth it.

WORDS AND NUMBERS TO PONDER

Studies show that children who are positively reinforced for their *effort* do better than children who are told they are talented.[191]

Students told that higher grades lead to higher pay in future jobs are eight times more likely to work harder.[192]

Women buy nearly seventy percent of kids' books, according to *Publishers Weekly*.[193]

Students who are physically fit get better marks in school.[194]

Studies show that napping helps memory.

In the typical American home with children, the television is on eight and a half hours per day.[195] Media guru James P. Steyer recommends that parents set a limit of two hours a day with exceptions for special agreed-upon events such as election returns, the Super Bowl, and New Year's Eve specials. "Kids often respond well to limits; once they know what they are, they learn to live with them." Some parents allow children to "earn" screen time by reading: for every *hour* of pleasure reading they do, they are allowed *half an hour* of media time. This sends a clear message that reading is valued more than electronic-media time.

SELF-QUIZ:
STRATEGIES FOR RAISING AN ACHIEVER

❑ I resist praising my son for being smart. Instead, I congratulate him on hard work and determination.

❑ I provide lots of different reading materials in the house.

❑ I read to my son even after he can read on his own.

❑ When we read together, I try to make it a social activity, not a quiet time.

❑ I set aside time for him to read for pleasure (not related to school assignments) every day, ideally fifteen to thirty minutes.[196]

❑ When my son chooses something I'd rather he didn't read (comic books, toilet humor, a book that seems too young for him), I bite my tongue rather than criticize.

❑ I set aside a time each day when all electronic entertainment must be shut off, and all the family (including parents!) reads—aloud or silently, together or separately.

❑ I encourage my son to read to his younger siblings or neighbors, or perhaps even pay or reward him for doing so.

❑ I occasionally reflect on any reading struggles I had as a child, and talk about how I overcame them.[197]

❑ (For moms): I encourage my husband (or a primary male role model) to do his own reading within sight of our son, and to read with him.

❑ I encourage a guy to take him to the library or bookstore on occasion—and to enter and select books at the same time!

❑ I tell him his brain is a muscle that gets stronger with use. (Kids told this do better on test scores.)[198]

- ❏ I remind him that good grades lead to better earning power.
- ❏ I buy my kids books or gift certificates for bookstores on occasion.
- ❏ I always give the kids a choice between several types of books and remember to let them hold the book and turn the pages.
- ❏ Sometimes, after a movie, I check out the book it was based on from the library and compare it with the movie version with my kids.
- ❏ I get my son to help me make shopping lists, read labels on food, write thank-you notes, clip coupons, read road signs and road maps—anything that uses his reading and writing skills.
- ❏ I encourage my son to make up stories, and I write some of them down as he tells them.
- ❏ I buy or borrow library copies of books on tape, or tape-record stories for him.
- ❏ I've helped my son create a special place for the books he owns.
- ❏ I keep a few favorite reading materials in the car.
- ❏ I've bought all my kids bedside reading lamps and turn a blind eye to late-night (but not super late-night) book or magazine reading. However, I'm aware that cell phone and Internet use late at night is vastly different; it robs kids of sleep.

IF ONLY I HAD BEEN AN AVID READER

"Reading is important because it opens up your mind to new possibilities. The imagination allows us to think outside the box. If I had been an avid reader as a kid, I would have achieved things a lot sooner in life—better grades and such.

"In making reading a chore, parents are making their kids into nonreaders. That's the number one thing parents do wrong. Do they have a misguided sense that if they force the kid to do it, eventually he will like it? The best thing you can do to make your kid read is to read yourself. And boys need men in their life who are reading, because boys want to be men.

"Remember that when your son is the only one reading and everyone else is watching television or going to a movie or playing outside, he feels like he's being punished and that is the wrong way to encourage reading.

"As a bookseller, I see the problem as being mostly the parents. Moms come up to me and say, 'I don't know what to do; my kid isn't reading at all. How can I get him to read more?' And I ask them what their kid is reading and they say magazines, and I say, 'Then your child is a reader.'

"Often when a parent says their child is not reading, it's because they're not reading what the parent wants them to: the classics. Your child might pick up classics as an adult, and he will have the life experience by then to enjoy them. But if he gets turned off reading before then, maybe he won't."

—JAMES MCCANN,

FORMER RELUCTANT READER, NOW A BOOK-

SELLER AND AUTHOR OF TEEN BOOKS

THE IMPORTANT PART WAS THE POPSICLE

"My dad didn't read with us much at all, but we had a huge collection of children's books in our house, and I remember my grandfather always reading the newspaper. I also have lots of fond memories of my sister, who is two years older than me, taking us to the library and reading to me. The important part was the popsicle afterwards.

"But really, my relationship with reading came through my grandfather's, father's, and uncle's storytelling; I wanted to understand these stories. Boys in particular need to not just read, but build a relationship with reading. There's a big difference."

—DHANOOK SINGH,

FORMER RELUCTANT READER,

NOW A SCIENCE TEACHER

HE KEPT ME READING TO HIM

"Our second son was not as eager to read as our first; he didn't find it as easy. He kept me reading to him. It was part of him trying to control me, until he was in grade four.

"I say do it as long as they want it. Until they've been bitten by the bug, you have to keep reading to them, preferably half an hour a day. And you have to surround them with so many books—so much richness—that they can't stand not to read."

—MARY LOCKE,

MOTHER AND TEACHER-LIBRARIAN

THE HOMESCHOOLING OPTION

"I always said that I'd rather homeschool my boys because I thought the school system discriminated against young boys. This was long before I learned anything about brain development. It was sheer observation: The teachers in lower elementary school demand that boys sit still and write neatly, and that just isn't a strength most boys have.

"So I homeschooled my boys for six years, our oldest benefiting through fifth grade, our second son through third grade. Our youngest had kindergarten at home. They entered the traditional classroom at ages eleven, nine, and almost seven. We lived below the poverty level, but I'd do it again, so great were the rewards.

"These were wonderful years: learning by doing, focusing on things they were interested in, having plenty of time to engage in community service and outdoor sports, including camping and hiking, traveling, and emphasizing character development. All three of our boys love to read, and I attribute that to many hours my husband and I spent reading books to them in an unhurried fashion.

"Here's what I learned during that time: Avoid reading practice at bedtime. They are tired, and the stress of decoding words will be magnified. Let the bedtime reading be pleasurable, as you want them to drift off into dreamland with good feelings and happy images floating through their heads.

"Bond with your son over a book: Laugh together over a silly story, picture, or joke. The endorphins released will not only bond the two of you together; it will impress your sons with the idea that books are a source of good. If they associate books with intimacy, they're more likely to succeed in the world of literacy."

—CYNTHIA GILL

DINNER DEBATES

In *The Purpose of Boys*, Gurian recommends that families institute a five-minute supper-table debate about something every night. Introduce it with a question such as, "What's the best way to help poor people?" and divide family members into teams if you like. According to Gurian, both male and female brains are ready for debate by fourth grade, and boy brains in particular benefit from this type of energy, acumen, and learning technique. To ensure that boys continue to enjoy this type of exercise, critique them on their delivery more than content of speech. "These memories are resources that they can mine later, as they develop a longing to be more concretely purposeful during adolescence and adulthood."

CAR TRIP FAMILY READING

"I'll never forget the car trip we took where we read some of the *Narnia Chronicles* aloud. After a particularly long day in the car—seven hours—we arrived home with only half a chapter left to read. The boys (ages ten, thirteen, and fifteen) did not want to get out of the car, they were so riveted by the story. We literally sat in the driveway for fifteen more minutes as we finished that book. A tribute to the power of well-written words."

—CYNTHIA GILL

HAPPY ENDING

"I didn't like reading initially because I preferred being outside. I was a reluctant reader up to age twelve. My parents didn't like it; they definitely wanted me to read, and wanted me to like reading. I told them it was boring. They tried giving me different books I might like: sports, fantasy.

"We never had a lot of magazines around the house, so I definitely thought reading meant reading fiction—the fiction assigned at school. The only nonfiction stuff I read was boring textbook stuff. At home, I was also intimidated by the fact that both my sisters were smart. I figured I'd get to be better than them at sports. Let them be smart.

"My dad read the paper and *Time* magazine. He never read a lot of fiction, but I noticed he often had a book by his nightstand. My mom definitely read to me more than my father. He'd never really sit down and read with me. If he had, he would have been more of an influence on my reading; I would have considered it more of a viable activity—not something associated only with schoolwork, something I had to do because it was good for me. We'd play sports together; that was the way we would bond.

"I remember my mom reading with me, and I remember my parents recording me reading a story at a young age. I still have it and I remember my dad being a main force in recording it.

"My sister, three years older than me, went through a stage with westerns; when I was in grade ten, she and I would read western stories together hanging out on the back patio. She even read aloud to me. I enjoyed that. Again, my family read to me, but when I was on my own, I didn't get into it, till I discovered a certain fantasy series. I'm glad they didn't give up on me."

—NEAL MICHAEL, A FORMER RELUCTANT READER, NOW A FRENCH TEACHER

CHAPTER SIX

SCHOOL SHORTCOMINGS: WHAT PARENTS CAN DO

"Throughout the whole nightmare of my school years, it was weird—I really wanted to like school. I just really wanted to."

—MIKE, SON OF KATHY STEVENS (LATE EXECUTIVE DIRECTOR OF THE GURIAN INSTITUTE)[199]

"I HAD ALL THE BOXES TICKED AGAINST ME: recent refugee, person of color, absent father. I was headed for big trouble," says Dhanook Singh, a former reluctant reader whose father had a grade-eight education and whose mother left school in grade ten.

"I had three things going for me: The male physical-education teacher let me latch onto him as a much-needed listener, mentor, and disciplinarian. The male school librarian let me hang out in the school library with my male buddies, messing around. And my male physics teacher encouraged my budding interest in science."

To kick off this chapter, we've chosen to let Dhanook—who is today an avid reader, high school science teacher, and poet—continue his story:

When I was fifteen, I got caught for shoplifting. My mom

wanted to leave me in the police station overnight, but my dad came and picked me up pretty quickly.

That's about the time my dad left our family for a while. It's also when my physical education teacher, George, started encouraging me, and straightening me out when I was out of line. He became a surrogate father.

I'd known him since ninth grade. He knew we were from subsidized housing. We were pretty poor when we came to this country, so gym became my hangout place at lunchtime. George always had a gaggle of boys around him, all of them into sports. I wasn't very good at sports but I was known for trying my best. He encouraged me, and he disciplined me.

I wanted to be like George. He was really serious, a strong personality, like a sergeant. He worked us hard but at the end of the day it felt good.

Then there was Mr. Schwartz, the librarian. He'd let me hang out in the school library with my friends, being a bit loud but respectful. We drove him crazy, but maybe he trusted that some of us would eventually discover books. It worked for me. It turned out the library was well stocked with books on the only topic that interested me: rockets. I soon devoured them all and little else. Mr. Schwartz didn't encourage me, exactly; he was just really friendly and allowed us a lot of freedom to goof around between bouts of reading. I became interested in the space program. I became a fixture in the library.

That got me involved in a science club in grade ten, where the male physics teacher basically gave us carte blanche to pursue making a rocket and launching it. Our group was mostly boys and it was a really good club to be in. It was like a hangout, and he was our sponsor.

I struggled with reading and writing, but I was so obsessed

with rockets that I read a lot. If I'd ever been allowed to write about rockets, I would have gotten an A easily, but I was forced to read and write about someone else's choice of topics. My writing really suffered for that.

Still, in grade eleven we had a course on science fiction, and I got into reading more. The teacher was male and he let me read *Dune* by Frank Herbert, a very boy-friendly book with action and a plot that moved almost like a video game. And when I discovered girls in grade twelve, I started writing poetry.

When I became a teacher I had my English-as-a-Second-Language students write about "the last ten days before you arrived in this country." I heard stories that brought tears to my eyes—about kids dodging Somalian gunmen who took everything the family had, but let them live. The English in the stories needed work, but the stories were so rich and passionate.

I knew to dwell on the passion, not the grammar and spelling, in order to encourage them to read and write more. I am very grateful to all my teachers, especially my male teachers. I was headed for trouble like a lot of poor immigrant boys but I was steered in the right direction by strong male role models. As a teacher now, I do my best to pay this forward by being a strong male role model myself.

Notice how Dhanook's most memorable school influences were male teachers? Notice how the science teacher and librarian allowed for a little more horseplay and rule-bending than the average teacher—perhaps partly because intuitively they understood what boys need?

When it comes to schoolwork, a teacher's skill is more important than his gender, but as we well know, there's also the gender role-model factor. Boys feel a need to look up to men, and with so few male teachers in the school system today, who could blame many boys for seeing school and academic achievement as a girl thing?

Given that a growing number of boys lack attentive males in their home life,[200] it's unfortunate that only twenty-four percent of teachers in the U.S. are male.[201] In elementary school, it's only seventeen percent.[202]

"Of all the theories offered to explain why boys trail girls in academics, the lack of male role models tends to lead the pack," concluded a series of articles in the Canadian newspaper, the *Globe and Mail*.[203]

A columnist for the same paper declared, "I think that if we had deliberately set out to ensure that as many boys as possible would wind up hating school, we could scarcely have done a better job...At an age when they crave initiation into manhood and the company of men, they're trapped in a world that's dominated over-whelmingly by women. At a time when they're experiencing their growing physicality, they're trapped indoors six hours a day and expected to sit still."[204]

So what's behind the dwindling number of male teachers? MenTeach.org did a national study and found three main reasons: 1) stereotypes about gender, 2) fear of false accusations, and 3) low status, low pay. It's not just one of those three items; it's the combination of all three, says MenTeach founder Bryan G. Nelson. "The biggest thing parents can do is to treat male teachers with the same warmth, friendliness, and thoughtfulness as they do female teachers. When men go to a school, particularly an elementary school, they aren't made to feel welcome."[205]

How ironic to compare that with an item from a U.S. government document in 1837: "There can be no doubt [of] a deep-seated prejudice against women teachers."[206] A massive flip-flop, but the pendulum has swung too far.

Happily, there's a movement afoot to put more male teachers back in schools as well as to ensure more training and resources for both male and female teachers eager to reach male students more effectively. Parents can help by pointing their sons' teachers to books and resources of which they may not be aware (see Appendix), advocating on the school-board level and checking out www.MenTeach.org.

"What's really significant is that children need diversity," Nelson says. "When you go in the classroom and you are a Latino or an African-American boy, and you look around and see primarily European-American women, why would you think education is a place for you?"[207]

Meanwhile, it's heartening to hear how some innovative schools are coping. For instance, there was the female reading teacher who each week pinned a plastic sheriff's badge on a boy in her class, handed him some dollar-store handcuffs, and sent him out into the hallways to "arrest" a man to read to the class. Sometimes the young volunteer returned with the principal, other times with the janitor or cook or a male teacher relaxing in the teacher's lounge. (Needless to say, staff had been warned and the scheme preapproved.) In any case, the kids loved having a surprise reader each week, and the teacher achieved her goal of a male role model for reading.

It would be far easier, of course, for parents to organize dads, uncles, or brothers to volunteer at the school, or to bring in local sports stars to read.

When Cynthia's boys were in junior and senior high school, the school gardener was an uneducated man in his eighties named Herb. He interacted a lot with the students, addressing each by name. He chatted with them about his family and gave the students attention they craved. He made such an impact on the kids that he showed up in their stories and drawings. When he passed away, Cynthia's oldest boy eulogized him as "one of the kindest, most loving men."

How can parents counter school shortcomings? They can provide extra support at home (see Chapter Five), communicate more with their child's teacher (see sidebar, "Do's and Don'ts of Dealing With Your Son's School," on page 119), volunteer at school (see other sidebars in this chapter), consider alternative schooling (see alternative school information in Chapter Four and the sidebar, "The Homeschooling Option," on page 102), and/or become an activist. Activists should strive to ensure the school has a school librarian, more boy-friendly books, more male teachers, and more awareness among both teachers and parents on boys' issues and programs like those we spotlight throughout this book. (See sidebar, "Do's and Don'ts of Dealing With Your Son's School," on page 119 and check out resources in our Appendix, including Richard J. Murnane and Frank Levy's *Teaching the New Basic Skills* and websites such as www.studentsfirst.com.)

On school involvement, educator and author Paul D. Slocumb says, "More fathers attend athletic events to watch their sons play sports than attend Parent Teacher Association or Parent Teacher Organization meetings. The unspoken message to boys is that physical prowess is valued more than mental prowess."[208]

Earlier we said that not all boys do the fourth-grade slump— in other words, lose interest in reading or start struggling with it around age ten. We've defined "elites" as those who embrace reading, schooling, and academic achievement continuously. Sadly, the gap between the elites and the discouraged is growing.[209] Indeed, fifty-six percent of grown children of university-educated parents have university degrees themselves, compared with just twenty-three percent of the children of the less educated. It's not clear whether this is a matter of money or culture, but it's certainly not a given or a destiny; this type of elite is defined by parental support, whether from a single mother in a poor neighborhood or an affluent couple forever taking their son to the bookstore.

Single mothers should be aware of Big Brothers Big Sisters (BBBS) of America's school-based mentoring program, where an assigned mentor meets weekly with kids during the school day or during afterschool programming. "Some days our Bigs and Littles may talk about school, work on homework or read, then play games, shoot hoops, or listen to music," says Cindy Mesko, a BBBS senior vice president.[210]

The key to converting an underachiever to an achiever is making time for, and role modeling, a love of reading. It also means structuring household rules to support schoolwork—for instance, no television in the bedroom and restricted screen time in general. There are even inexpensive ways to support children in households with little money and children with learning disabilities (www.keenreaders.org/detroit%E2%80%99s-parent-network-from-homework-kits-to-a-library).

Arguably one of the biggest school shortcomings is teachers who haven't recognized the need to gear their approach to boys as well as girls. Concerned, informed parents can gently push their son's teachers in this direction. What do boys want from teachers, anyway? You could suggest some of these to your son's teacher, or encourage your son to do so:

1) Read aloud to the class more; assign less silent reading.
2) Let boys dramatize their reading and writing more.
3) Give them more breaks to physically move around.
4) Do less nagging about squirming and talking.
5) Set up more buddy projects such as reading or writing with a partner, even though this may require more supervision.

6) Allow alternatives to book reports and journaling—for example, dramatization, drawing, and crafts.
7) Stock the school library with more boy-friendly books; give boys greater choice in book selection. (See Chapter Eight for more on this.)
8) Appeal to boys' love of competition. (See sidebar, "Set a Timer," on page 121.)
9) Learn how to encourage their self-esteem: Give positive feedback on character qualities (for example, honesty, respect, and enthusiasm) rather than merely on performance.
10) Avoid voice tones that don't work with boys. For example, instead of barking, "Sit down, be quiet, get to work," use "I'll be glad to listen to your questions when you are sitting down and using a calm voice." (See Chapter Ten for more on this.)
11) Role model reading. How can teachers instill a love of reading if they aren't reading themselves? (Teachers fare no better on adult reading behavior than the general population. In one study, 51.5 percent of pre-service teachers were unenthusiastic about reading.)[211]
12) Use more humor and tolerate more humor.
13) Consider getting involved in the "Drop Everything and Read" program (dropeverythingandread.com), a special reading celebration to remind and encourage schools and families to make reading together on a daily basis a priority.

Sommers in *The War Against Boys* tells of a mother who was shocked to learn that one of her sons had been punished for running during recess and later almost suspended after jumping over a bench. The principal told her, "He knows that jumping over benches is against the rules, so this constitutes defiance." Is "normal youthful male exuberance becoming unacceptable in more and more schools?" Summers wonders.[212]

Then there's what's happening in the classroom. "As long as education involves the teacher talking and the student listening, then school is set up for girls, who find it easier to listen than boys," say Liz Knowles and Martha Smith in *Boys and Literacy.* Can we as parents explain this respectfully to our son's teacher, requesting more breaks and more variety in activities?

Unfortunately, parents have little control over what textbooks their kids' teachers are using. They might be surprised to know that teachers don't have much control either; it's dictated by school boards. This is despite the fact that by some estimates, eighty-five percent of students can't read their textbooks independently and teachers often know it.[213] That puts the onus on parents to encourage their kids, help them with their homework (without actually doing it for them), or hire tutors. One tip: help kids find easier books on the same topic in the library to supplement assigned textbooks. There is also the option of becoming an activist at the school board on a state or federal level to ensure more appropriate textbooks, and speaking out against curricula overly driven by test scores.

Of course, the best school support is mom or dad. Yes, you are the best positioned to empower your child to learn to love reading, especially by ensuring reading choice. You more than teachers can give your kids permission to choose their own books. Sadly, too many books they love meet with disapproval at school and at home.

Washington, D.C., bookstore manager Dara La Porte told the *New York Times*, "I see children pick up picture books, and then the parents say, 'You can do better than this, you can do more than this.' It's a terrible pressure parents are feeling—that somehow, I shouldn't let my child have this picture book because she won't get into Harvard."[214] As we mentioned earlier, books with graphics can develop a child's critical thinking and the vocabulary is often more challenging than in chapter books.

Once in a fit of generosity, Pam took her eleven-year-old son to the local bookstore and told him he could choose any two books he wanted. To her chagrin, he chose an expensive coffee table book on astronomy and (in her opinion) a low-quality nonfiction book. She had intended for him to pick two novels, but had neglected to specify fiction. To her credit, she realized it was too late to back-track and she paid for the two books. As it turned out, he read and reread that astronomy coffee table book for years, which fueled an interest in reading much more about the topic.

Many schools are out of touch with what books appeal to kids these days, especially to boys. In their defense, schools often can't afford to keep up with the stream of books coming out of publishing houses. A growing number no longer have a full-time if any school librarian, and whoever is ordering books may not know about the many resources we list in our Appendix. (It's worth fighting for your school library. Studies show that students who attend schools with great libraries enjoy higher levels of literacy, are more confident readers, achieve higher test scores, have better communication skills, are better problem solvers, and navigate the Internet more safely and effectively.)[215]

Of course, many teens read blogs, wikis, magazines, and books that don't count at school. Wise parents encourage this reading at home, and let the teacher know their son may be reading more and at a higher level than he or she realizes.

How else can parents steer their sons toward success? Help them see themselves as leaders. Literally say, "You are a natural leader." You have more influence than teachers for encouraging your sons to get involved in extracurricular school activities that girls have begun to dominate. Encourage them to run for student government. Volunteer to help start a boys' book club, band, theater group, or school club (outdoor, arts and crafts, science, or community-service). Helping him initiate something he thought up himself would be ideal. For instance, point him to the Me to We website: www.metowe.com. Emphasize that such involvement will look great on his resume, attract more positive attention from peers and teachers, maybe even net him a better pick of girlfriends!

The jury is out on whether boys thrive more in all-boys' schools, but few would contest that occasional all-boy classes or clubs, especially involving reading and writing, benefit them.[216] [217] Several studies show that male-only classrooms have fewer discipline problems and lower numbers of at-risk boys, and that those attending show greater academic achievement, but the option must be voluntary.[218] Such research runs counter to the assumption that when boys get together they create problems.

How key is the teacher's gender? After polling librarians, teachers, and schoolkids, researcher Laura Sokal from the University of Winnipeg found that the sex of reading teachers made no difference if they were reading standard schoolbooks. Boys were equally uninterested. What did matter were the types of books being read. In other words, while hiring male teachers makes sense for the role-model factor, Sokal's study confirms that gender role modeling is not the only way to fix boys' underachievement problem. Schools don't need more male teachers so much as more good teachers, especially those who can advocate for what boys need, says Peg Tyre, author of *The Trouble with Boys*.[219]

Intuitively, male teachers should be able to empathize and understand boys' needs better than female teachers. But the bottom line is that both genders of teachers need to better understand and advocate for boys' needs.

SUMMER READING

Once every year, the school bell releases an eager torrent of kids into our arms for months of summer fun. They leave behind the homework hassles and school tensions. As we spend more relaxed time with them, they float comfortably back into our sphere of influence. So let's help them associate the magic of summer with the delight of reading.

Summer-reads outing. Create an early-summer tradition of visiting the library or bookstore (a used bookstore will do) so everyone (parents included) can emerge with a stack of summer reads. Give your son greater choice than ever—don't hover or suggest—but feel free to do a sneak visit to the librarian or bookseller beforehand. Fill her in on your son's reading level, topics, and favorite types of books and magazines. That way, she can make suggestions, or "happen to have" a pile of reads to push his way. You can also agree with your son beforehand that he gets to choose one book for you to read, and you get to choose one for him to read. Combine the trip with a stop for ice cream or pizza so he associates reading with a fun outing. Make sure each of you tucks a book or magazine into every backpack and beach bag headed out the door. If a book has a movie version, offer to pay your son's way into the cinema after he has read the book. Better yet, get everyone to read the book before the movie so you can have a lively discussion comparing the book and movie version later.

Summer projects. Summertime is a good time for projects ranging from kitchen science experiments to building a treehouse. So grab some reading on these topics. By letting him be the boss, you encourage reading without him even knowing it. "Read me those instructions again?" you might mumble around the nails you're holding between your lips.

Road-trip stories. Road trip coming up? Great! Stock up on audiobooks with your kids' input. During portions of the ride, too, try round-robin storytelling, where someone kicks off the first line of a made-up story, and each person adds a sentence or two. This builds an appreciation of storytelling and plot building.

Media blackout. What about all the movies and electronic devices you traditionally use on car rides to keep them occupied? That's a winter tradition! Make summer different. Announce a media "blackout" period, to be filled with audiobook or storytelling time.

Reading on the fly. Plane ride coming up? Buy or borrow some books or magazines you know he'll love and wrap each one up in colorful wrapping paper with ribbon. Tell him he gets to open one every hour, on the hour, during the plane ride. This can occupy kids for hours.

Camp reading. Serve up ghost stories with the roasted marshmallows around the campfire, read books aloud by kerosene lantern, or engage in round-robin family storytelling while hiking up a trail. Find booklets on the history of the region and read them together. While building memories that will last a lifetime, plant a lifetime reading habit.

Yard-sale finds. What better time than summer to hit yard sales together? Just make sure he knows you're after books as well as toys and gadgets. Summer is also a perfect time to organize a neighborhood book swap or book club.

Double the fun. Encourage your son to bring along a friend on your next trip to a bookstore or library. Buy or check out two copies of what interests them so they can read it together. This works especially well with a how-to book, as in, how to build a toy boat or backyard teepee. Buddy reading makes reading more social and "cool."

Reading credits. Your son may feel he's too old for the public library summer-reading lists or contests, but he's never too old to propose privileges he could earn for his summer reading.

READING CAN OVERCOME ADVERSITY

When Cynthia lived in Germany, she interviewed people who lived through World War II for a research project. Several women remembered sitting around in cold living rooms (firewood was scarce), while family members read aloud from various books that they all held dear. "This helped us get through those hard times, and forget that we were hungry, cold, fearful, and sad," explained these women.

Years later Cynthia put that advice into practice on a camping trip where it rained for days. The tent leaked, everyone's shoes and much of the gear got wet. After a day of hiking, the entire family crawled into their sleeping bags, and Cynthia's husband read aloud from the *Lord of the Rings*. The mesmerizing story transported everyone to a new world, and transformed a negative day to a wonderful memory.

DO'S AND DON'TS OF DEALING WITH YOUR SON'S SCHOOL

Do's:

Find a way to contribute to your school even if you have no time for volunteering. Studies show that children of parents who help at school have fewer behavior problems as a result.[220]

If you or your spouse help the school by, say, baking, building, or repairing something, involve your son so he feels part of this home/school connection.

Ask your son's teacher what kind of reading your son can check out at the library to supplement what he's learning at school.

Develop a positive relationship with the teachers so that when you contact them, they won't be expecting criticism.

Regularly thank them for what they are doing.

Mutual respect is the name of the game. Teachers are much more likely to listen if your tone is calm.

Use constructive comments. After pointing out a concern, focus on what can be done rather than overemphasizing the negative.

Back your concerns with research, perhaps from this book.

Offer examples of what has worked in other teachers' classrooms.

Ask about extra credit opportunities to show you are willing to help your son work hard.

Be open to the teacher's expertise; this will open him/her up to receiving ideas from you.

Use "I" messages like "I am concerned," "I am hopeful..."

Use "what" or "how" questions, which are more respectful than lecturing. Ask the teacher to collaborate with you to solve the problem.

Gift your son's teacher with this book, with Lazear's *Pathways of Learning,* or with Nelsen's *Positive Discipline in the Classroom.*

Be careful!

Don't come across as a know-it-all.

Try not to coddle or shield your son from school discipline; teachers are suspicious of such parents.

Remember to avoid blaming the teacher; much is out of his/her control.

Take care not to get overly involved; micromanaging parents come across as demanding and whiny.

If the teacher doesn't listen to you, consider that perhaps when you're stressed, you inadvertently resort to negativity. Also, steer clear of a "poor me" attitude.

SET A TIMER

Boys love to compete, especially with themselves. So set a timer for ten minutes then give him reading material you know he can read. Help him with any words he struggles with then join him in counting how many words he has read aloud at the end of the ten-minute mark. (Perhaps have him read the same section twice, and take the best score.) Do this weekly, and draw a chart that records his progress over time. He will notice he's improving. It's a great way to harness competitive energy.

VOLUNTEER DADS BECOME TOP "D.O.G.S."[221]

"Watch D.O.G.S." (Dads of Great Students—www.fathers.com/watchdogs) is a program that involves fathers and father figures in schools as volunteers to enhance school security, reduce bullying, and promote the importance of education. Fathers, stepfathers, grandfathers, and uncles are asked to spend at least one day per year at their student's school volunteering. They monitor the school property, read, help with flashcards and homework, and serve as sports referees.

"It is probably safe to say that every single Watch D.O.G. serving in an elementary or secondary school finds himself with a book in his hand at some point during his day," says Eric Snow, national director. "A man came to me one time after a workshop we ran and said, 'I want you to know what this program means to me. I have been trying for two years to gain the trust of my stepson, who was abandoned by his birth father, mother, and little sister. He obviously had trust issues. The first time he called me "dad" was when he introduced me to his teacher the day that I served as a Watch D.O.G.'"

"I think that volunteer and I both needed a Kleenex at that point. I gave him a hug and thanked him for sharing his story. Even among the tens of thousands of men in thousands of schools, it's funny how similar the stories are. Educators tell us that even though fifth-graders are normally very independent, when there is a Watch D.O.G. in the lunchroom, they suddenly can't seem to open their milk carton or Thermos without help. The way the kids respond is pretty humorous and touching. Even kids that have a great mom in their life respond differently when there is a man there during the day. They want to be noticed; they want someone to say 'good job, I'm proud of you, way to go.' Also, the guys who have great relationships with their kids tell us time and time again that it really changes the dinner conversation at home. Now their kids start talking about what's going on at school because dad has a new point of connection; he has been there. It opens them up because they know that dad knows where the water fountain is, where the principal's office is, what the playground looks like, where the lunchroom is."

HAPPY ENDING

"I was an underachiever until I entered sixth grade. It was one pivotal teacher who turned me around. Other teachers all punished me for my attention-seeking antics; they'd degrade and scold me. But Miss Dusic pulled up a chair and looked me in the eye.

"'Do you understand what you are reading?' she asked me. She seemed to know I had trouble retaining information; she didn't comment about how I was behind and she seemed to take a special interest in me. She stayed after school and encouraged me to try reading material that was simpler than what we were doing in class. And I remember her saying, 'Let's see what piques your interest.' She would listen to me and then say, 'I am seeing progress!' In other words, instead of giving me the sense that I was a bad kid, she instilled confidence in me. I did a dramatic shift in school after that. I began to read for fun, and maybe because of my new confidence, I became first-chair trumpet.

"Today, I run a home business, but I also spend lots of time encouraging my sons to read. I use Miss Dusic's approach with them. I ask them what they just read about, and if they can't seem to answer that, I encourage them to go back and reread. Today my oldest son is in advanced English and writing, and my second son is studying to become an elementary school teacher. I wish I could thank Miss Dusic for her encouragement, which has now reached another generation."

—PAUL

CHAPTER SEVEN

WISE GUYS: THE IMPORTANCE OF MENTORS

"When respected others believe in a boy's potential, he can believe in himself, in the possibility and reality of success."

—BARRY MACDONALD[122]

KYHRON HOWARD, AGE FIFTEEN, WAS STRUGGLING in school and regarded himself as a "knucklehead" when it came to homework. His mother was concerned her son was heading for trouble, so she phoned the Big Brothers Big Sisters office nearest to her Newark, New Jersey home. She asked the nonprofit organization (which has a long history of matching mentors with kids needing a mentor) if they could find a black man to be a Big Brother to her son.

The agency said it couldn't promise that, since only fourteen percent of volunteers are black, compared with thirty-eight percent of black boys waiting for a mentor. But she got lucky; Kyhron was hooked up with Dan Denose, a twenty-three-year-old professional from the area.

The two hit it off from the first meeting, Kyhron feeling that someone understood him, and Dan saying, "It's like we're the same person." They began hanging out together way more than their required one hour a week—going to movies or sporting events, or just sitting around and talking. Within months, Kyhron's mother noticed her son taking school more seriously: working on his grades, doing his homework, and paying more attention in class.

Dan says he volunteered to be a mentor because back when he was eleven, mentors diverted him from trouble. He recalls making poor grades, getting sent regularly to the principal's office for behavior problems, and being all too aware of crime and drug problems on his street.

"My family came from Haiti to America for the whole American dream to benefit their children, so that we can have somewhat of a better life," he reflects. Having finally achieved that with the help of intervention in his preteen years, he felt a need to give back. (This is one of many stories from "Start Something," a campaign sponsored by Big Brothers Big Sisters, www.bbbs.org.)

A role model is someone young people look up to and want to emulate, and all boys—whether or not they have an attentive dad—crave male role models in particular. That's why wise parents do their best to steer positive guys their kids' way: coaches, teachers, tutors, extended family members, community and religious leaders.

Several years ago, hockey coach Shane Doiron of Shediac, New Brunswick, Canada, decided to use his influence with the boys on his team to instill a love of books. He started an after-game reading circle to show that reading isn't a girly thing; he gets volunteer dads to help him. He lets the boys (mostly nine and ten years old) choose the books from a pile of mostly hockey and adventure books.

He also urges the boys to read at bedtime. "I tell them to finish the day with a good book. I explain that reading is part of exercise. The more you exercise your brain the better you think on the ice."[223]

Male role modeling works and in a variety of ways: National research by Big Brothers Big Sisters has shown that kids assigned mentors are more confident in their schoolwork performance, able to get along better with their families, forty-six percent less likely to begin using illegal drugs, twenty-seven percent less likely to begin using alcohol, and fifty-two percent less likely to skip school.[224]

More than half of boys failing in secondary school these days are being raised without a father;[225] their need to watch and mimic a man is even more intense than that of other boys, even if neither they nor their mothers consciously recognize it. Failure to find a man they look up to typically leads to a stronger identification with the kind of masculinity that television, electronic games, and movies promote—marked by impulsivity, aggressiveness, and unhealthy treatment of females. Such boys are reacting to a sense of being surrounded by females during their adolescence, which includes a natural phase of attempting to separate from females.[226]

If parents, mentors, and educators falter in providing secure love and intense training for adulthood, says Gurian, a boy "will enter adulthood dominating and being dominated by...lacking confidence in himself and hoping for others to save him from his sense that he is an imposter in life."[227]

Male mentors can help: guys who become a trusted counselor or guide, an encourager and motivator. Big Brothers Big Sisters partners young boys (ages six to sixteen) with carefully screened volunteers (nineteen or older). (We've listed other such organizations starting on page 281.)

The tricky part is figuring out what you're looking for in a mentor for your son, and how to monitor the relationship once he's on board. First, observe how he connects with your son. Is there rapport? Does he listen respectfully and encourage him? Do they have genuine fun together? Too many parents want their son and his mentor to spend all their time doing homework, reading, or discussing moral issues together. No way! Connecting requires laughter and fun, and a connection must be established before there's trust, sharing, or a willingness to engage in chats about issues. Our best advice is to resist monitoring your son's mentor. Back off once they've connected unless your son communicates serious concerns.

It's so crucial for moms to remember that guys relate differently. Micromanaging the relationship will sink it, and changing mentors frequently will quickly erode a boy's willingness to build a relationship with the next one. In other words, if the guy is honest, respectful, and moral, and your son likes him, continuity is better than perfection.

As for schoolwork and reading, one former "Little Brother" told us that he gained an appreciation for reading from his "Big Brother" even though they never actually read together. He liked that his Big Brother talked about what he (Big Brother) was reading and asked his Little Brother for his opinions on the topic. And he noticed that his Big Brother sometimes carried magazines and books around with him.

Be pleased if they play video games or shoot hoops together. Teen boys are often reluctant to open up until they are doing something else at the same time. Parents and other role models who spend relaxed time with kids—no wheedling information or lecturing or nagging—build an "emotional bank account," is how psychologist and author John Duffy puts it: "If you don't carry a positive balance of goodwill in that account, it is unreasonable to expect your teenager to respond to you in a positive way. Herein lies the reason that so many teens seem to blow off their parents."[228] So, first let your son and his favorite role model establish a connection. Then enjoy watching their mutual respect grow.

Some schools match an older and younger boy to boost the younger's reading skills. The goal is to create a warmer feeling toward reading and schoolwork. These are called reading buddy programs, with a "little buddy" and a "big buddy." If your school doesn't have one, it is easy enough to hire a boy up the street for the same purposes. (You can even barter baked goods or favors rather than pay him.) Or offer to help initiate one at your school with information from this website: www.classroomconnections. ca/en/readingbuddies.php.

If your son is a reluctant reader, it also works well to cast him in the role of older reader. Tell him that if he agrees to read to a younger neighbor or sibling, you'll reduce his household chore load, increase the amount of screen time he's allowed per day, or pay him. Suddenly, instead of feeling like a loser when it comes to reading, he experiences someone looking up to *him* for his reading skills, he reads on a regular basis, and he's also able to read material a level lower than school demands (without losing face). This can boost his confidence like nothing else, without his even realizing it. (See sidebar, "Reading Buddies," on page 137.)

Don't underestimate how much a reading-buddy experience can mean. After their six children had grown up and left home, Cynthia and Pam's parents volunteered in a local elementary school, where they read to youngsters. Five years later, they were strolling down a sidewalk when a seventh-grader walked up to them and said, "You were the ones who helped me read five years ago when I was struggling."

As we said earlier, without some type of positive male role models, boys are more likely to take their cues from the "hypermasculine" behavior depicted in electronic games, movies, and television.[229] Media basically offers kids the following messages:[230]

1) What we've got isn't enough.
2) It is wrong to wait for anything.
3) The notion of hard work and effort to gain satisfaction—that stinks.
4) Life and learning is all about fun.
5) Every problem has a fast solution.
6) All problems can be solved by buying something.

When today's movies and television shows are not playing on boys' fascination for male heroes amidst violence, they increasingly feature the "loser male"; think Homer Simpson or Oscar-nominated director Alexander Payne's movies (*Election, About Schmidt, Sideways, The Descendants*). Neither depiction of males is healthy, especially for boys watching films or television for too many hours, and for boys lacking a male role model to contradict some of the messages.

Not surprisingly, academic achievement drops sharply for children who watch more than ten hours a week of television,[231] and on average, boys watch thirty-three hours a week (girls, thirty). Boys also watch more movies than girls.[232]

Research indicates that boys are particularly susceptible to the allure of digital games, and many are becoming addicted.[233] Screen time increases kids' aggression, obesity, and impulsivity while decreasing their attention span, according to doctors. A study from the American Academy of Pediatrics even indicates that watching television or videos as a toddler may lead to ADHD, even though the damage may not show up until age seven. The overstimulation "rewires" the brain, causing permanent changes in developing neural pathways. For every hour watched as a toddler, a child has almost a ten percent higher chance of developing attention problems.[234] Meanwhile, the insistent noise can interfere with a child learning to resist impulsivity and think through problems and plans.[235] However, it's entirely unfair to assume that all kids with ADHD acquired it that way.

Here are some statistics to ponder:

"Tweens and teens are engaged with media each day, on average, for nearly twice as long as they attend school. Only *two hours a day* remain when they are not on media, at school, or asleep."—Bakan, *Childhood Under Siege.*[236]

The average time teenage boys in the U.S. spend playing video games: eighteen hours per week. The average time teenage girls in the U.S. spend playing video games: eight hours per week.[237]

Average time American kids spent with their parents in the mid-1960s: thirty hours per week. Average time American kids spend with their parents now: seventeen hours per week.[238]

Average time that parents spend in meaningful conversation with their children: three and a half *minutes* per week.[239]

The digital world has reduced average sleep by almost two hours.[240] Children four and under spend seventy-three to eighty-four percent of their waking hours being sedentary, whereas they should get at least three hours of physical activity each day.[241]

These factors are working against children learning how to reflect, which is crucial to maturity.

If you winced at any of the above statistics, be aware that the American Academy of Pediatrics recommends that parents limit children's total screen time to no more than one to two hours of quality programming per day.[242] (We offer more suggestions in the sidebar, "Screen Limits," on page 136.)

Duffy's advice is to express curiosity about what's happening on their screens, rather than trotting out judgment and lectures; be someone genuinely interested in what he's watching, what it's about, how popular it is in his crowd, and, most important, what he thinks of it. "Teenagers like to be experts and teachers—it fosters their sense of competence," Duffy says. "Show an interest by asking instead of telling."[243]

More than any other generation, today's kids are either out of the home or engaged in isolated activities within the home.[244] By putting a limit on their screen time *and* coaxing them to chat about their activities while they are home (without overdoing it), you can build goodwill and their self-confidence simultaneously.

Of course, before you lay down the law on kids' screen time, look at what you are modeling with your iPhone, iPad, Black-berry, and laptop. Pam recently saw a father plop down on the sofa beside his son, who was into his fourth hour of television that day. *Finally*, she thought: some quality father-son time. But the father pulled out his iPad and proceeded to catch up on work. Sadly, proximity does not qualify as attentiveness.

Perhaps make it a parent/kid challenge: Pin a chart on the wall with both yours and the kids' names over columns that track screen time. Use it to cut back screen hours simultaneously. Maybe even provide a family electronic-device drop-box at the front door for certain hours of the day—at least for dinnertime.

A school librarian who started up a boys' reading club was curious when he noticed that the majority of boys who signed up for it were from one large extended family in the community. He asked the parents why all these boys were such keen readers; their answer: "We have strict limits on screen time."

Darian, a former reluctant reader we interviewed, remembers losing interest in reading at around age ten. About the same time, he would rise at seven each morning and sneak down to the basement den to watch television before anyone was up. One day, he arrived to find a lock on the television. It turned out his parents were concerned about his slackening interest in reading and schoolwork.

"It took a couple of days, but I was determined, and I eventually managed to pick the lock," he says proudly. Even so, he got the message, and eventually returned to reading.

"Our family didn't have a formal reading hour or anything," Darian told us, "but from the youngest age, I remember my parents would let me gather my stuffed toys around me, and then we'd make up stories about them. We did that on camping trips too, and I remember it being a really nice thing. Also, I remember a particular teacher who would read aloud to us. She was very good with her voice, and I found my imagination could run more freely when I was being read to, than when the strain of reading distracted me. Anyway, you can only read for so many hours of the day, while listening to words is second nature once you're comfortable."

Sometimes the screen-versus-reading tug-of-war isn't kids' interest in what's on so much as busy, distracted parents giving in without really meaning to, and without realizing the implications. Many parents subscribe to one of the following statements, which we've followed up with a reality-check thought.

"I can't get them off of there." (Said with shrug of surrender.)

Yes, you can, and yes, you must if you don't want an underachieving boy. (We offer tips on how to do so in our sidebar, "Screen Limits," on page 136 and in Chapter Seven.) There's also a checklist in Steyer's *The Other Parent*, and excellent information in Jane Healy's *Your Child's Growing Mind* and Nelsen's *Positive Parenting*.

"Keeps them quiet. Keeps them out of my hair. I'm glad there's something to give me a break."

"Think about it," says Steyer. "If another adult spent five or six hours a day with your kids, regularly exposing them to sex, violence, and rampantly commercial values, you would probably forbid that person to have further contact with them. Yet most of us passively allow the media to expose our kids routinely to these same behaviors—sometimes worse—and do virtually nothing about it."[245]

"Better they're here at home where I can keep an eye on them than out carousing."

See response to "Keeps them quiet" above.

"All kids do it, so it's no big deal. The social media stuff especially: helps him keep in touch with his friends."

Check out www.parentfurther.com.

"I grew up on the boob tube and video games, and I'm fine, so it's no big deal."

Prior to the 1980s, there was a voluntary code among television programmers to keep shows family-friendly till 9 p.m. Parents who grew up then may be under the dangerous illusion it's still so. Not by a long shot, as Steyer outlines.[246]

"I kind of monitor what they're watching, so it's okay."

Excellent, except for the "kind of" and the issue of hours-per-day.

Again, all forms of media have long since shrugged off any sense of morals regarding what kids watch. Instead, corporations are pulling out all the stops to make money, including intensive research into precisely how to addict kids to material, regardless of how violent and sexualized it is.

"Campaigns, products, and media content are aimed at the unique, forming, and tumultuous emotions of childhood and adolescence...Digital media push parents to the margins of children's lives, as children become immersed in the endless enticement of worlds that not only exclude us but also deliberately undermine our values and concerns as parents."—Bakan, *Childhood Under Siege*[247]

When it comes to role models in your son's life, electronic games, movies, television, and other media are not the ones you want to dominate. Happily, you can reverse the "other parent's" hold on your child. It's never too late to steer him to healthier role models.

We can use kids' interest in technology today to coax them to read, says children's author and Internet entrepreneur Mark Jeffrey. "Kids are used to using Facebook and Twitter and 'reading' online; get these kids a Kindle or a Kindle app for their iPad or iPhone—the line between what's a webpage and the page of a book can blur easily, and it may seem more natural to them than an actual bound paper volume."[248]

He's right, and here are more insights:

Twenty-one percent of adults read an e-book in 2011.[249]

Readers of e-books read an average of ten books more per year than readers of print books.[250]

Online reading increased seventeen percent between 2009 and 2011.[251]

Those who buy magazines in digital form are twice as likely as the average reader to buy more magazines each month.[252]

SCREEN LIMITS

Limit screen time to the widely recommended maximum of two hours per day, with exceptions for agreed-upon specials.

Allow your child to earn more screen time through reading. This sends the message that reading is more important than screen time in your family.

No screens in the bedroom for elementary children. It can adversely affect brain development. Technology is all but robbing younger people of their ability to concentrate and learn.[253]

Check labels of games and movies for age recommendations and stick to them.

Password protect your computer, lock your TV, or whatever else it takes to enforce your limits.

When possible, "co-watch" programs and "co-listen" to music lyrics with your children, and when you come across objectionable material, ask them what they think about it. Rather than lecture them, ask them for permission to give your opinion, or say, "What do you think I am thinking right now?" Research shows that children who co-view programs with their parents do better in school.[254]

Turn off the TV and don't allow cell phone usage during dinner. Research has shown that children who talk with their parents over dinner get higher grades in school.[255]

READING BUDDIES

A reading buddy program involves older kids paired with younger kids for one-on-one reading time. Or adults paired with children for the same. Such programs are organized by schools, public libraries, community centers, or religious institutions, or by parents who hire the kid next door to read to their kid on a regular basis. (Aim for a buddy of the same gender, experts suggest.)

Here's the best-kept secret about reading-buddy programs: The teens who saunter into a room wary of reading to some restless youngster, typically end up gaining as much as their "little reading buddy." They gain self-confidence, reading skills, academic growth, and a new desire to read.

Why? Because they thrive on having someone look up to them, and they're able to read easy books that boost their own confidence. Sometimes backing up to an easy book is just what a struggling preteen or teen reader needs, but won't do on his own.

More than that, they're sitting down and reading *for leisure* each week, something they may not have done for a long time. That's why being a big reading buddy can unexpectedly attach rocket boosters to someone's ability and desire to read, as well as build self-confidence about relating to another age group. All while the little reading buddy gains the same.

Where schools or local libraries don't have such a program, often it's parents who get them to initiate one.

How effective are they? With just fifteen hours of reading-buddy contact, one group of fourth- and sixth-graders in Oregon gained the equivalent of more than two-and-a-half years in reading abilities (www.rainbowreaders.com). Even students with as few as five hours of contact gained the equivalent of a year and a half.

HERE ARE ANSWERS TO COMMONLY ASKED QUESTIONS

Q: How can I start one?

A: www.classroomconnections.ca/en/readingbuddies.php offers two free booklets, twenty and twenty-four pages respectively, with everything you could possibly need to set up a program.

Q: How old are big and little buddies?

A: Typically, big buddies are sixth grade and up, and little buddies are fourth grade and below, while fifth-graders can fall either side of the divide. The exception is English-as-a-Second-Language (ESL) students, who benefit from being little buddies to non-ESL big buddies or peers, right through high school.

Q: How often should buddies meet?

A: It's best to meet consistently—the same day, time, and place— whether that's monthly, twice-monthly, weekly, or twice-weekly. Most reading buddy programs opt for weekly sessions of thirty to forty minutes, but anywhere from twenty minutes to an hour is common.

Q: How should book selection work?

A: Ideally, involve a librarian in this. Big reading buddies some- times bring a basket full of options and then let the little buddy choose. Studies have found that giving the little buddy options is key to the program's success.

Q: What are some tips for pairing up buddies?

A: Some programs match by hobbies, some by personality, some by reading abilities. Some hold a "get to know each other" session and then let little buddies submit three names of people they'd most like to be assigned to. Too often, coordinators take the "logical" route of assigning strong readers to weak readers, but pairing older weak readers with younger weak readers not only offers a more likely personality match; it will build confidence on the part of the older weak reader.

Q: How long should the program run?

A: Experts suggest several months.

Q: How should the reading work?

A: Sit beside one another and allow the little buddy to hold the book and turn the pages. Talk about the title, study the pictures, and pause to talk about what you've read now and again. Talk about your favorite parts when you've finished.

Q: What's the difference between a reading buddy, a tutor, and a mentor?

A: Reading buddies just read; big reading buddies aren't trained to be reading tutors and are not meant to deal with homework or academic issues.

More Tips

Let them hang out on cozy spots on the floor, rather than stick to desks. (Or, be innovative like the man who found that his little reading buddy was obsessively interested in motorcycles and totally uninterested in reading. He took the boy outside, lifted him onto his motorcycle, and read to him there. It worked!)

Meet in a place surrounded by books.

Try skits, songs, or field trips as an occasional break from reading.

Sometimes big buddies write books for their little buddies, or the two write and illustrate books together.

Remember that the bonding and role modeling is at least as important as the reading, so cut some slack to partners not reading every moment of their time together.

A QUARTER FOR THEIR THOUGHTS

Here's how to help your child learn to become an independent thinker, someone who thinks for himself and develops discernment. Cynthia taught her boys to do it using this strategy: For every "lie" they heard on television and reported to her, she would pay them twenty-five cents. One son collected a quarter for the Pringles potato chips ad, "Once you pop, you can't stop!"

He said, "Of course I can stop; I have self-control!"

Her sons still remember the game and use it in their own parenting. They're proud of their ability to engage in critical thinking.

FATHERLESS, YES, BUT NO STATISTIC[256]

"Every time I hear about another study telling me that, as a boy, especially a fatherless boy, I may be destined to fail in school, it makes me cringe and more determined to prove the researchers wrong.

"I'm one of those statistics discussed in [such studies]. Raised by my mother alone, I'm a fatherless boy (well, that isn't quite accurate; he's apparently alive and well, but I haven't seen him in more than a decade). I'm also an avid video gamer so, according to research, I should be failing in school, a nonreader, and basically a loser. And though not discussed in the articles, I have what other studies have said is also a risk factor for dropping out of school: I'm black. Hell, I should just throw in the towel. It worries me that other fatherless kids might think it's hopeless, too.

"Although I don't think the studies are always right, I agree that growing up without a father (especially if your family is also poor) can be a real challenge. And since we know this, we should be working hard to intervene before failing is a done deal.

"That's what my mother did. And though I have lots of time yet to screw up, today, I'm a happy, well-adjusted sixteen-year-old who really loves to read, already has a university scholarship waiting, and is a published writer.

"It wasn't always like this, though. When I was eight or nine, I was bullied as the only black kid in my class. I was full of anger and getting into lots of trouble. I felt really lonely and lost after my father left. My mom was called to my school all the time, and she kept telling me how afraid she was for me.

"So one day, she went to the principal's office and the two of them developed a plan, a sort of intervention to ensure I didn't end up as one of those statistics. This was the plan:

"Find other role models. My mom made sure I was surrounded by very positive adults, male and female. I'm lucky to have two big brothers who've been great father figures, and one of my uncles sort of took me under his wing. And I was lucky to have teachers, two women in particular, who really believed in me.

"Create a community family. Big Brothers Big Sisters provided a great Big Sister for me. We waited for a Big Brother for a year, but there weren't enough men willing to join up, they said. And now I have a mentor through their program, too. My mom also enrolled me in programs offered by the school, community center, church, and public library that all helped me to feel accepted.

"Nurture a love of reading. Instead of banning me from video games, my mom got me games that also required me to read (like Pokémon) and encouraged me to get books (even comics) that interested me. Gradually, I wanted to read books and, eventually, I wanted to read everything, all the time.

"Do community service. My mom and I volunteered in our community because giving back makes you feel good about yourself. I've already finished the required volunteer hours to get my high school diploma by helping kids read at the public library, and working at a homeless shelter and for the Raptors Foundation.

"Eventually, with the help of our battle plan, I grew wiser and realized I had great potential (as do all children, no matter the circumstances). I started to try harder in school, I found better friends, and became a role model myself. Suddenly, before I realized it, my life was right side up."

—HAILLE BAILEY-HARRIS

POSTER BOYS

Figuring that boys would read more if they saw more male role models reading, a library media specialist named Tori Jensen at Spring Lake Park High School in Spring Lake Park, Minnesota, convinced male school staffers (teachers, administrators, coaches, and technology staff) to pose with a book, magazine, or newspaper in their hands for photos she would turn into posters. Jensen then hung the posters around the school. The results were startling. In less than a year, the number of boys checking material out of the school library tripled, many of them students never before seen in the library.[257]

Though it was a school staffer who initiated the program, there's nothing to stop a parent from taking the idea and running with it. Especially since the program's success inspired some of the guys in the posters to do more toward encouraging boys to read. One volunteered to start a book discussion group for boys, others blogged about their favorite books and how they got started reading, and someone designed T-shirts that read "Real Men Read" on the front, and "Be One" on the back. Meanwhile, the poster idea grew until dozens of men had posed and the posters were being displayed throughout the district.

HAPPY ENDING

The staff at a small New Hampshire public library was concerned about boys not reading enough, so they decided to introduce a program to encourage boys to attend with their fathers, uncles, grandfathers, and brothers. Playfully, they named it "No Girls Allowed!"

They thought people would be amused by the title, but the local middle school turned out to be so offended that it refused to publicize the event, claiming it was discriminatory. That stirred up so much discussion that the matter became a huge news story.

As Michael Sullivan, the guest storyteller, arrived at the evening event, he feared low attendance, if not a horde of protesters. Instead, he was astonished to find a large contingent of boys and men waiting eagerly to partake of the evening's entertainment.

"It was a grand night. The children's librarian who organized the event warmed up the audience with interactive games that got the crowd shouting, laughing, and jumping up and down until the bookshelves themselves were swaying," recalls Sullivan. "We told and listened to stories for more than an hour, and by the time we were done my ears were ringing as if I had been at a rock concert."[258]

CHAPTER EIGHT

REAL BOYS READ: WHAT AND HOW DO THEY WANT TO READ?

"I stopped reading books when I was twelve or thirteen and started again when I got to the age that people weren't trying to make me read."

—CHRIS CRUTCHER, YOUNG ADULT AUTHOR[259]

GLEN AND PATTI BOTH WANTED THEIR TWIN SONS to be avid readers, so they started a family reading time when the boys were babies. At first, the infants were happy to sit on their parents' laps as board books were turned. Later, they were content to lean against their parents on the sofa as the sound of reading mesmerized them.

As preschoolers, they started wandering around the room during reading time; nearby blocks or toys distracted them. Glen, a sports coach, convinced his wife that he and she should keep reading anyway; the boys were hearing and enjoying the story even if they were pretending not to. As the boys grew older, he looked up websites that reviewed the latest books particularly popular with boys, and negotiated with his wife over objections she raised about the books' toilet humor or fighting scenes. "Boys like that stuff. If it keeps their attention, that's what counts."

When they were in elementary school, Patti let the kids swing on the backyard swings while she sat on a lawn chair and read to them. She and Glen also encouraged them to make mini-plays out of their favorite books for evening family performances complete with costumes. By middle school, Glen (for the role-model factor) took the two to a local kid's book club every week.

Long after most parents dropped reading aloud, Glen and Patti offered the story-hour option and sometimes got taken up on it. When Patti joined the school's parent-teacher association during her boys' middle school years, she helped raise funds for author visits, and pushed the idea of bringing in male authors as much-needed role models. She also volunteered in the school library and introduced the school librarian to books and websites of particular interest to boy readers.

Glen and Patti's twins are now among the minority of boys in their high school who read avidly and comfortably, and get good grades in most other subjects as a direct result.

Who has the time and energy for all that? Ah, but we need to take only a few of the lessons from above to help our boys stand out from others, and to stop or slow their slippery slide down the "I hate reading" slope.

Boys prefer different types of books *and* different ways of reading than girls. They do best when they're allowed more squirming and noisemaking during reading, and more say in the book choice. They thrive on being read to and on dramatizing their reading. They do well when no one shuts down their phases of liking the kind of reading to which highly educated (especially female) teachers and parents may object.

Boys prefer to read or be read to with others around, and more than girls, they take to audiobooks[260] and reading on computer screens. They love boys-only reading clubs. And they enjoy exchanging book recommendations with other guys.

Above all, to discover the joy of reading, boys need to find reading material they like. So what is it that they like? Adventure, thrillers, suspense, sports, horror, fantasy, and humor: also comic books and graphic novels (a classy version of comic books, as discussed in Chapter One). Nonfiction including biographies, magazine and newspaper articles, instructional manuals, business books, books on hobbies, blogs, Internet information sites, and books with lots of glossy pictures—of animals, disasters, and so on. Reluctant readers especially get drawn in by the pictures and move on to the text.

Until their brains finish maturing in their twenties, boys actually need more pictures in books than girls in order to stay engaged. No point fighting it, especially since as adults, males continue to reflect this preference.[261]

Boys are also known for favoring a fast-moving story line, lots of dialogue, and heroic quests. Boys like to collect things, including comics and series books, and when they stand around discussing and swapping them, it is a form of male bonding[262] that reinforces reading. Parents who frown on comics and series books are often missing that point. Instead, when boys request a book or magazine, buy or do a library checkout of two, so they can read it at the same time as a friend.

"Parents often scorn the type of reading that boys most enjoy," laments Miller in *The Book Whisperer.*

How can we get boys who would rather be playing electronic games to sit down and read? Make household rules that restrict screen time, and provide them with books that are just as action-packed and rewarding as electronic games. That means parents anxious for their boys to be at a higher literary level may need to slow down and be more flexible.

Scieszka, teacher-turned-children's-author, says that boys like biographies and books on science or random facts, like the *Guinness Book of World Records*. They also like books with action, especially portraying brave males facing danger or demonstrating loyalty. And they like comic books, graphic novels and funny books. "Especially irreverent humor or books that mention bodily functions...We shouldn't make [boys] wrong for liking to read what they like to read."[263]

Scieszka founded GuysRead.com, which features books that guys have told the site they like. Its mission is to help boys become self-motivated, lifelong readers. (Similar sites, such as keenreaders.org and readkiddoread.com, are listed in our Appendix.)

Gurian says guys have an "unspoken envy for warriors—soldiers, policemen, firefighters." That's why they often love fantasy landscapes, knights, television cops and detectives. "Men want to fight the good fight," he explains.[264]

Parents who are open to letting their sons read what interests them should know that a growing number of publishers specialize in young adult books, more and more of these targeted at boys. Likewise, more than fifteen publishers today (listed in our Appendix) specialize in books for "reluctant readers," also known as "high-low books" for "high-interest and low vocabulary." (Smart librarians display them as "Quick Reads" instead.)

Typically, reluctant-reader novels are written in first-person (more engaging) with lots of action and dialogue, and protagonists and subject matter that don't match the actual vocabulary level (say, sixth-grade material at a fourth-grade reading level). They feature short sentences, short chapters, and catchy covers (boys have been known to tear off the covers of books that they want to read but fear are uncool to be caught with). They're half the length of most books and many are designed to fit in the back pocket of a pair of jeans.

But here's what makes parents nervous: Reluctant-reader books often tackle edgy topics like peer pressure, conflicts with parents, relationships, teen pregnancy, sexual identity, school violence, terrorism, and global warming. Why? Because so many reluctant readers are at-risk kids uninterested in anything that doesn't reflect real life as they or their friends know it. Or they're normal teens who want a quick, exciting read that gives them insight into today's (not our day's) teen issues.

Should we let them crack such covers? First, keep in mind that many "parent-approved" classics deal with similar issues. Second, reading encourages reading, and because young adult books hook teens, they often serve as a bridge to other kinds of reading, including classics. (Just not on parents' preferred timeline.) Third, such books can offer an "in" to difficult topics of conversation between parents and teens. And precisely because they're edgy, they can force teens to think about consequences and multiple layers of meaning, which is part of growing as a reader *and* as an individual. Certainly, these books pose more questions than answers, and it's a teen's job to question and explore.

The key is to discuss the values of the books that they're reading. For example, is there any justice done in the violent story? Does the bad guy get his due reward? And if your son is reading something that includes sex, we might ask him whether it teaches respect toward women. Just be sure not to talk at him. Rather, ask him, "What do you think about this situation?" (More on how to talk to boys in Chapter Ten.)

A caution to parents: If boys aren't allowed to choose the reading that appeals to them, they will opt for other media. "If a boy gets bored with one of my novels, in all likelihood he will put it down and play a video game where he can make people's heads explode. That's my competition," says John Wilson, author of war novels for teens.[265]

If your son is reading something you are really worried about involving sex, harsh language, etc., there are ways to deal with it besides trying to ban the book. He may have brought it home purely for shock value, says Duffy.[266] "But if we as parents don't ask openly, carefully, and without judgment, we don't really know. At the very least, such a book opens the door for parents to talk with their children about the subject matter. I suggest parents read some of the same books as their children to open the door to easy discussion, seamlessly."

That worked for children's author Katherine Paterson. "Sometimes all you have to do is invoke the name of a character, and the other person knows how you feel."[267]

Beyond life experience, there's something else that reading has going for it with boys in particular: It exposes them to emotion and empathy, sometimes helps them feel less alone in dealing with an issue, and can even provide positive role models they don't have (or won't give access to) in real life. This is vital.

"Many of us, particularly those in the at-risk category, do not seek, or cannot afford, professional help," says Marilyn Reynolds in *I Won't Read and You Can't Make Me.* "We muddle through on our own, trying to heal the scars and fill in the empty spaces. Friends help us do this. Love helps us do this. Books help us do this."[268]

Keep in mind that biographies, magazines, and material on history can do this as well as fiction. Throughout history, says Gurian, males have not only learned through stories, but been "gentled or civilized" by them: "Primal stories teach boys what true manhood is," he says in *What Stories Does My Son Need?*[269]

"Especially until about age sixteen, the greater the exposure a boy gets to stimuli that do not teach compassion and self-restraint, the more difficult it becomes for him to learn such things."[270]

Moral lessons can even prevent problems, preparing children for emotional experiences before they occur, says Roger Sutton in *A Family of Readers: The Book Lover's Guide to Children's and Young Adult Literature*.[271]

Yet reading can also be therapy after the fact. Immediately following the devastating earthquake in Haiti in 2010, officials established sixty reading points in camps where children were read to or encouraged to read to help them deal with their trauma.[272]

Still, mothers who hope that pushing more novels at boys is the way to change their personalities need to temper their hopes. Our ancestors never had the intense emotional expectations of males we have today, says Gurian.[273] In fact, only twenty to thirty percent of boys like reflection as well as action in their reading.[274]

It's not that males are afraid of emotions or that they always reject books with female protagonists,[275] although one study found that boys remembered stories with male protagonists better.[276] It's that the emotions have to involve high stakes, "like a gun or mutiny," says Sutton. Maybe that explains why men's favorite fiction author is Jack London, who is rated only ninth or tenth by women.[277]

Many of the boys and men we interviewed for this book told us that it was the discovery of one particular book that converted them from reluctant to keen reader. In other words, as parents, we need to enlist all the websites, librarians, and friends we can to keep presenting possibilities to our sons, and we need to keep inviting our sons to explore options.

Unfortunately, boys have relatively fewer quality books to

choose from than girls, because some eighty-five percent of children's and young adult authors are females,[278] and they are more inclined to write fiction and topics that interest girls than sports, adventure, horror, and fantasy. (Yes, we know that some boys like to read beyond these, and that some girls like to read these topics too, which is a good thing.)

Certainly, many female authors try their hand at writing for guys, but if their sales on these books fall flat, it may be because they fail to write in a style that boys like. Offering up a male protagonist isn't enough; boys typically reject the touchy-feely characters and dialogue that make male characters "sound like chicks," as Pam's teen son once informed her while editing one of her early manuscripts. (Thereafter, he was assigned to go through each of her finished manuscripts with a "chick detector," to ensure that her writing appealed to boys. At one point, she also asked one of her publishers for a male editor, as she found that female editors were more inclined to object to the risk-taking behavior in her novels that attracted boy readers.)

In the 1980s, Sutton says a wave of women writers tried their hand at a male perspective, but their male characters sounded too much like female characters.[279] "It was as if the goal of these books was to take these tough characters and turn them into women... and I wasn't convinced."[280]

Whether it was her own long involvement in adventure sports or her pushy teen editor's feedback, Pam managed to publish numerous bestselling novels particularly popular with boys. Then she told her literary agent she wanted to write a novel for girls. Her agent's response stunned her: "Forget it. You're in an underserved niche and you've built a solid reputation. I recommend you stay with adventure books for boys." On reflection, Pam decided to take the advice, not so much for marketing strategy as because she is passionate about getting boys to read. But the comment serves to show that the industry needs more male writers, editors, and publishers, and women who can check their biases at the door.

In general, fiction popular with boys tends to have more action, faster pacing, more dialogue, and a subject and genre that intrigues. Boys are so suspicious of female authors being able to pull off a genuine boy book that publishers sometimes ask female authors of "boy books" to publish under their first initials rather than first names. That's why J. K. Rowling's Harry Potter series runs under "J. K." rather than "Joanne." On the bright side, more boys than girls have read the Harry Potter series, and sixty-one percent of boys compared with only forty-one percent of girls say they did not read books for fun before they discovered Harry Potter.[281]

Given that not only most children's book authors, but also most children's book editors and literary agents are female (never mind the children's book-buying public of teachers, librarians, and mothers), if there's a shortage of quality boys' books, it gets insufficient attention. One children's book publisher with whom we spoke acknowledged that it had never occurred to him to be more proactive in hiring male editors and authors, but that it was a good idea he'd act on in the future. Of course, that would involve finding and developing more male writers, which in turn means a real need to encourage more boys to write, the topic of Chapter Nine.

Here's more inside information: When they are choosing a book, preteen and teen boys look for an interesting title, a cover that doesn't embarrass them, relatively large print, and photos or illustrations. If there is a film tie-in, all the better.[282] And more so than girls, boys like to feel that they are reading for a reason, hence their love of technical manuals and nonfiction.[283]

In encouraging your son's say in books, take care not to make an issue of the length. Pam once received a letter from a young boy saying, "I love your books, but I only get credit at school for books over 200 pages and the one I'm reading of yours right now is only 199 pages." How sad that teachers sometimes inadvertently discourage reluctant readers from reading a book chosen partly for its unintimidating length! Which is more important, pages read or encouragement toward becoming a lifetime reader? (Pam notified her publisher, who has since ensured that her books come out to at least 200 pages!)

Again, adults trying to persuade boys to read more need to ensure that they're not defining reading as books, and especially not as merely fiction. Any kind of reading—food labels, road signs, cookbooks, menus, baseball cards, magnetic letters on a refrigerator—helps build their reading confidence, and parents have many opportunities daily to encourage it. "Son, can you read out the road signs for me while I'm driving?" In fact, Mary F. Rogers, author of *Novels, Novelists, and Readers*, says that when all types of reading are considered, men do more reading than women.[284]

Keep in mind that many boys read only to get information: fifty-six percent of boys compared with thirty-three percent of girls.[285] And adult men form only twenty percent of the fiction market,[286] so why should we expect boys to be different?

"When you're not one hundred percent confident in your reading ability, nonfiction is more accessible," teacher Kirsty Murray has blogged.[287] "You can read a short bite of something and come away feeling you've learned something. Boy readers are particularly hungry to know about the world and feel empowered by reading that informs them of how it works."

Besides, there's that empathy factor we touched on earlier: "Cognitive psychologists have found that women are more empathetic than men, and possess a greater emotional range—traits that make fiction more appealing to them," says Eric Weiner of National Public Radio.[288]

Of course, it's not useful to dwell on a fiction/nonfiction divide. After all, the two can serve as great bridges to one another, especially if an adult takes the time to pair some books (for instance, a nonfiction book on skateboarding with a skateboarding novel, or a history fact book with a novel set during World War II). Some librarians place such pairs in a Ziploc bag so kids can browse and select them at leisure. An idea parents can try at home?

"Easily half my reading as a young child was nonfiction: history, science and technology, sports," one blogger has written.[289] "I was interested in those subjects largely because I had come across them in works of fiction and wanted to learn more."

Does your son have a bookshelf in his room? Here's a thought: Arrange the books with covers out and it may encourage his reaching for them. Libraries have found that this can increase circulation for fiction by ninety percent, and for nonfiction by twenty-five percent.[290]

The bottom line is that both fiction and nonfiction are reading. Also, our goal is not just to get boys to read, but to get them to enjoy reading. Some seventy-five percent of people who *can* read choose not to. Let's keep our boys in the "choose to" club.[291]

MALE VERSUS FEMALE TASTES

Nonfiction books checked out at primary school libraries: seventy-five percent to boys, twenty-five percent to girls.[292]

Book readers overall: men, forty-six percent; women fifty-four percent.[293]

Literary readers: men, thirty-seven percent; women, sixty-three percent.[294]

Heavy readers: men, twenty-nine percent; women, seventy-one percent.[295]

Readers of science fiction and horror: men, seventeen percent; women, eight percent.[296]

Readers of mystery and suspense: men, fourteen percent; women, twenty-four percent.[297]

Readers of history and war: men, nine percent; women, negligible.[298]

Readers of science and technology: men, seven percent; women, negligible.[299]

Readers of romance: men, negligible; women, twelve percent.[300]

Readers of personal growth: men, negligible; women, eight percent.[3091]

CREATIVE WAYS TO GET BOYS TO READ

Create "whisper phones" from plastic piping in hardware stores, and read to your son with your lips at one end of the tube and his ear at the other. Teachers swear it endears youngsters to reading time!

While they're being read to, let boys draw, write about, or dramatize characters and settings. Legos or clay work, too.

Let them read the same passage several times; it can work wonders for struggling readers' understanding and confidence.[302]

How do you know if a book is too hard for your son? Have him raise a finger for each word he doesn't know on a page. Three fingers or more per page (or five percent) means he's not ready for that particular one; trade it in for easier reading.[303]

In one study, children whose parents read with them fifteen minutes per day *more than tripled* their reading improvement each month.[304]

Watching television shows with captions on the screen, including Manga cartoons, improves reading skills.[305]

Place books you think might interest him beside where he uses his computer.

In one town, parents volunteered to read spooky books at the public library on Halloween. Some of the kids who showed up ended up getting library cards and checking out books for the first time.[306]

While audiotapes are a good way to get story structure, vocabulary, and information into them, don't overdo the option of handing them the tape and accompanying book in hopes they'll boost their reading skills by reading and listening simultaneously. Sometimes they need to just enjoy the story.[307]

When a boy "owns" a book (be it from a bookstore or garage

sale), he's more engaged with reading than someone who has only borrowed school and library books.

While it's great to read to all your children at once, you can really boost a child's enjoyment of reading by giving him some one-on-one reading time on occasion. Also, avoid comparing one sibling to another for reading skills; it encourages the more accomplished one to put the other down when you're not around.

They like to read in a comfortable, fun place, preferably somewhere they're not usually allowed, like under a table.

Try taping your son as he reads at the beginning of the school year, and then again near the end of the school year. He'll hear his improvement and feel a surge of confidence and initiative to continue improving.

One mother, who almost gave up when her son refused to have anything to do with books, had an inspiration that ended up working. She wrote short sentences on flashcards and read those to him. This interested him, eventually wearing down his resistance to reading such that she was able to transition to magazines and books.

When it comes to reading, the subject matter is more important to boys than to girls. That's why adults need to put special effort into finding books boys may like while letting him have the final say (which ensures he's more engaged).

Magazines related to a hobby or special interest often kick-start reluctant readers.

The types of books boys like are often catalogued in the adult book section.

One good way to find quality boys' books is to search current and past lists of Caldecott Medal and Honor Books. For no apparent reason, these carry more illustrated male than female characters.[308]

FIVE WAYS TO READ
(PARENT WITH SON, OR SON WITH A
YOUNGER READING BUDDY)

Reading aloud: Older reader reads while younger reader follows along.

Echo reading: Older reader reads a sentence, paragraph, or page, and then younger reader reads the same section.

Choral reading: Older and younger reader read everything together.

Popcorn reading: Older reader reads most of the material, pausing occasionally to let younger reader read a few words.

Seesaw reading: Older and younger reader take turns reading, by sentence or paragraph or page.

Judge which your son enjoys most, but also vary it!

HAPPY ENDING

"'My kid doesn't read,' is a complaint I hear working as a bookseller and also as a published author, from parents. I can identify with this frustration, as I was also once considered a 'reluctant reader.' I usually ask parents one of two things: What topics is your child interested in, and what are you reading right now?

"When I was a teenager, I read dozens of comics. I also read every Dungeons and Dragons manual from cover to cover, often more than once. But because these books were not 'the classics,' they were not considered 'real reading,' and so I was forced to read books in school such as *Tale of Two Cities* or, shudder, *Tess of the d'Urbervilles*.

"There's a funny thing about forcing a teenager to read. Our good intentions tell us that if we do so, he or she will magically come out the other side of the book with a love of reading: richer culturally, and with improved grades, of course. Eventually, reality has to replace good intentions and we have to admit to ourselves that all we've done is turn reading into a chore that the teenager will avoid.

"I read two of the probably two-dozen books required in high school: *Cue for Treason* and *Lord of the Flies*. Each of the other books I convinced a classmate to summarize for me, and I wrote my essays based on those summaries. From an educational viewpoint, I was not a reader.

"Now as an adult, I ask parents if their reluctant reader is interested in comics or magazines. 'That isn't reading,' they'll often respond. When I ask what they themselves are reading, they tell me they just don't have the time for reading anymore. I wonder how we can expect our kids to engage in something that we not only have turned into a chore, but also refuse to do ourselves by example?

"At sixteen, I discovered the first novel that I enjoyed so much that I had to read more just like it. *The Druid's Tune* by O. R. Melling, now out of print, was that magical novel that turned reading from a chore into an enjoyable pastime. When I moved on to the series *The Belgariad* by David Eddings, I even took my mother along for the ride. When I finished a book, she picked it up. When she finished, we had something to talk about—to connect with. This was the step missing by everyone else who had tried to force me to enjoy reading: allowing me to read what interested me, and then taking an interest in it themselves. Eventually, I was willing to try exploring other genres.

"I grew up in a household that never discouraged me from reading comics, and my mother saw Dungeons and Dragons as a blessing that kept me from getting into trouble. All of this reading eventually turned me on to novels, and those novels eventually inspired me to write my own. So now when parents tell me that they are discouraged that their teen reads only comics and magazines, I tell them that I was the same way. When they ask when I stopped reading comics and magazines, I tell them that when it happens, I'll let them know. Then I thank my mother for giving me the freedom to enjoy reading as a teen, whether or not she considered it actual reading."

—JAMES MCCANN,
FORMER RELUCTANT READER,
NOW A BOOKSELLER AND AUTHOR
OF TEEN BOOKS

CHAPTER NINE

REAL BOYS WRITE: MAKING IT HAPPEN, MAKING IT FUN AND EFFECTIVE

"The largest achievement gap between boys and girls occurs in writing."

—RALPH FLETCHER, *BOY WRITERS*[309]

LAURA'S OLDEST SON WAS IN SECOND GRADE WHEN his teacher took her aside and told her point-blank, "Paul is getting behind in writing—in processing it, in learning the concept of it. He needs a tutor or eventually he'll get further and further behind."

Laura, wanting to heed the advice and be a conscientious mother, tried twice to get Paul into a special education class for writing, but both times her son was turned away because he "wasn't bad enough."

"To qualify, he had to be considered two or more years behind," Laura says, shaking her head. The trouble was, every project in school involved writing, and Laura (a stay-at-home mom with the demands of two younger boys as well) had enough on her hands coaxing Paul to finish homework without becoming a writing coach.

Paul soon grew to hate writing and everything to do with it.

"He did everything to avoid it; he'd become belligerent and start fights so that we'd send him to his room, and then he'd feel he'd won," says Laura. This lasted for several years. "At one point, he became so hostile that we went to a counselor, who said just let him fail and he'll learn from that. But it didn't work." (See sidebar, "Tackling Chronic Underachievement," on page 48.)

Ironically, Paul was a voracious reader; he read two to three years ahead of his classmates, and was getting decent grades in everything except writing (where he got D's, F's, and "incompletes"). But Laura felt he was underperforming in non-writing classes, and that all his grades were being pulled down by his lack of organization, poor writing skills, and resistance to writing. Almost every assignment that required writing was returned with the comment, "Expand; write more." Worse, he often "forgot" to turn projects in.

At one point, Paul was diagnosed as having ADHD and went on medication, which helped his ability to focus and organize and thus curtailed some family tension. Eventually, Laura and her husband hired a writing tutor, a children's writing-club coordinator recommended by the school. But the tutor and Paul failed to hit it off. In fact, the tutoring seemed only to entrench Paul's resistance, which led Laura to do some soul searching.

"The tutor encouraged him, but never gave him a road map for organizing his writing. Because Paul was a good reader, he knew how good writing *should* sound, and he had thoughts on what he wanted to write. He just needed to know how to outline a story, and he needed to learn some 'in the trenches' practical stuff, tricks like how to combine sentences for better flow. It was as if I'd hired an artist instead of an art teacher, someone who only supplied an empty easel and words of encouragement. Paul needed someone willing to whip out a paint-by-numbers kit, so to speak.

When I tried to talk to the tutor about this, she responded, 'I know what you're looking for but I don't teach writing that way. It's too formulaic.'"

Laura decided to search for a new tutor, and this time hired a former home-schooling mom of a boy with Asperger's Syndrome. This woman, Becky, took Paul into her house for three hours per month. The result? Paul's D's and F's turned into A's and B's. "He still claims to not love writing, but he is clearly proud of many of his writing assignments," Laura says. She hopes Paul will continue seeing his tutor right through high school.

We asked Becky what she did that worked, as in, what approaches she could recommend any parent adopt for similar success. She boiled it down to six points:

1) "I think writing is and should be formulaic! I would never throw a list of algebra problems at a child and say, 'Be creative. Just come up with anything that comes into your head.' But that's how they teach writing. I like to start with the basics and then remind them of the basics as we are writing together.

2) "I start every session by reading the teacher's directions aloud. This is key. If a child understands, truly, what he is being asked to do, it demystifies the task.

3) "An outline is essential to success; a messy outline in any form is better than no outline at all. Without this road map, writing is frustrating and difficult.

4) "When Paul brought a paper for revision, I'd read and reread his paper aloud to model a habit I wanted him to take on himself.

5) "I always hold a pencil in my hand as I talk. As I catch mistakes (and many times, Paul catches them before I say anything, because we are reading the paper aloud), I mark them in red

immediately. Again, this models the behavior he should be using when writing. Editing is a process, not an event.

6) "Lastly, I compliment anything I find compliment-worthy because students, no matter how poorly they write, need to feel successful. That way, when there are tough things to work through, they at least feel they have budding talent."

Paul's struggles with writing are more typical than atypical of boys. You thought the reading gap between boys and girls was wide? *The writing chasm is three times the size.*[310] [311] In fact, for all the attention that the math gap between boys and girls has received for decades (girls at a disadvantage and therefore needing special resources), the reading gap (boys at a disadvantage) is twice the math gap, and the writing gap (boys at a disadvantage) is six times the math gap.[312] [313]

As mentioned in Chapter Two, the average eleventh-grade American boy writes at the same level as the average eighth-grade girl. And this writing-achievement gap applies to boys in every socioeconomic and ethnic group.[314]

There are those who would say "So what?" If writing is primarily a girl thing and boys can get through school with good-enough writing competence, maybe it's unnecessary to push them beyond basics. But lack of writing skills not only loses applicants jobs; it hurts the economy. A Statistics Canada study indicates that raising literacy levels by a mere one percent would raise the nation's literacy scores by two-and-a-half percent and worker output by one-and-a-half percent.[315]

Dr. Brian R. Haig and Jeffrey D. Haig, twin brothers who founded www.MaximizeYourEducation.com, say the importance of writing skills is underrated. "Many students don't realize that the ability to write effectively can determine how successful they become, not only in school, but also in their social and career endeavors."[316] Writing skills determine employment and promotion because comfort with writing assures more effective communication, necessary for both good work relationships and getting work projects done.

Besides, in today's technological and information age, employees spend a large percentage of their day writing: emails, instant messaging, blogs, discussion boards, chat rooms, letters, and memos.

The Haig brothers say that misspelling words, using bad grammar or awkward sentence structure, using run-on sentences, and failing to clearly articulate your message all give an impression of "who you are, your thought process, and your ability to effectively convey information. Regardless of whether it's accurate or fair, your ability to write determines how people perceive what type of person you are, how intelligent you are, and how seriously you should be taken."

If you're the parents of a troubled boy, there's another reason to encourage him to write: it can be therapeutic, an outlet for emotions that boys vent with greater difficulty and in a different manner than girls.

Award-winning novelist Joseph Boyden (*Three Day Road, Through Black Spruce*) told an interviewer that writing saved his life. The youngest of eleven children who lost his father at the age of eight, he describes his teenage self as highly sensitive, deeply unhappy, and self-destructive. "I was traveling down a pretty dangerous road, getting in trouble a lot. Like a lot of teens, especially teen boys, I suffered pretty hard. I had a deep anger that was really sadness disguised as anger. Instead of turning that outward on others, I turned it in on myself and attempted suicide seriously a couple of times, once even throwing myself in front of a moving car."

Then he discovered poetry, and found that it helped him express himself. "It was very angst-ridden, bad teen poetry, but writing it totally helped." From that, he built a highly successful writing career.[317]

Writing can help kids find a much-needed emotional connection, agrees Schultz, in *My Dyslexia*. Fear of facing one's own vulnerabilities is the main reason why students stop writing, he says, and why others avoid topics they're passionate about.[318] "My poetry, like my dyslexia, serves as a giant filter for my darkest feelings and ideas."[319]

Writing in a humorous, even sarcastic vein allows some youth to get comfortable with writing before they venture into more personal or passionate topics. It's also less risky for boys fearful of being teased. Newkirk even says that action writing utilizing slapstick, parody, exaggeration, and comedic exchanges is "key to popularity among young writers."[320]

Where some (especially males) love slapstick and some (especially females) disdain it, this may be all about how their brains are pre-wired, says Daniel H. Pink in *A Whole New Mind*.[321] He adds that humor represents one of the highest forms of human intelligence. It quickly reduces hostility, deflects criticism, relieves tension, improves morale, and helps communicate difficult messages,[322] and as we'll see in Chapter Eleven, that makes it a people skill vital in today's workplace.

Unfortunately, teachers are often less open to the kind of humor boys like than parents are. In fact, school is as likely to turn boys off, as on, to writing. It depends so heavily on how it's taught, and the teacher's flexibility and training. But the best programs and teachers need parents to back them up—to encourage boys to write at home. And make no mistake: Parents have tremendous influence on whether their kids take to writing or not, especially dad, granddad, an uncle, or male tutor. Yes, as with reading, the male role-model factor is key. In fact, one Harvard study indicates that fathers influence their sons' writing skills more than their sons' reading enthusiasm.[323]

Whoever is encouraging them at home should contemplate how to go about it differently than at school. That's because too many boys get teachers who dwell on errors in their work, and address how to make it better, rather than supplying the encouragement boys need. "Children need encouragement like a plant needs water," says Dreikurs in *Children: The Challenge*.[324]

As we've long since established, with ninety percent of elementary schoolteachers being women, classrooms often inadvertently favor girls, including their writing-topic tastes and learning styles.[325] One fifth-grade female teacher admitted, "I think I respond more empathetically to girls because they are choosing topics that appeal to me, using language that I appreciate, responding to authors I admire, and so it is easier for me to be drawn into their writing."[326] A teacher surveyed on boys and writing agreed that girls tend to write for the teacher, and boys write to entertain other boys. "But I still think that if we teach, model, and practice, boys [will] abandon this grandstanding opportunity."

"Grandstanding!" the male who conducted the survey responded. "Grandstanding, which means performing to impress an audience, is a negative way to describe something that could have been described as a real strength."[327] That's an example of a bias against boys at school that parents can eliminate from the home.

While girls may throng to a writing teacher in hopes of encouragement, boys who do so can lower their status in the eyes of other boys.[328] Again, there are no such restrictions when boys step through the door after school. If only mom and dad made the time and knew how to encourage their writing at home!

Parents should also consider the fact that because teachers need a break from class boisterousness, reading at school is typically assigned as silent, solitary work, and only rarely as a discussion topic or partner/team project. Besides, teachers know that in general, girls and "elite boys" respond well to reading as quiet time.

So parents might introduce a writing session that's livelier—one that pairs their son with a friend or sibling. It might involve a writing activity particularly popular with boys: writing songs for a rock band or a script for a play or movie (to be performed for you later, of course).

Parents can also spearhead a boys' writing club at school or in a community facility. School writing clubs tend to be heavily dominated by girls whose more advanced abilities leave boys in the dust.

When Delhi Middle School in Cincinnati, Ohio, launched an all-boys' book club, it drew in more than one-third of the boys in the school by its fifth year.[329] But all-boys' book clubs need to change the approach, not just separate the boys and girls.[330] Preferably with more tolerance for their moving about and working together; more input from the guys themselves on how it should be run; less heavy-handedness on writing guidelines; structure where it's asked for (such as "how many words?"); more tolerance on the topics and styles chosen; more male role models involved (teachers, dads, volunteers); and more flexibility on their supplementing the writing with artwork and dramatic readings.

Fletcher explains that girls' brains are wired for language while boys' brains are stronger when it comes to spatial-mechanical functioning. Allowing boys to include artwork with their writing plays to that strength.

At school, not only is writing often used as a way to punish, test, or quiet kids, but poetry isn't introduced in a boy-friendly way.[331] "Through over-teaching and ill-advised homework (write a haiku about your grandfather), kids learn to loathe it," says Sutton.[332] So, how to play with poetry at home? You can model your own attempts by composing a poem for his birthday card. You can buy blank cards and help him compose appropriate rhyming messages for other occasions. You can even introduce "treasure hunts" in poetry form: He has to interpret the next destination from the poem's message until he reaches the prize. Make it fun enough that he soon begs to be the writer for a treasure hunt with friends or younger siblings.

Parents can also be more lenient than school with what their boys want to write about, especially when it comes to violence or edgy humor. As we've mentioned before, school sensibilities frequently discourage the very topics that get boys enthused: swordplay, heroic action, death and destruction.

When Cynthia taught high school history, she noticed that boys' favorite four topics were heroism, battle strategies, spies, and weapons. One sixteen-year-old in particular did not like school at all. He was smart, but did only enough work to get by. When Cynthia assigned the class a research paper, however, he decided to try rounding up information on his family's role in World War II. Although he ended up finding little specifically on his ancestors, that assignment got him pursuing information on the country from which his grandparents had immigrated, which led him to a lot of reading about the resistance movement there.

When he turned his paper in, Cynthia was astonished: It was one of the best papers she had ever read, with impressive research. After marking it with the A-plus he deserved, she noticed him suddenly convert to a real achiever in school. By term's end, she was amused and delighted to read his end-of-class evaluation: "Assign more big research papers!"

"How many high schoolers write that?" she reflected. Last she heard, this boy was succeeding in college, a direct outgrowth of the month in which he was allowed to pursue his own identity and topic of interest—heroism in war—with full passion.

"Men often do not see aggression as the same moral issue women do," says Gurian in *What Could He Be Thinking? How a Man's Mind Really Works.*[333] Women tempted to try to change that might pause and ponder a question we introduced earlier: Is our lack of understanding of brain science causing boys these days to be regarded as faulty girls? And, which is more important, controlling our sons' every interest, or helping them get comfortable with writing?

Of course, if your son is consistently writing truly angry material, that's less about his writing than about what's going on in his life, and it offers a perfect opportunity to communicate. Say disparaging words about the writing, and you give him a perfect excuse to back off of writing *and* conclude that you don't care and he can't talk to you.

It's not unusual for teens trying to capture their parents' attention to read or write edgy material, use harsh language, refer to drugs, or talk openly about sex. "Don't take the bait," says Duffy, the psychologist. "Don't just get angry and dismiss them." Instead, talk with them (not at them). Listen carefully and openly without judgment in order to discover who he is and how he thinks. In the process, you may discover strengths of character you hadn't previously recognized—something on which to offer him positive feedback.[334] Cynthia suggests saying, "Sounds like you're having a tough time, but seems to me you're pretty good at standing up for yourself when you feel strongly, son. That is a strength you have.

And I'm proud of how well you are working at writing. So what's your thinking about (whatever the issue is)?"

A pair of researchers found that sixty-one percent of boys' stories contain some reference to violence and crime, which is higher than in girls' writing.[335] Also, boys are more inclined to create protagonists who act alone, whereas girls focus on joint action that serves the community. Yet by sixth grade, even girls fold some type of violence into their stories (forty percent of them, anyway).

Researchers typically move from findings about vaguely defined "violent" themes in boys' writing to a sense of alarm, says Newkirk.[336] Yet, given how much violence there is in the media, and the amount of media time that most households allow their kids to watch, what else do parents expect their kids to write about? Besides, do we really believe that writing about violence means they'll act on it? Again, discuss the issue of justice with your son, wrapping the conversation in understanding and encouragement.

Fiction lets kids assume powers they don't possess in real life. Remove too much independence on writing-topic choice and boys will walk. They'll walk away from writing, from reading, from overall literacy. The deck is stacked enough against them. Their interest in words is already fragile.

Beyond the violence and humor, teachers often object to students including their friends in their writing, especially if the friend's head gets blown off or something else occurs that teachers fear will offend the schoolmate. In fact, however, this is a common way young people bond and even flirt with one another. Adults are far more likely to be offended than the young people themselves.[337]

"I remember writing stories that starred my classmates as main characters," says Andrew Auseon, today an acclaimed writer of novels for young people, "and each day I would add new twists to the tales depending on how people reacted to what I'd done the day before. It was very interactive, and very satisfying."[338]

So next time your son Ted makes up a story in which little brother Wally suffers a dramatic fate, don't scold or rush in to erect new rules about writing. Instead, assess whether Wally is half-smiling behind his protests, and make a neutral comment like, "Wow, Wally, Ted included you in his story! Isn't that nice! And what great action!"

If you decide that Wally is truly hurt, you can have a quiet talk with both boys later, separately. In other words, help Wally toughen up and see things differently ("Don't you think it means Ted really loves you, to include you in his story like that?"), and urge Ted to give Wally a more heroic role the next round, "because Wally is younger than you and can take things the wrong way, even though I know you didn't mean any harm. I loved how much imagination you put into that story, by the way!" This teaches empathy, if you refrain from lecturing. The bottom line is that parents have an opportunity to encourage writing and storytelling to flourish in their home, and their approach need not resemble what schools are doing.

NOTES AND LETTERS

Smart parents write lots of notes to their kids, and set things up so their children need to reply in writing. At school, notes often take the form of criticism. Parents can counter this association by leaving him notes to compliment him on a job well done; notes are often more powerful than spoken words.

Notes allow for privacy and reflection and allow people to communicate without anyone else listening in or waiting their turn, says Harvey "Smokey" Daniels, author of thirteen books on language, literacy, and education.[339] He suggests buying a cheap mailbox at the local home improvement store, letting your son personalize it, then kicking off a correspondence with him.

Through notes, parents can model strong writing. But make sure your letters aren't polished; use occasional slang or abbreviations, circle a word and write "sp?" beside it, and occasionally cross out a phrase and substitute another. That way you allow him to relax about not being perfect. And never, ever mark, circle, or correct his errors. Leave the red pen stuff to his school; dare to be the one who is focused entirely on encouragement.[340]

Require him to write thank you letters, and encourage him to send ideas or complaints to a company whose products he uses. Kids also can write letters to their favorite authors in care of the publisher's address at the front of the book or through their website.

When Pam's son was in high school, he was passionate about mountain biking. After several of his favorite places for biking became threatened by city bylaw changes, he began writing passionate letters to politicians. Pam and her husband encouraged him, and taped the published ones on their refrigerator.

If you can't think of an issue likely to inspire your son to try his hand at persuasive letter writing, make it into a game instead. Organize a family "play" in which one person is king, queen, president, or mayor, and the others have to write letters to influence him/her to change a decision. Have participants (including parents) read the letters with fanfare. Remember to compliment some aspect of each impassioned letter. Another way to coax letters from boys is to require them to "apply" with a persuasive letter when they want something, say, a new gadget or an extension on their curfew.

A BOY'S WRITING TOOLBOX

Tools such as storyboards, writing frames, scaffolds, and templates allow boys to draw on their analytical skills. For instance, if your son can remember the acronym POWER, it will help get him started: P is for plan, O is for organize, W is for write, E is for edit, and R is for revise.[341]

Another visual prompt: Draw a hamburger and then lines pointing to the upper and lower buns, and the meat. On those lines write: "*the topping*: introduction, topic sentence, or introductory paragraph." Under that: "*The filling*: the details and supporting ideas." And under that: "*The ending*: the conclusion or summary."

Proofreading and editing are other stumbling blocks for some kids, especially those with dyslexia and dysgraphia.[342] Here, a memory trick might work: Have your son go through his piece four separate times, each time looking for a different type of error (to maintain maximum focus). He could do this using any of the following acronyms: "COPS" (capitalization, organization, punctuation, spelling) or "STOPS" (sentence structure, tenses, organization, punctuation, spelling).

All these visual organizers, along with self-feedback checklists, are available from www.retctrpress.com and www.linguisystems.com.

WHAT DO BOYS WANT, ANYWAY?

"I like writing without having any guidelines to follow, just where you have to do your own thing. I might not mind having a guideline as how long it has to be, but I don't like having a topic to write about, just to make up my own story."—Guy, quoted in *Reading Don't Fix No Chevys* by Michael Smith and Jeffrey D. Wilhelm.[343]

MacDonald, the teacher and therapist, recalls a former student who, like Guy, preferred to know the exact number of words required before he'd start in on an assignment. When a boy makes a special request like that, MacDonald says accommodate it if it might motivate them to write, because once they are motivated, they eventually shed the need for such artificial confidence-boosters.[344]

Parents could take a cue from a group of fourth- and fifth-grade boys at Albert S. Hall School in Waterville, Maine. The boys approached teacher and literacy specialist Jennifer Allen and asked her to volunteer one lunch hour per week just to be present in a room so they could have a writing club. They wanted no rules, no assignments and no lectures, not even an expectation they had to finish anything. It was simply an opportunity to write together and share their writing if and when they wanted to.

Allen was largely invisible; the boys set their own rules. "It is not what she would have envisioned for a writing program, but she was thrilled with the results," says Sullivan in *Connecting Boys with Books 2.*[345]

PARENTS' BAG OF TRICKS

There's only one way to develop writing skills, and that is practice and repetition.[346] Happily, parents are in a perfect position to coax their child to practice and encourage him on anything he seems to be doing right. Here's a list of tricks:

When your son seems totally stuck for getting started on a school writing project, seat yourself at the computer and offer to be his scribe as he dictates.[347]

Help him write an outline on a vertical plane (blackboard, whiteboard, paper pinned to the wall) to help get him unstuck.[348]

Introduce your son to scrapbooking by helping him gather material on his favorite topic, be that racecars or nature. Or start a family photo album or Flickr project, and challenge your kids to write captions. Introduce different types of prizes to reward different talents, including "best description," "funniest" or "most action."

When you write at home, do it within view of your child. Talk about your job's writing demands, what you like about the challenges, and how you've learned to think through ideas.

When discussing fiction, refrain from asking boys to comment on the emotions and relationships of characters. If boys are willing to reflect at all, "it has to do with how protagonists can handle a situation, not how an experience has affected them," says Newkirk.[349]

Let them plot their writing through drawings beforehand. Refrain from saying, "Shouldn't you stop drawing and start writing now?"

Let them illustrate their stories, act them out, videotape them.

On family vacations, instead of asking each child to keep a

journal (something boys rebel against more than girls), start a family journal that all family members (including parents) take turns contributing to. Establish early on that art, poems, songs, and photo captions count. This will draw the more reluctant writers into the process.

When visiting relatives, suggest he conduct some interviews as part of a family history. Help by brainstorming questions to ask them.

TOPICS

Kids often go through a stage of seeming to fixate on one topic, and to write about it so repeatedly that adults think they're "in a rut." Stop worrying. It's a natural phase. Experts call it "tunnel vision." Allow whatever it takes to win boys over to reading and writing in the first place. They'll diversify eventually, especially if no one tries to force them to do so.[350]

Ever heard yourself utter something like, "Why don't you write about something more realistic?" Oops. That can discourage budding writers, especially boys. Lots of writers make a living from writing fantasy, science fiction, and horror books. Don't clip his wings before he has had a chance to spread them; encourage him to write about anything that interests him.[351]

HAPPY ENDING

Colin used to enjoy making up stories, especially about space-ships, robots, and dramatic heroes. He wrote them down and added vigorous illustrations. Occasionally he showed them to his mother, but mostly he stuffed them in a drawer.

His mother, a professor, always took a pencil to them so he'd learn better spelling and grammar. When Colin's interest in writing sagged, Colin's mother shrugged. "Wasn't really his thing, I guess," but she wondered.

The next school year when Colin submitted one of his robot-hero stories as a class project, a different teacher had the following reaction: "Colin, you need to do this kind of writing at home. At school, we don't allow violence, okay? I just know you can write something good that fits the rules."

Colin all but stopped writing stories altogether then; he submitted only short, bland material to his teacher. "She didn't seem to notice. It was like that's what she expected of me. She only ever praises the girls."

When Colin turned nine, he took up ice hockey, a sport whose rules and action left his mom so confused that she often embarrassed the family by cheering at the wrong moments. One Mother's Day, Colin presented her with a guide to hockey rules and action. It was a manual with concise descriptions and a glossary, all neatly stapled and fully illustrated in colored pencil. She was impressed; she was delighted. And for once, she didn't critique or edit it, because roles had been reversed and she recognized that her son was reveling in being the expert.

"Finally!" she said. "Now I can follow the game." And she let him see her studying it, and showing it off to fellow hockey moms.

Soon after, Colin took up writing again but nonfiction this time: real-life stories of his favorite sports heroes, summaries of best hockey strategies. Once again, the drawers of his desk at home bulged with self-styled booklets, and gradually he regained the confidence to show his work to people—even to his mother.

"Took me awhile, but I got it," she says. "At home, I'm not a professor and my kids aren't my students. At home, I need to relax and just show pride."

CHAPTER TEN

REAL BOYS TALK: WINNING WITH WORDS

"An 'attitude' in most cases stems from a dearth of words. It's a nonverbal means of expressing one's feelings, thoughts, and ideals."

—PAUL D. SLOCUMB, EDUCATOR[352]

THE "TERRIBLE TWOS" ARE NAMED FOR THE TEMPER tantrums that toddlers have as a result of not having the words to communicate what they want. As they gain vocabulary, their frustration subsides. But even when they're older, not all kids have the words they need to negotiate themselves out of a tight spot. Too often, their one-word answers land them in trouble, especially if it's a female adult who doesn't realize that "boy culture" uses fewer words, and that one-word answers or a delayed response need not be interpreted as defiance.

"Struggling to connect in the face of male silence, women will sometimes say more, say it in a different way, or say it louder. Mounting frustration can sometimes erupt into anger or sometimes even despair," writes MacDonald.[353]

Happily, there are win/win ways to communicate with boys,

from accepting their silence as "processing time" to resisting the urge to shame them. It's important to listen beyond their bravado, not lecture them, respect their desire to chat without eye contact, and replace sarcasm with humor.

Not only do parents need to communicate better with boys, they need to help their boys use words better to sidestep trouble. Luckily, many boys love playacting and drama, so there are ways to make it fun.

One day when Pam's son Jeremy was in third grade, he returned home crying after having been confronted by bullies. She and her husband sat him down, had him recount every word said, and chatted about how it might have gone better. Pam's husband in particular introduced the notion of using humor to defuse situations. Jeremy grinned as they role-played together to test his new skills; it was like a game, a lighthearted family acting class.

Below are before-and-after examples of conversations that Cynthia has devised from her decades of experience as a mother, teacher, and therapist with at-risk teens and their families. The "before" scripts showcase typical talk that shuts down communication and prompts angry exchanges. The "after" is that same conversation re-scripted in a way that builds trust and communication.

Before:

Mom: "I want your room cleaned up before you leave for school tomorrow. I'm not putting up with this filth any longer."

Son: "Whatever."

Mom: "Don't sass me."

Son (mimicking her voice): "Don't sass me."

Mom: "That's it! You're grounded! I've had enough of your attitude!"

Son: "I'm outa here."

After:

Mom: "I know you've been really busy with school and soccer this week. Must be tough finding time to clean your room as well. But it does need to be cleaned by tomorrow, so what do you suggest?"

Son: "You clean it for me?"

Mom (laughing): "Nice try. Next idea?"

Son: "It's not a big deal, mom. I'll get around to it after the soccer tournament."

Mom (winking): "Soccer stars all have neat rooms. I'm proud you're doing all that practice. Now, about your room, do you want to clean it by tomorrow's game or pay me (or the housekeeper) to do it for you?"

Son (sighing): "Okay, I'll do it right after soccer practice today, I promise."

Mom: "Good choice. And I'll cut you some slack for how neat it has to be between now and the tournament. Deal?"

Son: "Deal! Thanks, Mom."

MacDonald tells the following story about navigating a tough spot as a father: "When our oldest announced that he was sick and tired of school and wanted to quit, my impulse was to say 'not on your life.' Instead, I remarked that it was an interesting suggestion. Had he thought about what he would do instead? What ensued was a thoughtful exchange about life goals during which he eventually expressed his frustrations with school. I withheld any impulse to tell him what to do but respected and trusted that he would figure it out—with guidance. We both left the conversation without conclusion and the next day he announced that he wouldn't quit but that he needed help to figure out how to work around a teacher with unreasonable expectations."

One study shows that welfare children hear 500 words of encouragement versus 1,100 of discouragement per week. In contrast, working-class children hear 1,200 words of encouragement versus 700 of discouragement, and professional-class children hear 3,200 words of encouragement versus 500 of discouragement.[354][355]

The lesson is that *any* parents who want their sons to get ahead and stay out of trouble need to work on more positive talk. Parents who are willing to work on their own attitudes, not responding in anger, will make much more headway with their sons. A famous saying states, "A gentle answer will calm a person's anger, but a harsh word will stir it up."

Children have several basic needs, and parents aware of these can understand where their kids are coming from when they "ask" for things, whether the asking takes the form of a simple request or a temper outburst.

According to William Glasser, world-renowned psychiatrist and consultant for schools, children who misbehave are trying to meet one of their five basic needs: survival, love, power, fun, or freedom.[356] Nelsen in her *Positive Parenting* books says they are aiming for attention, power, or revenge, or they want to show us that they're inadequate. Following are scripts to help parents meet these needs and divert the mistaken goals and assumptions more effectively.

Scenario: Charlie has a meltdown when told he can't play his electronic games.

Before: "How many times do I have to tell you homework comes first? You are so disrespectful! You're grounded for a week!"

After: If possible, simply ignore the outburst. Close your mouth and refuse to be pulled into an argument. Or say, "Love you too much to argue!"[357] Keep your voice calm, because your son will react not to your words but to your tone. The left side of the brain (rational thinking, processing what has been said) shuts down when the right side (emotions) is out of control. This is one reason lectures don't work. Remember, it's okay to say no to your children, and it's okay for them to be angry. It's not okay for them to hurt property, themselves, or others.

After they calm down, say, "Okay, you are learning how to calm yourself down. Now let's have a redo. I'll ask you to put your game away and you respond with respect." That avoids shaming the child. Kids learn to manage their own emotions much more readily if they are not shamed and overwhelmed through parental lectures, anger, and threats. Nor will they achieve maturity if parents give in to their emotional tirades. After all, kids do what works for them. If it works to have a temper outburst, they'll certainly do it again.

Another scenario: Billy refuses to do his homework. Every night seems to be a battle, and he is falling behind at school.

Before: "I'm so tired of fighting with you. You are so irresponsible! You can forget using your cell phone or Xbox for a month until I see you showing a real change of attitude, young man!"

After: "Your teacher called me to tell me you had three missing assignments in math. What are you going to do about it?" (Better yet, when the teacher calls, put Billy on the phone to talk with her.)

When Billy says he doesn't know what he's going to do, ask him to brainstorm with you. Ask him for permission to suggest things that might work, as they've worked for other kids. (Avoid comparing him with others, however.) Solutions might include: setting aside a time with no television or social networking allowed, creating a homework nook, or setting up times you are available for consultation.

Listen to his suggestions to help determine what will work best for him. Allow him to try his ideas for a week, resisting the temptation to nag or say, "I told you so" when they don't work. Instead, listen empathetically ("Wow, that must be frustrating for you") and encourage him to try another idea. Stay in touch with the teacher to let him/her know that you are working on teaching your son responsibility. Enlist the teacher's help in administering natural and logical consequences, as often there are things that school can implement when homework isn't completed. Collaboration between home and school is something most teachers welcome. It certainly sets the child up for success on both fronts.

"L-O-V-E"

To help meet children's needs, use this acronym to remember how to encourage positive parenting: **LOVE**.

L is for Listening. Parents do way too little of this, and kids feel powerless and angry as a result. We listen to respond, not to hear their heart. Be honest: Aren't most of us already formulating our retort before they are done speaking? This is very discouraging for a child, and does not nurture a good relationship. Practice this phrase: "I heard you say _____, and you're feeling _____."

O is for Order. Children are not supposed to be in control. It is parents who need to set reasonable guidelines and expectations. Such leadership is vital to raising a secure child. When the child knows he can get his way through angry outbursts, manipulation, charm, or arguing, then it's a chaotic world he is living in and his anxiety will increase drastically.

V is for Voice. A child needs to be heard. It is disrespectful of parents to lecture and flood a child with words, or to demand unquestioning obedience (especially as they get older) without simultaneously nurturing a relationship. Rules without relationship breed rebellion. Give him voice by providing him simple choices. "Do you want to read now or after dinner? Never? But that's not one of the options. Now or after dinner?" Ask their help in solving problems. "How do you think we should deal with this problem of the dog needing to go out early on Saturday morning when we all want to sleep late?" Family meetings (see sidebar, "Family Meetings," on page 197) are excellent forums for each family member to exercise their voice.

E is for Empathy. Empathy means understanding the child's feelings, listening for his heart, not just judging the content of what he is saying. Let him know you struggle too. Be emotionally available and honest. "When _____ happens, I feel _____ because _____. Does that describe how you are feeling in this situation?"

VOICE TONE IS EVERYTHING

New brain research shows that the way we speak to our kids—the voice tone, volume, and rhythm/speed—affects their responses.[358] A parent's threatening tone may trigger a fight-or-flight reflex. A rhythmic, lighter voice will go a long way in calming the child, playfully engaging him. So will gentle, firm words, spoken slowly with eye contact. How much better to be proactive and stop the temper outbursts before they begin!

Scenario: Johnny doesn't write a story due at school the next day. "I'm not going to write a stupid story!"

Before: (Angry, threatening tone) "Son, how dare you refuse me! You know better than that. Do it right now or there will be consequences!" (Note: this is a misuse of the word "consequences," presenting it is a punishment, as we'll discuss later.)

After: "Oops!" (playful tone) "Are you asking me or telling me you won't sit down and write it?" Boy says, "I'm telling you!" Parent in a playful tone, a little more slowly: "When you tell me, that doesn't work for me. Can you ask again with respect?"

If he persists with a defiant attitude, lower your voice, so it's firmer, and use eye contact at the child's level. "Johnny, my energy level goes down when there's disrespect in the family." (Notice you are choosing not to react in anger, which is very important!) "In order to restore that energy, there will need to be some consequences. You may have your cell phone back when the story is done."

If that doesn't work, he needs to be given a "time-in." This differs from a time-out in that the parent is nearby, available to talk with the child when he/she has cooled off.

"Johnny, it's very important that you learn to respect us. So you can sit here until you're ready to talk; I'll be over here. When you've calmed yourself down and are ready to talk, say 'ready' and I'll come over." When Johnny is ready, explain in as *few* words as you can that you love him, and it's your job to teach him to learn how to cooperate. Someday when he is a dad, he will do the same for his kids. Invite him to learn the art of negotiating and compromising. Then offer him a redo: *no* shaming, just practice, with liberal doses of praise. When he does it, say, "Good job asking for a compromise with respect!"[359]

Compromise: This is a great skill to teach your son. "What do you have in mind?" When you ask that, be ready to listen nonjudg-mentally. Also, beware of your first reaction. You feel like saying, "What? That's outrageous!" but such a disrespectful response will derail the process; he will probably shut down. Acknowledge what he has said. "I hear you saying that you don't think a twelve-year-old boy should have to load the dishwasher." Validate him by nodding (after all, you were twelve once). If your tone is peaceful, you may then push back: "That won't work for us; our family needs everyone to contribute. But, perhaps we can negotiate. Here are three other chores that need to be done: taking care of the garbage, raking the yard, and washing the car. Would you prefer one of those instead?"

Anyone who truly understands human behavior knows that the goal of discipline is to help a child learn self-control rather than to try and control him. Logical and natural consequences mean focusing on solutions and problem solving. This offers mutual respect, which is so vital to growing his courage. Punishment stems from a vindictive attitude, while consequences can be deliv-ered with a calm, empathetic tone, and are not designed to hurt a person back, but rather to allow him to learn cause and effect in real life.

The following examples illustrate some common mistakes parents make in relating to their children. We all know that we need to correct such errors; how we do it makes all the difference.

Before:
Mom: "Josh, it's time to do your homework!"

Josh: "Aw, Mom, can't I play for fifteen more minutes?"

Mom: "How many times have I told you that procrastination only makes things worse? You know the saying 'Work first, then play.' Now, let's lick that bad habit right away, and make yourself do what you know you should do."

Josh: "You are so unfair!"

Mom (angry): "How can you say that? We work so hard to put a roof over your head, feed you, and wash your laundry, and we go to your games. Now get busy, before I think of some other punishment for you."

Josh: "I hate homework, and I'm *for sure* not going to college."

After:

Mom: "Josh, what is your plan for this evening?"

Josh: "I'm going to work on my model, then Facebook for twenty minutes, then go to bed."

Mom: "What do you think I am wondering about that list?"

Josh: "Homework?"

Mom: "You guessed it!"

Josh: "Well, I just have a little bit of math and one essay to write. I can do that in study hall."

Mom: "And what happens if for some unforeseen reason things don't work out in study hall?"

Josh: "No problem."

Mom (calmly): "I'm not comfortable with that. How about we compromise: You get the essay done tonight."

Josh: "You never let me manage my own affairs! Besides, I need you to wash my football uniform tonight for the game tomorrow."

Mom: "Love you too much to argue!"

Josh: "You always say that!"

Mom: "I'll be glad to wash your uniform when I see the rough draft of the essay."

Josh: "Okay, fine."

All too often parents allow their kids to pull them into power struggles. A rule of thumb is "We don't need to attend every argu ment we are invited to!" The best way to avert power struggles is to offer the child *choices*. They need power; that is what they are craving. Isn't it more in line with our goals to teach them to think for themselves? In the second example above, the wise mom used "what" questions to require her son to think for himself. She then engaged in some *collaborative* problem solving. Compromise is a problem-solving skill that this mom both models and teaches. She expressed her need, thus not allowing him to be in charge. Sharing power actually has the effect of increasing respect rather than (what parents fear) decreasing the children's respect.

The following exchanges illustrate the need for parents to speak in a respectful manner with their children. How can we teach our kids respect if we do not model it? If they can get us mad, or if we retort to them in the same manner in which they spoke to us, we teach them nothing. The first rule of effective discipline is to calm yourself down! Anger begets anger. *Take a few deep breaths; remind yourself that you can regain composure.* Notice the positive tone of the "After" parent in the following examples.

Before: "That is it, I've had it! No more Facebook till your home-work is done!"

After: "You guys are welcome to Facebook as soon as your homework is done."

Before: "Don't use that tone of voice with me, buster! Don't diss me!"

After: "I will be happy to continue discussing this with you when your voice is calm, dear."

The second rule is to express *confidence* in him.

Before: "You'll probably end up like your dad, lazy and out of control. You don't deserve to go anywhere for the next week!"

After: "I have confidence that you will learn from your mistake, honey. That is why I'm enforcing these consequences."

The third rule is to work on the *connection*. Refuse the temptation to rescue or attack him. Engage in mutual respect, empathy, and collaborative problem solving.

Scenario: Boy is mad at his teacher for what he considers unjust punishment. *"I worked so hard on that paper. And all I got was a B because the teacher said that I didn't use paragraphs! Stupid teacher! I'm never taking his classes ever again. He just doesn't like me; he prefers the girls."*

Before: "Hey, I won't tolerate such disrespect coming out of your mouth. How dare you criticize your teacher. Of course you need to use paragraphs. You are in ninth grade! I want an apology from you right now for bad-mouthing your teacher!"

Another Before: "You are right; he is being way too picky. I bet your paper was better than lots of the others, and paragraphs are just a technicality. I will go talk to him tomorrow."

After: "That sounds really frustrating. You worked hard, and that B sure must be disappointing. What do you think is the best thing to do in a situation like this?"

(If he says "I don't know"): "Want to know what some kids do to solve problems like this? Let's look at some options."

After you brainstorm together, help him evaluate each option: "How well do you think this one would work for you? How's this one likely to turn out? Would this cause a problem for anyone else?

What will matter most in twenty five years, this grade, the skill of using paragraphs, or learning how to be honest and responsible?"

(If he wants you to fix it): "Sounds like you want me to fix it, but I believe in you, buddy. I believe you are capable. Let's brainstorm together on some ways you can solve this. You could...."

After you've discussed various options, say, "Will you let me know how this turns out?" (Taken from www.loveandlogic.com.)

Scenario: Your boy comes into the living room and says, "We got assigned to make a video for a school project. Jim and I are going to skateboard off the garage roof for ours!"

Before: "Don't you two dare! What are you thinking? Stop talking so foolishly!"

After: "Wow, a creative idea! Are you trying to make us all laugh? Or are you trying to get us to worry? You're pretty good at entertaining people; tell us where you got that idea. Then let's see if you can come up with a safer idea."

Scenario: Your son demands that you carry his books home from the library. "You made me come here. I don't want to carry these, and they are too heavy. You carry them!"

Before: "What do you mean you didn't want to come? I didn't tell you that you had to pick out so many books. Now stop being lazy."

After: (with empathy, calmness) "Are you asking me or telling me?"

If he says *asking*, then say, "Can you say it again with respect?" (Use a fairly lighthearted tone.)

If he says *telling*, then say, "If you are telling me, then of course the answer will be no. Do you want to try again, asking?"

If he asks with respect and you decide you don't want to carry the books, then say, "Would you like to ask for a compromise?" Wait to see if he comes up with a compromise. If he struggles too long, suggest one: "How about you carry one half and I carry one half?" Or you can give him two choices: "Would you rather carry half the books in your backpack or in a bag?"

Scenario: Your son throws a ball too hard and it knocks down your prized artwork, breaking the glass and the frame.

Before: "I've told you so many times to watch what you are doing in the house with your stuff! Now, you'll be grounded from your ball for a month, and you'd better clean up the mess right now."

After: "Oh, crumb! What are we going to do about this?" (If he is scared and you are mad, then take a few minutes and breathe deeply to cool down before problem solving.) "I am disappointed that my frame is broken. How are you feeling? Sad or scared? You know, I bet you can come up with a solution to help solve this problem. You're a pretty responsible kid." (Then work out a plan for his helping to clean it up, or for his paying for it—*without shaming or lecturing him.*)

Let's look at another potential power struggle.

Situation: Your eleven-year-old doesn't want to wear his coat outside in the cold.

Before: "Do you want to get your privileges taken away for a week? Now get over here and get this coat on now!"

Before: "I don't know why I even try! I work so hard for you! The poor kids in the street don't even have coats, and you don't appreciate yours!"

After: "Okay, do you want to wear your blue sweatshirt or your green jacket?"

(If child still insists he doesn't want to wear anything): "Oh, that wasn't one of your choices."

If he persists in defying you, you have several options. 1) If you're brave enough to let him experience the cold without a coat, you could let him go outside in the cold, expecting him to return in a few minutes after he has experienced the consequences of his foolishness. Most kids won't get sick from five minutes out in the cold. Then let him try again. "Let's have a redo: Do you want to wear your blue sweatshirt or your green jacket?" Or, 2) You could just toss him the jacket without saying anything. Then, if he challenges you, say, "Bring it with, just in case." (*Notice: no arguments, no lectures, no threats.*)

FAMILY MEETINGS

An excellent way to improve self-esteem, build character, teach collaborative problem solving, and give children voice is to hold family meetings. Here are several ways to conduct them:

1) Start with appreciations or compliments. Each person tells other family members something they appreciate about them in the past week. *"I appreciate how you helped me with the dinner last night." "I think you were generous when you gave your cookie to Joey."*

2) Choose a topic to discuss and ask for input on how to solve it. *"Let's talk about how to deal with the problem of computer time. How can we stop the fighting that happens after school when everyone wants to use it?"*

3) Each family member takes a turn suggesting solutions to the

problem. Treat each other with respect, regardless of whether you agree with their idea.

4) Set ground rules: no interrupting, no put-downs, keep a calm voice. Everyone needs to feel safe and heard. The goal is to solve the problem (if possible) but even more importantly, to teach mutual respect.

5) Brainstorm! This is a valuable skill to teach. Can you collectively come up with eight possible solutions? The key is to refrain from judging or evaluating the potential solutions until you are done brainstorming. It's fun and energizing to let the creative juices flow.

6) If a problem cannot be solved in a meeting, table it until the next one.

7) End the meeting with a treat and a fun activity if possible.

8) Remember, meetings are more effective if you have them every week, not on the parent's whim or when there is a crisis.

9) Rather than engaging in an argument in the heat of the moment, say, "Let's put this on the agenda for the next family meeting." That gives you and the kids the opportunity to cool down, and they will look forward to being heard. Keep the family meetings a forum for thoughtful discussion.

10) Start and end the meetings on time. Set a timer so the kids know it will not drag on. Keep them short (fifteen minutes if you have preschoolers, thirty to forty minutes maximum if you have teens).

More family meetings advice is offered in Nelsen's *Positive Discipline* books.

THE GREATEST GIFT

What's the greatest gift parents can give their child? Taking care of their own emotional health. When a parent struggles with anxiety, depression, or anger issues, there is a hundred percent chance the children will be affected by it. On the other hand, when parents choose to deal with their own internal "stuff," they become more able to guide their children to emotional maturity.

Cynthia treated one boy who struggled with anxiety. "Ben" was eleven, his parents had recently divorced, and he frequently had meltdowns when stressed. Cynthia gave the parents (who, to their credit, both attended the first session) her usual opening advice: "I've worked with a lot of kids. The kids who make the most progress are the kids whose parents are willing to change. Everyone in the family plays a role in helping the child get better." These parents were willing to work with her to learn positive parenting skills. It took only two months for Ben to gain a new sense of self-control. His parents said, "What a relief!" The key was their willingness to change.

In contrast, a mother and father brought fourteen-year-old "Zach" in because he had been running away and using marijuana. As Cynthia gave them her perspective on how vital it is for family to support a discouraged son, and to be willing to consider changes in their parenting, the mom exploded, "He's fourteen and I'm forty-two! He needs to change, not me!" Sadly, their son did not receive the encouragement he needed. The last Cynthia heard, he had been sent away to a facility for help. The mother refused Zach the greatest gift she could have given: the courage to address her own imperfections, which would have allowed the input that would have helped her son.

One little guy, "Jesse," struggled with ADD. His mom expressed her frustration at his disrespect, failure in school, and impulsive behavior. As Cynthia worked with the family, it came out that their main forms of discipline were threatening and yelling. Cynthia suggested replacing ineffective parenting techniques with effective techniques. "The old ways are not working here, folks!" Under her guidance, the parents began to work on controlling their own anger, calming themselves down before correcting the child; limiting words to ten maximum if they or the child were angry; using natural and logical consequences instead of excessive words (to which he had grown deaf anyway); administering the consequences with empathy, using a kind and firm tone; and learning how to encourage effectively (see sidebar, "How to Encourage Effectively," on page 202), problem-solve together (see sidebar, "Family Meetings," on page 197), and aim for mutual respect.

The process was not without its challenges; after all, it involved parenting, which is not for the faint of heart. But, as the parents implemented these changes in their home, the mother said she was reminded continually of her own father's harsh treatment of her, as she admitted that she had not known anything else growing up. Because she had the courage to face this about herself and get the help she needed, her son blossomed both at home and at school.

WISDOM FROM THE AGES

In many cultures, elders are respected and younger people are taught to glean wisdom from them. Sadly, in the West we have lost a great deal by abandoning this tradition. Recently Cynthia interviewed a number of parents over fifty, asking them, "Knowing what you do now, what would you have done differently in raising your children?" Here are some of the responses:

Listen more. Really listen!

Play with them more. Slow yourself down and try not to accomplish so much in a day; spend time with them instead.

Say "no" less.

Have more conversations.

Pray more with them.

Be more present in the little day-to-day moments and conversations.

Listen, teach, and encourage them more.

Laugh at yourself more often (rather than trying so seriously to be the "perfect" mom and wife).

Spend more time in nature, less indoors.

Live for the moment and be present when your kids learn and discover new things.

Teach them what's behind bad behavior.

Worry less what others think.

Make a lot of memories together.

Where respondents most agreed was that time spent listening and playing with kids trumps what we so often think is important. Sons appreciate us most for the recreation, fun, silly games, and laughter we enjoy together. These are what forge connections, and are one of the greatest gifts we can give our family.

HOW TO ENCOURAGE EFFECTIVELY

Focus on effort rather than talent.

Point out character qualities as more valuable than performance.

Remind them that character is who we are deep inside: integrity, perseverance, unselfishness, consideration, forgiveness, self-control, cooperation, and hard work.

Be transparent with your own mistakes: "I remember when I learned the hard way..." Fill in with a personal story.

Use feeling words to go along with your encouragement: "When you _____, I feel _____, because _____."[360]

Be specific. The sentence "I like how you showed teamwork when you passed the ball to Joe!" is much more powerful than "Good game!"

HAPPY ENDING

Cynthia often served as a chaperone on camping trips with youth. Once when tent camping with some teen boys, she and the other adults found themselves frustrated that the guys wouldn't settle down to sleep even after a full day. Her female coworkers tried various approaches: asking, begging, threatening. Finally, Cynthia rose from her sleeping bag, wandered to the boys' tent and said, "Hey you guys, *we are exhausted*!" This message seemed to reach them because they felt neither threatened nor ordered around. They felt respected, and responded respectfully. Mutual respect and "I"-messages work wonders with people of all ages.

"What a problem-solver you are!" This is one of the most useful phrases Cynthia has found for dealing with boys. Somehow, these words resonate with them; perhaps it sounds more believable than other compliments adults try out. Sometimes she uses it after play therapy, during which a child uses puppets, toy dinosaurs, stuffed monsters, or robots to create a story with a hero solving the problem. (That's an idea parents can try with their children.)

When working with troubled kids, Cynthia tries to teach them two sets of phrases that help them cope with life: "truth talk" and "stinkin' thinkin'." Truth talk includes such phrases as: "I can learn to control my temper," "Life isn't fair but I can learn to handle it!" and "I can't control other people but I can control myself." Stinkin' thinkin' includes phrases such as: "I'm really stupid," "My family is all messed up and it's my fault," and "Life should be fair/easy/fun..." Kids can be encouraged to get creative about adding some examples of their own, telling stories and drawing pictures using these concepts.

Courage is a word that rings with depth and positivity. "What courage you are showing by sitting here when you don't want to be here!" Cynthia likes to say to her young clients. If they are reticent to talk directly about their problems at home, she often gets them to chat about a story they've read or a movie they've seen. Engaging them about plots and characters makes it easier to broach the topic of emotions: fear, sadness, humor, excitement, and danger. Stories involving heroic deeds are especially popular and useful, because they're about overcoming adversity, finding courage, and moving from a place of powerlessness to one of personal power. The kids who deal most successfully with their problems are those who get comfortable telling stories. And she has found that storytelling is one of the best ways to connect with kids, especially when humor is involved.

CHAPTER ELEVEN

SCHOOL'S OUT: TRANSITIONS TO ADULTHOOD

"Most men are capable of swift and important change when they understand and see their course clearly."

—ANTHONY J. IPSARO, PH.D., PSY.D.[361]

THE GOOD NEWS IS THAT BOYS WHO STRUGGLE IN high school or college often thrive in the workplace. Why? Either because the workplace suits their skills and approach to life better than the school system—it offers a more natural fit—or because they experience a spurt of maturity and responsibility (in part a result of the brain completing its development).

But, as the workplace changes, that natural fit gets ever less comfortable. Parents whose career advice to their sons is based on what worked last generation need to read this chapter carefully. They need to judge how they can maximize their son's chances of success by a) helping him realign career aspirations with what the changing economy is actually offering, and b) engaging him in conversations about how the workplace is changing and what employers are looking for these days.

As we've said before, many high-wage jobs traditionally snapped up by men with lackluster grades and/or no college degree are disappearing. Manufacturing jobs have been moving overseas for decades, sales jobs are morphing into degree-requiring careers, and even white-collar positions are being outsourced with greater ease these days.[362]

A former machinist reduced during the recent recession to working part-time for minimum wage as a Walmart cashier spoke of how neighbors passing through the cash register lineup avoided his eyes, pretending not to know him. "I know they knew me; I've been in their home," he said. He appreciates that his wife has a higher-paying job but he admits that there's a toll on their relationship as a result.[363]

Men suffered roughly three-quarters of the eight million job losses between 2008 and 2010. That's because male-dominated industries (construction, finance, manufacturing) were particularly hard-hit, while female-heavy sectors (education, healthcare) did relatively well. The result? In 2010 for the first time in history, women were on the brink of holding a majority of jobs in the U.S.[364]

Are men ready to accept earning less than their fathers and the women in their lives, and to experience longer periods of unemployment? Knowing the score makes it easier for parents to talk with sons about these issues and to devise ways of avoiding their being sucked into a place of resentment and defeatism.

Here are the messages parents need to get across. Consider introducing them as family conversations, topics for family meetings or debates.

Today's workers need more education. College admissions boards scrutinize high school grades, and a college degree remains the primary ticket to high-paying jobs. As the percentage of males obtaining university degrees dwindles, more and more women will earn as much or more than men, which can negatively impact females, as we saw in Chapter One's sidebar, "Why Tackling Boys' Issues Helps Girls Too," on page 9. (Women's overall salaries remain lower than men's so far, but that's in part because women often choose less lucrative occupations than men, and opt for part time work to care for children.)[365]

"The good jobs—the jobs that pay enough to support a family—continue to become more complex and to require employees with greater levels of skill," say authors and professors Richard J. Murnane and Frank Levy. "And so, economic change hits hardest at the least educated."[366]

Here's how the job market has shifted in the United States:[367]

	1950s	1990s
professional jobs:	20%	20%
skilled labor:	20%	more than 60%
unskilled labor:	60%	less than 20%

The transition from unskilled to skilled labor demands more education and training, but worryingly, the skilled-labor sector is seeking skills not traditionally valued by males, as we'll discuss in a minute. That begs for new perspective and an attitude change, something parents can help their son achieve more easily than educators or peers can.

It's worthwhile to remind our sons that not only are they competing against females, but against newcomers whose attitudes (not just aptitudes) will be compared closely to theirs. In the 1970s and 1980s, when males transitioning from manufacturing to service work overtly showed resentment and "displayed less flexibility on the job than, for instance, first-generation immigrant workers...employers began to prefer hiring women and immigrants, and a vicious cycle of resentment, discrimination, and joblessness set in."[368]

Schools typically haven't kept pace with training kids for what the workplace needs. "Many of today's schools continue to educate children for an economy that no longer exists, and many of today's parents are just beginning to recognize the problem," say Murnane and Levy.[369]

There are ways for parents to supplement what the schools are missing, steer their boy toward extracurricular activities that will add value to his resume, and (in an activist's role) improve his high school's effectiveness. (Read Murnane and Levy's *Teaching the New Basic Skills*.)

Doing all you can to ensure that your son gets quality teachers is also key. "Three good teachers in a row, and the student is going to be a year-and-a-half to two years ahead of grade level. Three bad teachers in a row and the average student's going to be so far behind it's hard for them to ever catch up," U.S. Secretary of Education Arne Duncan has said.[370] Of course, getting the grades to get into an elite university is an ideal solution, as such graduates are the least likely to suffer.[371]

What else can parents do? We know three sets of parents who pooled their expertise to tutor one another's boys for a college entrance exam. And a mom who helped her son research what a local employer was looking for after he was turned down. (She did this because she was distressed by how depressed the rejection made him.) When he learned that "international experience" was a major plus at the company, she said she'd support his efforts to select an overseas charity work stint. He chose to build houses in Peru for Habitat for Humanity. He came back a new man—energized, motivated, and eventually accepted by the employer who'd previously turned him down.

The workplace has changed. Lifetime employment, company loyalty, and a "safe career" are largely entities of the past. To borrow a phrase from the music industry, most employees these days are only as good as their last gig. In fact, roughly forty percent of the workforce has been with their current employer for less than two years.[372]

Workers need to be prepared not only to change jobs, but to change careers several times in their lifetime, and college graduates are the best positioned to do this.[373]

It's also true that as manufacturing jobs shrink, as service jobs grow, and as women move into ever more industries and job levels, men are taking on traditionally female roles. They're becoming nurses, librarians, kindergarten teachers, paralegals, typists, and secretaries.[374]

Service work requires different interpersonal skills and different ways of presenting one's self than blue-collar work demands.[375] If an applicant knows this going in, and stays open-minded to some coaching from a mentor, colleague, or book on job interviewing (perhaps one you find for him), that need not be a barrier.

One way to help make our sons more open to these jobs is to introduce them to dynamic men who've become comfortable in such roles. For instance, help a local community center pull together an evening roster of male speakers: a male nurse who emphasizes how his work allows him to live overseas; a male librarian who relates his thrill at getting to attend a sci-fi writers' conference as part of his job. Or invite such men to your home for dinner.

The type of worker in demand has changed. "A young man shuffled into the interview room and slumped into a chair. He had jumped through the hoops of postsecondary education and seemed to be, at least on paper, a promising candidate. Yet he was unable to convince an employer desperate to fill the job that he was the right person. He lacked communication skills, and didn't pass the reading comprehension test. The position went unfilled..."[376]

How could that be? Why do experts say that a lack of applicants with "people skills" is the largest challenge facing employers these days, even those having difficulty filling jobs? Most importantly, how can parents ensure that their son passes muster in this area? First, get him involved in volunteer work or jobs that entail working with people (camp counselor, retail, etc.). Second, restrict his time on electronic gadgets. Anything that involves communicating, working with others, and thinking abstractly is important.[377]

Also, drive home the message that where individualism and competition were once applauded, now employers look for collaboration and teamwork, and inclusion rather than exclusion.[378] Those in the hiring seat also want fewer "dominant, self-interested, and tough" leaders, and more "people of principle, vision, and humanity."[379]

Here's how author Pink puts it in *A Whole New Mind*: "The last few decades have belonged to a certain kind of person with a certain kind of mind—computer programmers who could crank code, lawyers who could craft contracts, MBAs who could crunch numbers. But the keys to the kingdom are changing hands. The future belongs to a very different kind of person with a very different kind of mind—creators and empathizers, pattern recognizers and meaning makers. These people—artists, inventors, designers, storytellers, caregivers, consolers, big-picture thinkers—will now reap society's richest rewards and share its greatest joys."[380]

Big-picture thinking and empathy tend to reside in people with a variety of experiences, Nicholas Negroponte of the Massachusetts Institute of Technology has said.[381] In other words, parents should encourage their kids to work a variety of jobs and volunteer positions and travel if possible.

Today's employers are also on the lookout for[382] 1) hard skills: basic mathematics, problem-solving, and reading abilities at levels much higher than many high school graduates now attain; 2) soft skills: the ability to work in groups and to make effective oral and written presentations, skills many schools do not teach; and 3) computer skills.

The workplace has diversified, and employers want hires who work well with a diversity of cultures, genders, and age groups. It's never too late to encourage this. Boys need to learn how to connect. This is best taught by activities such as laughing and roughhousing, especially involving dads, uncles, or grandpas. Have fun with them in a way that involves eye contact, conversation, and listening, says Jean Mavrelis, a corporate consultant on gender and culture.[383]

Finally, the workplace values employees with perseverance, adaptability, humility, and entrepreneurialism[384] and is wary of those who need almost constant direction, which Ron Alsop, author of *The Trophy Kids Grow Up*, says micromanaged children become. Positive parenting (see Chapter Ten), with its emphasis on family meetings, collaborating, and mutual respect, equips boys to think for themselves, which is the opposite of micromanagement.

Men and women bring different approaches to the table. Knowing this allows our sons to present themselves to employers in the best light, and to vigorously pursue working on any shortcomings. Here's what experts say:

Men are more comfortable in a hierarchical, process-driven world, which means they formerly had an advantage, but as more and more workplaces stress a creative and synergistic approach, women may come to have the upper hand.[385]

Men tend to have a thicker skin and they're more invested in "knowing" than listening and learning.[386] Many white guys in particular "freely engage in competition and conflict without preoccupation or concern with how that might undermine the group or how others are feeling," say the authors of *Corporate Tribalism*.[387] If we enlist male mentors to help our boys understand that this can work against them in today's work environment, might they work at moderating such tendencies?

When a particular plan isn't working out, women tend to be faster at changing course in midstream; men tend to work the same plan harder. In other words, in a global environment that demands flexibility and speedy decisions, men may have something to learn from women.[388]

Finally, men's identities are far more defined by their work than women's;[389] perhaps just being aware of this tendency may help men present themselves in whatever light is most advantageous.

IT'S NEVER TOO LATE

"I didn't read much as a kid. My mom read voraciously and I have some vague memories of my father, a medical doctor, reading. But I didn't read much more than comic books and Hardy Boy novels. School destroyed reading for me, especially book reports and assignments, like 'memorize this poem.' I'm a very slow reader and long books still get on my nerves because I just want them to end. Once my friends and I got hauled into the principal's office because we had supposedly bullied a girl. We were forced to read a story about a bully. I remember that all my friends finished it but me; I remember the frustration I felt.

"I might have been dyslexic; it was never diagnosed. I read as little as possible in high school and college. If I got an assignment to read six chapters of a textbook in college, I'd divide it into however many nights there were before the reading had to be done, and I'd read that little bit each night. I absorbed a ton by listening instead, and asking questions. I'd much rather listen to someone than read something.

"As an adult, I started working with an author who would go around to schools and talk to kids about the importance of reading. Through him, I came to understand the value of reading, and I wanted to become part of that world. So I finally started reading at the age of fifty-four, and writing, in a diary I now write in every night. I do that for the discipline and brain stimulation, and also as a record.

"I believe that if I'd had more role models who had encouraged me to read, I'd have read more. I think reading is a great life experience and now when I talk to people, I'm a real pusher of books. I love the accomplishment, the dialogue, the description, the life experience. It's never too late to embrace reading."

—CHRIS, AGE FIFTY-EIGHT

THE GIRLFRIEND FACTOR

"Books were forced on me when I was young, and they were boring ones. As a result, I developed a negative attitude toward reading and followed my parents' example of watching television and playing video games instead.

"Only when I hooked up with a girlfriend who was into reading did I discover that reading could be enjoyable. She made a deal with me to read certain books that she was reading and it aroused my competitive spirit. Reading gives my imagination power and I learn a lot about myself. Books carry a weight that movies or speakers don't, because you can reread them and do additional research on a topic that catches your interest.

"Because my girlfriend is now into 'speed reading,' I am currently trying to master that, so that I can take in even more books in a shorter time."

—JASON, AGE TWENTY-FIVE

HAPPY ENDING

"I wasn't an outcast, because I had friends, but my learning disability and ADHD sure made school hard. It didn't help that I had four brothers who were all very high achievers in school. My mom tried everything to get me to read and succeed; I even remember her reading something onto a tape, and I was supposed to read along in the book as I listened. Usually I just listened, as reading was such a struggle for me.

"My turning point involved taking classes at a nearby technical college; that's when I found my niche. I literally fell in love with horticulture, and learned how to manipulate the environment to make plants flourish. For the first time, I read books I was interested in: books on horticulture. Reading is still a struggle, and I still read more slowly than I'd like to. It took lots of dedication and focus, but I've achieved my goal of becoming an international certified arborist."

—JON, AGE THIRTY-TWO

APPENDIX

ENDNOTES

Introduction

1   Michael Sullivan, *Connecting Boys with Books 2* (Chicago: ALA Editions, 2009), 99.

Chapter One

2   Peg Tyre, *The Trouble with Boys* (New York: Three Rivers Press, 2009), 33.

3   John Pryor et al., *The American Freshman: National Norms for Fall 2011* (Los Angeles: Higher Education Research Institute, UCLA, 2011).

4   U.S. Department of Education, National Center for Education Statistics, *The Condition of Education 2011*, by Susan Aud, William Hussar, Grace Kena, Kevin Bianco, Lauren Frohlich, Jana Kemp, and Kim Tahan. NCES 2011–033 (Washington, DC: United States Government Printing Office, 2011), Table A-26-2.

5   Rudolf Dreikurs, *Children: The Challenge* (New York: Plume, 1991), 36.

6   Tyre, *Trouble*.

7   Statistics Canada, *Public Postsecondary Graduates by Institution Type, Sex, and Field of Study*, Table 477-0020, www.statcan.gc.ca/tables-tableaux/sum-som/l01/cst01/educ70b-eng.htm.

8   *Condition of Education*, Table A-26-2.

9   Tyre, *Trouble*.

10 Torkild Hovde Lyngstad, "The Impact of Parents' and Spouses'

Education on Divorce Rates in Norway," *Demographic Research* 10 (2004): 121–142, www.demographic-research. org/volumes/vol10/5/10-5.pdf.

[11] Tyre, *Trouble.*

[12] Ibid.

[13] Don Peck, "How a New Jobless Era Will Transform America," *The Atlantic*, March 2010.

[14] Ibid.

[15] Michelle Conlin, "Look Who's Bringing Home More Bacon," *BusinessWeek*, January 28, 2003, www.businessweek.com/ careers/content/jan2003/ca20030128_9891.htm.

[16] Tyre, *Trouble.*

[17] Peck, "Jobless Era," 53.

[18] Ibid.

[19] Michael Gurian, *The Purpose of Boys: Helping Our Sons Find Meaning, Significance, and Direction in Their Lives* (Hoboken, NJ: Jossey-Bass, 2009), 174.

[20] Jean M. Twenge, *Generation Me: Why Today's Young Americans Are More Confident, Assertive, Entitled—and More Miserable Than Ever Before* (New York: Free Press, 2007), 66–67.

[21] Christianne Hayward, interview by Pam, www.keenreaders. org/book-club-maestro-christianne-hayward.

[22] Barry MacDonald, *Boy Smarts: Mentoring Boys for Success at School* (Surrey, BC: Mentoring Press, 2005), 100.

[23] Daniel Egeler, *Mentoring Millennials: Shaping the Next Generation* (Colorado Springs, CO: NavPress, 2003), 47.

Chapter Two

[24] Walter Dean Myers, "Letter to Readers," *Handbook for Boys: A Novel* (New York: Amistad, 2003), n.p.

25 U.S. Department of Education, National Center for Education Statistics, *Highlights From PISA (Program for International Student Assessment) 2006*, by Stephane Baldi, Ying Jin, Melanie Skemer, Patricia J. Green, and Deborah Herget. NCES 2008-016 (Washington, DC: United States Government Printing Office, 2007).

26 National Dropout Prevention Center/Network, "Early Literacy Development," www.dropoutprevention.org/effective-strategies/early-literacy-development.

27 National Institute for Literacy, *Fast Facts on Literacy & Fact Sheet on Correctional Education* (National Institute for Literacy, 1998).

28 Paul Kropp, *How to Make Your Child a Reader for Life* (New York: Random House, 2000), xv.

29 Ibid., xiii.

30 Paul Kropp, interview, www.keenreaders.org/hip-help-from-paul-kropp.

31 Michael Gurian, *A Fine Young Man: What Parents, Mentors, and Educators Can Do to Shape Adolescent Boys into Exceptional Men* (New York: Tarcher, 1999), 186.

32 Kropp, *How to Make*.

33 Nancie Atwell, *The Reading Zone: How to Help Kids Become Skilled, Passionate, Habitual, Critical Readers* (New York: Scholastic Teaching Resources, 2007), 130.

34 MacDonald, *Boy Smarts*, 134.

35 Michelle M. Garrison, Kimberly Liekweg, Dimitri A. Christakis, "Media Use and Child Sleep: The Impact of Content, Timing, and Environment," *Pediatrics* 128, no. 1 (2011): 29–35, DOI: 10.1542/peds.2010-3304.

36 *Globe and Mail*, "Probing the Problem: Why Are Boys Falling Behind in School?" October 16, 2010.

37 Kropp, *How to Make*, 36.
38 Ibid., 37.
39 *Guys Read Pilot Program: Final Report* (Fairbanks North Star Borough Library in Alaska, 2007), 1.
40 MacDonald, *Boy Smarts*, 134.
41 Kropp, *How to Make*, 40.
42 Ibid., 40, 179.
43 Michael W. Smith and Jeffrey D. Wilhelm, *Reading Don't Fix No Chevys: Literacy in the Lives of Young Men* (Portsmouth, NH: Heinemann, 2002), 16.
44 Thomas Newkirk, *Misreading Masculinity: Boys, Literacy, and Popular Culture* (Portsmouth, NH: Heinemann, 2002), xxi.
45 David Ward, interview, www.keenreaders.org/literacy-expert-david-ward-what-is-a-reluctant-reader.
46 "Kids and Family Reading Report" (New York: Scholastic, 2006), 3, www.scholastic.com/aboutscholastic/news/reading_survey_press_call_2.pdf.
47 Shari Frost, interview, www.keenreaders.org/shari-frost-is-red-hot-on-reading.
48 Ron Jobe and Mary Dayton-Sakari, *Reluctant Readers: Connecting Students and Books for Successful Reading Experiences* (Portland, ME: Stenhouse Publishers, 1999), 12–13.
49 Cathy Fleischer, *Reading and Writing and Teens: A Parent's Guide to Adolescent Literacy* (Urbana, IL: National Council of Teachers of English, 2010), 43.
50 Marilyn Reynolds, *I Won't Read and You Can't Make Me: Reaching Reluctant Teen Readers* (Portsmouth, NH: Boynton/Cook, 2004), 21.
51 *Globe and Mail*, "We Need Tool-Savvy Teachers," October 20, 2010.

[52] Adi Bloom, "Girls Go for Little Women but Boys Prefer Lara," *Times Educational Supplement*, March 15, 2002, 18.

[53] U.S. Department of Education, *The American Freshman*, 61, 87.

[54] U.S. Department of Education, National Center for Education Statistics, *Trends in Educational Equity of Girls and Women*, by Yupin Bae, Susan Choy, Claire Geddes, Jennifer Sable, and Thomas Snyder, NCES 2000-030 (Washington, DC: United States Government Printing Office, 2000), 18.

[55] U.S. Department of Education.

[56] Ward, interview.

[57] Frost, interview.

[58] Gurian, *Fine Young Man*, 180.

[59] Ibid., 14–16.

[60] Atwell, *Reading Zone*, 114.

[61] Gurian, *Fine Young Man*, 15–16.

[62] Michael Rutter et al., "Sex Differences in Developmental Reading Disability—New Findings from Four Epidemiological Studies," *Journal of the American Medical Association* 291, no. 16 (2004): 2007–12.

[63] Michael Gurian, *The Minds of Boys: Saving Our Sons from Falling Behind in School and Life* (Hoboken, NJ: Jossey-Bass, 2005), 180.

[64] Gurian, *Fine Young Man*, 15.

[65] David Jackson and Jonathan Salisbury, "Why Should Secondary Schools Take Working with Boys Seriously?" *Gender & Education* 8, no. 1 (1996): 105.

[66] Gurian, *Fine Young Man*, 15–16.

[67] Ibid., 14.

[68] Ibid., 15–16.

[69] Dan Kindlon and Michael Thompson, *Raising Cain: Protecting*

the Emotional Life of Boys (New York: Ballantine, 1999).

[70] *Globe and Mail,* "Are Boys Merely Misunderstood?" October 20, 2010.

[71] Sullivan, *Connecting,* 21.

[72] National Institute for Literacy, *Fast Facts.*

[73] U.S. Department of Education, National Center for Education Statistics, *The Nation's Report Card: Reading 2007,* by Jihyun Lee, Wendy S. Grigg, and Patricia L. Donahue, NCES 2007-496 (Washington, DC: United States Government Printing Office, 2007).

[74] Anne Cunningham and Keith Stanovich, "What Reading Does for the Mind," *American Educator* 22 (1998): 8–15.

[75] Kropp, *How to Make,* 217–18.

[76] Simon Burgess, Brendon McConnel, Carol Propper, and Deborah Wilson, "Girls Rock, Boys Roll: An Analysis of the Age 14-16 Gender Gap in English Schools," *Scottish Journal of Political Economy* 51, no. 2 (2004): 209–29.

[77] MacDonald, *Boy Smarts,* 134.

[78] The Boys Project, "Helping Boys Become Successful Men," www.drjonherzenberg.com/The-Boys-Project.html.

[79] Ibid.

[80] U.S. Department of Education, *The American Freshman.*

[81] *Globe and Mail,* "What's Your Degree Worth?" September 26, 2011.

[82] Michael Gurian, *Boys and Girls Learn Differently! A Guide for Teachers and Parents,* (Hoboken, NJ: Jossey-Bass, 2001), 37, 57.

[83] Aaron Kipnis, *Angry Young Men: How Parents, Teachers, and Counselors Can Help "Bad Boys" Become Good Men* (Hoboken, NJ: Jossey-Bass, 2002), 55.

[84] *Literacy Awareness Resource Manual for Police* (Literacy and

Policing Project of the Canadian Association of Chiefs of Police, 2008), 20.

[85] Olena Hanivsky, "Cost Estimates of Dropping Out of High School in Canada," *Canadian Council of Learning* (2008): 28.

[86] U.S. Department of Education, *Condition of Education 2011*.

[87] "Civic Report No. 48: Leaving Boys Behind: Public High School Graduation Rates," (New York: Manhattan Institute for Policy Research, 2006).

[88] "Average High School GPAs Increased Since 1990," *U.S.News*, April 19, 2011, www.usnews.com/opinion/articles/2011/04/19/average-high-school-gpas-increased-since-1990.

[89] U.S. Department of Education, National Center for Education Statistics, *Digest of Education Statistics, 2010*, NCES 2011-015, nces.ed.gov/programs/digest/d10/tables/dt10_199.asp.

[90] Ibid.

Chapter Three

[91] U.S. Department of Education, National Center for Education Statistics, *Science 2011: National Assessment of Educational Progress at Grade 8*. NCES 2012-465 (Washington, DC: United States Government Printing Office, 2011).

[92] Marilyn Burns, *Math: Facing an American Phobia* (Sausalito, CA: Math Solutions Publications, 1998), ix.

[93] "A Developmental Perspective on College and Workplace Readiness," *Child Trends*, by Laura Lippman, Astrid Atienza, Andrew Rivers, and Julie Keith (Bill and Melinda Gates Foundation, 2008), 13–14.

[94] Leslie Minton, *What if Your ABCs Were Your 123s?: Building Connections Between Literacy and Numeracy* (Thousand Oaks, CA: Corwin Press, 2007), 7.

[95] Burns, *Math*, 78.

[96] Pam's husband Steve Withers, award-winning chemistry professor, University of British Columbia, Canada.

[97] Ibid., 6.

[98] Clive Thompson, "How Khan Academy Is Changing the Rules of Education," *Wired Magazine*, August 2011.

[99] U.S. Department of Education, *Science 2011*.

[100] Burns, *Math*, 139.

[101] Ibid.

[102] Minton, *What If*, 1.

[103] Ibid., 69, 77.

[104] Burns, *Math*, 134.

[105] Danica McKellar, *Math Doesn't Suck: How to Survive Middle School Math without Losing Your Mind or Breaking a Nail* (New York: Hudson Street Press, 2007), 265.

[106] Ibid., 277.

[107] Ibid., 266.

[108] Ibid., xiv.

[109] Sander Marcus, "Personality Styles of Chronic Academic Underachievers," SelfGrowth.com, August 9, 2007.

[110] Ogbonnia Chukwu-Etu, "Underachieving Learning: Can They Learn at All?" *ARECLS* 6, no. 4 (2009), 91.

[111] Michael Whitley, *Bright Minds, Poor Grades: Understanding and Motivating Your Underachieving Child* (New York: Berkley Publishing, 2001).

[112] Douglas Varvil-Weld, "Your Child's Underachievement and What to Do About It," Pauquette Center, www.pauquette.com/archive9.htm.

[113] Whitley, *Bright Minds*, 13.

[114] Ibid., 35–36.

[115] Ibid., 179.

[116] Sylvia Rimm, *Why Bright Kids Get Poor Grades and What You Can Do About It: A Six-Step Program for Parents and Teachers* (New York: Crown Publishers, 1995), 161–162.

[117] Ibid., 146, 390.

[118] Steve Chinn, *The Trouble with Maths: A Practical Guide to Helping Learners with Numeracy Difficulties* (New York: Routledge, 2012), 25.

[119] Ibid., 24.

[120] Ibid., 31.

[121] Ibid., 37.

[122] Ibid., 20.

[123] Ibid., 21.

[124] Burns, *Math*, 78.

[125] Chinn, *Trouble with Maths*, 27.

[126] Bruce Upton, "World's Greatest Tutor," Forbes.com, March 12, 2012, 52.

[127] Chinn, *Trouble with Maths*, 113.

[128] Burns, *Math*, 140.

[129] Upton, "World's Greatest Tutor," 52.

[130] Gerald Wheeler, interview, www.keenreaders.org/dr-gerald-wheeler-on-youth-and-science.

[131] Linda M. Gojak, interview, www.keenreaders.org/linda-m-gojak-on-youth-and-math.

Chapter Four

[132] Philip Schultz, *My Dyslexia* (New York: W.W. Norton, 2011), 51.

[133] Ibid., 26–7.

[134] Aribert Rothenberger and Tobias Banaschewski, "Informing the ADHD Debate," *Scientific American* 17 (Nov. 2004): 36–41.

[135] Schultz, *My Dyslexia*, 74.

[136] KidsHealth.org, "Auditory Processing Disorder," kidshealth. org/parent/medical/ears/central_auditory.html#cat138.

[137] Robert Farrald and Richard Schamber, *A Mainstream Approach to Identification Assessment and Amelioration of Learning Disabilities* (New York: Adapt Press, 1973).

[138] College of Pathologists and Audiologists of Quebec, www. ooaq.ca.

[139] The Franklin Institute, "The Human Brain," www.fi.edu/ learn/brain/head.html.

[140] Ibid.

[141] Ibid.

[142] The Brain Injury Association of Canada, "Males Are Twice as Likely to Sustain a Brain Injury," (2008), biac-aclc. ca/en/2008/09/21/males-are-twice-as-likely-to-sustain-a-brain-injury.

[143] Los Angeles Caregiver Resource Center, "Fact Sheet: Traumatic Brain Injury," (2003), lacrc.usc.edu/damcms/sitegroups/ SiteGroup1/files/fact-sheets/DMH%20Funded/Traumatic% 20Brain%20Injury.pdf.

[144] Guy Manaster and Raymond Corsini, *Individual Psychology: Theory and Practice* (Chicago: Adler School of Professional Psychology, 1982).

[145] Thomas Armstrong, *In Their Own Way: Discovering and Encouraging Your Child's Multiple Intelligences* (New York: Tarcher, 2000).

[146] Rita Dunn and Kenneth Dunn, *Teaching Secondary Students Through Their Individual Learning Styles* (Toronto: Allyn and Bacon, 1993).

[147] Marie Carbo, Rita Dunn, and Kenneth Dunn, *Teaching Students to Read Through Their Individual Learning Styles* (Upper Saddle River, NJ: Prentice-Hall, 1986), 13.

[140] VARK. A Guide to Learning Styles, www.vark-learn.com/english/index.asp.

[149] Christina Hoff Sommers, *The War Against Boys: How Misguided Feminism Is Harming Our Young Men* (New York: Simon & Schuster, 2001), 91.

[150] Sullivan, *Connecting*, 25.

[151] Debby Zambo and William Brozo, *Bright Beginnings for Boys: Engaging Young Boys in Active Literacy* (Newark, DE: International Reading Association, 2008), 5.

[152] Sullivan, *Connecting*, 25.

[153] Ibid., 37.

[154] Learning Disabilities Association of America, "One in Seven," www.ldanatl.org/new_to_ld/index.asp.

[155] Zambo and Brozo, *Bright Beginnings*, 38.

[156] MacDonald, *Boy Smarts*, 40.

[157] National Early Literacy Panel, *Developing Early Literacy* (National Institute for Literacy, 2008), www.nichd.nih.gov/publications/pubs/upload/NELPReport09.pdf.

[158] MacDonald, *Boy Smarts*, 41.

Chapter Five

[159] Gurian, *Fine Young Man*, 74.

[160] Gina Panettieri and Philip S. Hall, *The Single Mother's Guide to Raising Remarkable Boys* (Avon, MA: Adams Media, 2008), 34.

[161] Michael Gurian, *What Could He Be Thinking? How a Man's Mind Really Works* (New York: St. Martin's Press, 2004), 254.

[162] Gurian, *Fine Young Man*, 49.

[163] Newkirk, *Misreading Masculinity*, 42.

[164] Mihaly Csikszentmihalyi, "Education for the 21st Century,"

Education Week, April 19, 2000, www.edweek. org/ew/articles/2000/04/19/32csikszentmihalyi.h19. html?qs=education.

165 Gurian, *What*, 255.

166 U.S. Census Bureau, www.census.gov/newsroom/releases/ archives/facts_for_features_special_editions/cb06-ffse07. html.

167 Kropp, interview.

168 Nermeen E. El Nokali, Heather J. Bachman, and Elizabeth Votruba-Drzal, "Parent Involvement and Children's Academic and Social Development in Elementary School," *Child Development* 81, no. 3 (2010): 1001.

169 *Globe and Mail*, "How to Build Your Child's Learning Brain," November 19, 2010.

170 Vivian Gadsden and Aisha Ray, "Fathers' Role in Children's Academic Achievement and Early Literacy," *Eric Digest*, 2003, ceep.crc.uiuc.edu/eecearchive/digests/2003/ray03.pdf.

171 Newkirk, *Misreading Masculinity*, 43.

172 U.S. Census Bureau, *Living Arrangements of Children: 2009*, by Rose M. Kreider and Renee Ellis, P70-126 (United States Government Printing Office, 2011), 4.

173 *Globe and Mail*, "The Sins of the Fathers Are Visited on Black Youth," December 2, 2005.

174 Ibid.

175 MacDonald, *Boy Smarts*, 89.

176 Gurian, *Fine Young Man*, 55–6.

177 Ibid., 48–9.

178 Gurian, *Fine Young Man*, 49.

179 Panettieri and Hall, *Single Mother's Guide*, 3.

180 Newkirk, *Misreading Masculinity*, 38.

181 Ibid., 39.

[182] Ibid., 41.

[183] Gurian, *What*, 249.

[184] Jean M. Twenge and W. Keith Campbell, *The Narcissism Epidemic: Living in the Age of Entitlement* (New York: Free Press, 2009), 77.

[185] Ibid., 34.

[186] Ibid.

[187] Ibid.

[188] Ibid., 30–31.

[189] Kevin Leman, *Have a New Kid by Friday: How to Change Your Child's Attitude, Behavior & Character in Five Days* (Grand Rapids, MI: Revell, 2012), 182.

[190] Twenge and Campbell, *Narcissism*, 83.

[191] *Globe and Mail*, "How to Build Your Child's Learning Brain," November 19, 2010.

[192] Ibid.

[193] *Publishers Weekly*, "What Do Children's Book Consumers Want?" January 31, 2011. www.publishersweekly.com/pw/by-topic/childrens/childrens-industry-news/article/45943-what-do-children-s-book-consumers-want-.html.

[194] *Globe and Mail*, "How to Build Your Child's Learning Brain," November 19, 2010.

[195] James P. Steyer, *The Other Parent: The Inside Story of the Media's Effect on Our Children* (New York: Atria, 2002), 191.

[196] Kropp, *How to Make*, 6.

[197] Donalyn Miller, *The Book Whisperer: Awakening the Inner Reader in Every Child* (Hoboken, NJ: Jossey-Bass, 2009), 110.

[198] *Globe and Mail*, "How to Build Your Child's Learning Brain," November 19, 2010.

Chapter Six

199 Gurian, *Minds*, 12.

200 Csikszentmihalyi, "Education."

201 National Education Association, *Rankings & Estimates: Rankings of the States 2011 and Estimates of School Statistics 2012* (National Education Association, 2011), www.nea. org/assets/docs/NEA_Rankings_And_Estimates_FINAL_ 20120209.pdf.

202 National Education Association, *Status of the American Public School Teacher, 2005-2006* (National Education Association, 2010), 112, www.nea.org/assets/docs/HE/2005-06StatusTextandAppendixA.pdf.

203 *Globe and Mail*, "Failing Boys Part 2: The Endangered Male Teacher," October 18, 2010.

204 *Globe and Mail*, "No Wonder They Turn Away from School," October 15, 2005.

205 MenTeach.org, "Children Learn Best from Role Modeled Behavior and Approaches," www.menteach.org/news/ menteach_interview_children_learn_best_from_role_ modeled_behavior_and_approaches.

206 Rhey Boyd Parsons, "Men and Women Teachers in Tennessee," *Peabody Journal of Education* (1935): 89.

207 Bryan G. Nelson, interview, www.keenreaders.org/bryan-g-nelson.

208 Paul D. Slocumb, *Hear Our Cry: Boys in Crisis* (Highlands, TX: Aha! Process, 2004), 7.

209 Keith E. Stanovich, "Matthew Effects in Reading: Some Consequences of Individual Differences in the Acquisition of Literacy," *Reading Research Quarterly* 21 (1986): 360–407, web.mac.com/kstanovich/Site/Research_on_Reading_ files/RRQ86A.pdf.

210 Cindy Mesko, interview, www.keenreaders.org/cindy-mesko-senior-vp-of-big-brothers-big-sisters-of-america-reading-together-at-school.

211 Anthony Applegate and Mary Applegate, "The Peter Effect," *The Reading Teacher* 57, no. 6 (2004): 554–63.

212 Sommers, *War Against Boys*, 94.

213 Yvette Jackson and Eric J. Cooper, "Building Academic Success with Underachieving Adolescents," in *Adolescent Literacy: Turning Promise into Practice*, ed. Kylene Beers, Robert E. Probst, and Linda Rief (Portsmouth, NH: Heinemann, 2007), 247.

214 Megan Gibson, "Children No Longer Reading Children's Books," *Time News Feed*, October 9, 2010, newsfeed.time.com/2010/10/09/children-no-longer-reading-childrens-books.

215 BC Coalition for School Libraries, www.bccsl.ca.

216 Gurian, *Fine Young Man*, 75.

217 MacDonald, *Boy Smarts*, 216.

218 Sullivan, *Connecting*, 32–34.

219 Tyre, *Trouble*, 133.

220 People for Education, Ontario Trillium Foundation, *Parent Inclusion Manual* (People for Education, 2009), 15.

221 Eric Snow, interview, www.keenreaders.org/parents/interviews.

Chapter Seven

222 MacDonald, *Boy Smarts*, 88.

223 *Globe and Mail*, "Young Hockey Players Hit the Ice, Then the Books," March 12, 2011.

224 Mesko, interview.

225 Gurian, *Purpose*, 173.

226 MacDonald, *Boy Smarts*, 93–95.

[227] Gurian, *Fine Young Man*, 69.

[228] John Duffy, *The Available Parent: Radical Optimism for Raising Teens and Tweens* (Viva Editions, 2011), 84.

[229] MacDonald, *Boy Smarts*, 96.

[230] Dr. David Walsh, www.parentfurther.com.

[231] U.S. Department of Education, Family Involvement in Learning, *Strong Families, Strong Schools* (1994), www.eric.ed.gov/PDFS/ED371909.pdf.

[232] Kaiser Family Foundation, *Generation M²: Media in the Lives of 8- to 18-Year-Olds* (2012), 16, 32, www.kff.org/entmedia/upload/8010.pdf.

[233] Robert Weis and Brittany Cerankosky, "Effects of Video-Game Ownership on Young Boys' Academic and Behavioral Functioning," *Psychological Science* 21, No. 4 (2010).

[234] Dimitri A. Christakis, Frederick J. Zimmerman, David L. DiGiuseppe, and Carolyn A. McCarty, "Early Television Exposure and Subsequent Attentional Problems in Children," *Pediatrics* 113, no. 4 (April 2004): 708–13.

[235] Jane M. Healy, "Early Television Exposure and Subsequent Attention Problems in Children," *Pediatrics* 113, no. 4 (April 2004): 917–18.

[236] Joel Bakan, *Childhood Under Siege: How Big Business Targets Your Children* (New York: Free Press, 2011), 53.

[237] Harris Interactive, www.harrisinteractive.com/news/allnews-bydate.asp?newsid=1196.

[238] Steyer, *Other Parent*, 4–5.

[239] Gurian, *Fine Young Man*, 210–11.

[240] Gary Small, *iBrain: Surviving the Technological Alteration of the Modern Mind* (New York: Collins Living, 2008).

[241] *Globe and Mail*, "More Activity, Less Screen Time Urged for Young Kids," March 27, 2012.

[242] Bakan, *Childhood*, 53.
[243] Duffy, *Available Parent*, 2., 75.
[244] Ibid., 4.
[245] Steyer, *Other Parent*, 5.
[246] Ibid., 6.
[247] Bakan, *Childhood*, 16–17, 34.
[248] Mark Jeffrey, interview, www.keenreaders.org/mark-jeffrey.
[249] PEW Internet and American Life Project, www.pewinternet. org.
[250] Ibid.
[251] Ibid.
[252] Periodical Marketers of Canada, www.thclipc.ca
[253] Small, *iBrain*.
[254] Steyer, *Other Parent*, 197.
[255] The National Center on Addiction and Substance Abuse, *The Importance of Family Dinners* (New York: Columbia University, 2003, 2005, 2011).
[256] *Globe and Mail*, "Fatherless, Yes, but No Statistic," October 21, 2010.
[257] "Male Teachers Show That Real Men Read," *Education World*, www.educationworld.com/a_admin/admin/admin551. shtml.
[258] Sullivan, *Connecting*, 8.

Chapter Eight

[259] Chris Crutcher, interview, March 2011, www.keenreaders.org/ chris-crutcher.
[260] Guys Read, www.guysread.com.
[261] Gurian, *Minds*, 138–39.
[262] Roger Sutton and Martha V. Parravano, *A Family of Readers: The Book Lover's Guide to Children's and Young Adult*

Literature (Somerville, MA: Candlewick, 2010), 113.

263 Tyre, *Trouble*, 150.

264 Gurian, *What*, 64.

265 Carolyn Hart, "Engaged by History: Bringing History to Life for Young Readers," *Canadian Children's Book News* 14, no. 2 (2011): 10.

266 John Duffy, interview, www.keenreaders.org/john-duffy.

267 Sutton and Parravano, *Family*, 285.

268 Reynolds, *I Won't Read*, 41.

269 Michael Gurian, *What Stories Does My Son Need? A Guide to Books and Movies That Build Character in Boys*, (New York: Tarcher, 2000), 9.

270 Ibid., 2.

271 Sutton and Parravano, *Family*, 281.

272 *Globe and Mail*, "Every Child a Reader," January 3, 2011.

273 Gurian, *Fine Young Man*, 36.

274 Gabrielle Bauer, "Why Boys Must be Boys," *ReadersDigest.ca*, www.readersdigest.ca/health/family/why-boys-must-be-boys.

275 Sutton and Parravano, *Family*, 256–7.

276 William G. Brozo, *To Be a Boy, To Be a Reader: Engaging Teens and Preteen Boys in Active Literacy* (Newark, DE: International Reading Association, 2002), 19.

277 Mary F. Rogers, *Novels, Novelists, and Readers: Toward a Phenomenological Sociology of Literature* (New York: SUNY Press, 1991), 76–77.

278 Calculated from www.cwill.bc.ca and www.scbwi.org membership lists.

279 Sutton and Parravano, *Family*, 309.

280 Ibid.

281 Eric Weiner, "Why Women Read More Than Men," NPR.org,

September 5, 2007, www.npr.org/templates/story/story.php?storyId-14175229.

[282] Lawrence Baines, "Cool Books for Tough Guys: 50 Books Out of the Mainstream of Adolescent Literature That Will Appeal to Males Who Do Not Enjoy Reading," *The ALAN Review* 22, no. 1 (1994), n.p.

[283] Boys Project, "Boys in School: What Every Teacher and Parent Should Know," www.drjonherzenberg.com/The-Boys-Project.html.

[284] Rogers, *Novels*, 76.

[285] www.literacytrust.org.uk.

[286] "Why Women Read More," NPR.org.

[287] Kirsty Murray, "How Is Non-Fiction Different?" *Education Web Forum*, September 2, 1999, forum.education.tas.gov.au/webforum/education/cgi- bin/ultimatebb.cgi?ubb=print_topic;f=102;t=000003.

[288] Weiner, "Women Read More."

[289] "Aristotle Was Not Belgian," *Tomemos*, May 21, 2007, tomemos.wordpress.com/2007/05.

[290] Colorado State Library, Department of Education, University of Denver, May 1, 2002.

[291] Oak Lawn Patch, "Real Boys Read," October 18, 2010, oaklawn.patch.com/articles/real-boys-read.

[292] Rogers, *Novels*, 76–77.

[293] Hill Strategies Research, *Who Buys Books and Magazines in Canada?*, by Kelly Hill (2011), www.hillstrategies.com/docs/Who_buys_books_magazines2008.pdf.

[294] Ibid.

[295] Ibid.

[296] Ibid.

[297] Ibid.

[298] Ibid.

[299] Ibid.

[300] Ibid.

[301] Ibid.

[302] Timothy V. Rasinski, *The Fluent Reader: Oral and Silent Reading Strategies for Building Fluency, Word Recognition, and Comprehension* (New York: Scholastic Teaching Resources, 2010), 88.

[303] Harvey Daniels and Nancy Steineke, *Mini-Lessons for Literature Circles* (Portsmouth, NH: Boynton/Cook, 2004), 95.

[304] Rasinski, *Fluent Reader*, 36.

[305] P. S. Koskinen, R. M. Wilson, L. B. Gambrell, and S. B. Neuman, "Captioned Video and Vocabulary Learning: An Innovative Practice in Literacy Instruction," *The Reading Teacher* 47, no. 1 (1993): 36–43.

[306] "Real Boys Read."

[307] Daniels and Steineke, *Mini-Lessons*, 164.

[308] Becky Ray, In Langerman 2004, www.booklistonline.com/Caldecott-Medal/pid=5306371, cited in thesis by Kathleen Hunter.

Chapter Nine

[309] Ralph Fletcher, *Boy Writers: Reclaiming Their Voices* (Portland, ME: Stenhouse Publishers, 2006), 12–13.

[310] James M. Royer and Rachel E. Wing, "Making Sense of Sex Differences in Reading and Math Assessment: The Practice and Engagement Hypothesis," *Issues in Education* 8 (2002): 77.

[311] Smith and Wilhelm, *Reading*, 1.

[312] Royer and Wing, "Making Sense," 77.

[313] Smith and Wilhelm, *Reading*, 1.

314 Judith Kleinfield, "Five Powerful Strategies for Connecting Boys to Schools" (presentation, White House Conference on Helping America's Youth, Indianapolis, IN, June 6, 2006).

315 *Globe and Mail*, "Literacy in Canada," March 26, 2012.

316 Brian R. Haig and Jeffrey D. Haig, *Unlock Your Educational Potential: What Every Student Needs to Know to Succeed!* (Irvine, CA: THF Publishing, 2008), 148.

317 Eric Friesen, "A Spirited Voice," *Nuvo Magazine*, Spring 2011, 87–88.

318 Schultz, *My Dyslexia*, 103.

319 Ibid., 103, 112.

320 Newkirk, *Misreading Masculinity*, 177.

321 Daniel H. Pink, *A Whole New Mind: Why Right-Brainers Will Rule the Future* (New York: Riverhead Books, 2006), 198.

322 Fabio Salio, "Laughing All the Way to the Bank," *Harvard Business Review* (September 2003), cited in *A Whole New Mind: Why Right-Brainers Will Rule the Future* (New York: Riverhead Books, 2006), 24.

323 Caroline Snow, *Unfulfilled Expectations: Home and School Influences on Literacy* (Cambridge, MA: Harvard University Press, 1990).

324 Dreikurs, *Children*, 36.

325 Fletcher, *Boy Writers*, 22.

326 Ibid., 23.

327 Ibid., 113.

328 Leonard Sax, *Why Gender Matters: What Parents and Teachers Need to Know About the Emerging Science of Sex Differences* (New York: Three Rivers Press, 2006), 85.

329 Sandra Lingo, "The All Guys Book Club: Where Boys Take the Risk to Read," *Library Media Connection*, April/May 2007, 24.

[330] Sullivan, *Connecting*, 34.

[331] Daniels and Steineke, *Mini-Lessons*, 2.

[332] Sutton and Parravano, *Family*, 184.

[333] Gurian, *What*, 56.

[334] Duffy, *Available Parent*, 129.

[335] Mary Ann Gray-Schlegel and Thomas Gray-Schlegel, "The Investigation of Gender Stereotypes as Revealed Through Children's Creative Writing," *Reading Research and Instruction* 35, no. 2 (1995–1996): 160–70.

[336] Newkirk, *Misreading Masculinity*, 119.

[337] Ibid., 179.

[338] Andrew Auseon, interview, www.keenreaders.org/andrew-auseon.

[339] Harvey Daniels, "One Teacher to One Student with One Powerful Strategy," in *Adolescent Literacy: Turning Promise into Practice*, ed. Kylene Beers, Robert E. Probst, and Linda Rief (Portsmouth, NH: Heinemann, 2007), 132.

[340] Daniels and Steineke, *Mini-Lessons*, 138–9.

[341] Regina G. Richards, *Learn: Playful Strategies for All Students* (Riverside, CA: RET Center Press, 2001), 75.

[342] Regina G. Richards, "Understanding Why Students Avoid Writing," LDOnline (1999), www.ldonline.org/article/5892.

[343] Smith and Wilhelm, *Reading*, 33.

[344] MacDonald, *Boy Smarts*, 141.

[345] Sullivan, *Connecting*, 54.

[346] Regina G. Richards, "The Writing Road," Colorín Colorado, 2008, www.colorincolorado.org/article/5608.

[347] MacDonald, *Boy Smarts*, 142.

[348] Richards, "Writing Road."

[349] Newkirk, *Misreading Masculinity*, 179.

350 Ibid., 184.

351 Ibid., 87.

Chapter Ten

352 Slocumb, *Hear*, 26.

353 MacDonald, *Boy Smarts*, 101.

354 Slocumb, *Hear*, 27.

355 Betty Hart and Todd Risley, *Meaningful Differences in the Everyday Experience of Young American Children* (Baltimore, MD: Brookes Publishing, 1995).

356 William Glasser, *The Quality School: Managing Students Without Coercion* (New York: HarperCollins, 1990), 46.

357 Loveandlogic.com

358 Karyn Purvis, David Cross, and Wendy Sunshine, *The Connected Child: Bring Hope and Healing to Your Adoptive Family* (Toronto: McGraw-Hill, 2007).

359 Karyn Purvis and David Cross, "Trust Based Relational Intervention," Institute of Child Development, www.child.tcu.edu.

360 Tina Feigal, *The Pocket Coach for Parents: Your Two-Week Guide to a Dramatically Improved Life with Your Intense Child* (Edina, MN: Beaver's Pond Press, 2008).

Chapter Eleven

361 Anthony J. Ipsaro, *White Men, Women, and Minorities in the Changing Workforce* (Denver, CO: Meridian Associates, 1997), 214.

362 Peck, "Jobless Era," 46.

363 Ibid., 52.

364 Ibid.

365 *Globe and Mail*, "Women Make the Grade, but Not the

Money," September 8, 2010.

366 Richard J. Murnane and Frank Levy, *Teaching the New Basic Skills: Principles for Educating Children to Thrive in a Changing Economy* (New York: Martin Kessler/Free Press, 1996), 228.

367 Ibid., vii.

368 Peck, "Jobless Era," 54.

369 Murnane and Levy, *Teaching*, 229.

370 *Globe and Mail*, "To Sir, with Love: U.S. Schools Seek Role Models for Boys," October 18, 2010.

371 Peck, "Jobless Era," 56.

372 Peter Cappelli and Rocio Bonet, "What Happened to the 'New Deal' with Employees?" in *Workforce Wake-Up Call: Your Workforce Is Changing, Are You?*, ed. Robert Gandossy, Nidhi Verma, and Elissa Tucker (Hoboken, NJ: Wiley, 2006), 120.

373 Murnane and Levy, *Teaching*, 229.

374 "Preface," in *Workforce Wake-Up Call: Your Workforce Is Changing, Are You?*, ed. Robert Gandossy, Nidhi Verma, and Elissa Tucker (Hoboken, NJ: Wiley, 2006), xvi–xvii.

375 Peck, "Jobless Era," 54.

376 *Globe and Mail*, "Mind the Gap: No 'People Skills,' No Job," March 5, 2012.

377 Ibid.

378 Ipsaro, *White*, 253.

379 Nigel Nicholson, "Organization as Nature Intended: Human Universals and the Employment Experience," in *Workforce Wake-Up Call: Your Workforce Is Changing, Are You?*, ed. Robert Gandossy, Nidhi Verma, and Elissa Tucker (Hoboken, NJ: Wiley, 2006), 267.

380 Pink, *A Whole New Mind*, 1.

[381] Ibid., 136

[382] Murnane and Levy, *Teaching*, 9.

[383] Jean Mavrelis, interview.

[384] Peck, "Jobless Era," 48.

[385] Mavrelis, interview.

[386] Thomas Kochman and Jean Mavrelis, *Corporate Tribalism: White Men/White Women and Cultural Diversity at Work* (Chicago: University of Chicago Press, 2009), 194.

[387] Ibid., 113.

[388] Ipsaro, *White*, 221.

[389] Peck, "Jobless Era," 53.

BIBLIOGRAPHY

Applegate, Anthony, and Mary Applegate. "The Peter Effect." *The Reading Teacher* 57, no. 6 (2004): 554–63.

"Aristotle Was Not Belgian." *Tomemos.* May 21, 2007. tomemos. wordpress.com/2007/05.

Armstrong, Thomas. *In Their Own Way: Discovering and Encouraging Your Child's Multiple Intelligences.* New York: Tarcher, 2000.

Atwell, Nancie. *The Reading Zone: How to Help Kids Become Skilled, Passionate, Habitual, Critical Readers.* New York: Scholastic Teaching Resources, 2007.

Auseon, Andrew. Interview. www.keenreaders.org/andrew-auseon.

Baines, Lawrence. "Cool Books for Tough Guys: 50 Books Out of the Mainstream of Adolescent Literature That Will Appeal to Males Who Do Not Enjoy Reading." *The ALAN Review* 22, no. 1 (1994).

Bakan, Joel. *Childhood Under Siege: How Big Business Targets Your Children.* New York: Free Press, 2011.

Bauer, Gabrielle. "Why Boys Must be Boys." *ReadersDigest.ca.* www.readersdigest.ca/health/family/why-boys-must-be-boys.

BC Coalition for School Libraries. www.bccsl.ca.

Bloom, Adi. "Girls Go for Little Women but Boys Prefer Lara." *Times Educational Supplement,* March 15, 2002.

The Boys Project. "Boys in School: What Every Teacher and Parent Should Know." www.drjonherzenberg.com/The-Boys-Project. html.

—. "Helping Boys Become Successful Men." www.drjonherzen-berg.com/The-Boys-Project.html.

The Brain Injury Association of Canada. "Males Are Twice as Likely to Sustain a Brain Injury." 2008. biac-aclc.ca/en/2008/09/21/males-are-twice-as-likely-to-sustain-a-brain-injury.

Brozo, William G. *To Be a Boy, To Be a Reader: Engaging Teens and Preteen Boys in Active Literacy.* Newark, DE: International Reading Association, 2002.

Burgess, Simon, Brendon McConnel, Carol Propper, and Deborah Wilson, "Girls Rock, Boys Roll: An Analysis of the Age 14-16 Gender Gap in English Schools," *Scottish Journal of Political Economy* 51, no. 2 (2004): 209–29.

Burns, Marilyn. *Math: Facing an American Phobia.* Sausalito, CA: Math Solutions Publications, 1998.

Cappelli, Peter, and Rocio Bonet. "What Happened to the 'New Deal' with Employees?" In *Workforce Wake-Up Call: Your Workforce Is Changing, Are You?* edited by Robert Gandossy, Nidhi Verma, and Elissa Tucker. Hoboken, NJ: Wiley, 2006.

Carbo, Marie, Rita Dunn, and Kenneth Dunn. *Teaching Students to Read Through Their Individual Learning Styles.* Upper Saddle River, NJ: Prentice-Hall, 1986.

Children's Writers and Illustrators of British Columbia. www.cwill.bc.ca.

Chinn, Steve. *The Trouble with Maths: A Practical Guide to Helping Learners with Numeracy Difficulties.* Second Edition. New York: Routledge, 2012.

Christakis, Dimitri A., Frederick J. Zimmerman, David L. DiGiuseppe, and Carolyn A. McCarty. "Early Television Exposure and Subsequent Attentional Problems in Children." *Pediatrics* 113, no. 4 (April 2004): 708–13.

Chukwu-Etu, Ogbonnia. "Underachieving Learning: Can They

Learn at All?" *ARECLS* 6, no. 4 (2009): 84-102.

"Civic Report No. 48: Leaving Boys Behind: Public High School Graduation Rates." New York: Manhattan Institute for Policy Research, 2006.

College of Pathologists and Audiologists of Quebec, www.ooaq.qc.ca.

Colorado Department of Education. Colorado State Library. www.cde.state.co.us/cdelib.

Conlin, Michelle. "Look Who's Bringing Home More Bacon." *BusinessWeek*, January 28, 2003. www.businessweek.com/careers/content/jan2003/ca20030128_9891.htm.

Crutcher, Chris. Interview. March 2011. www.keenreaders.org/chris-crutcher.

Csikszentmihalyi, Mihaly. "Education for the 21st Century." *Education Week*, April 19, 2000, www.edweek.org/ew/articles/2000/04/19/32csikszentmihalyi.h19.html?qs=education.

Cunningham, Anne, and Keith Stanovich. "What Reading Does For the Mind." *American Educator* 22 (1998): 8–15.

Daniels, Harvey. "One Teacher to One Student with One Powerful Strategy." In *Adolescent Literacy: Turning Promise into Practice*, edited by Kylene Beers, Robert E. Probst, and Linda Rief. Portsmouth, NH: Heinemann, 2007.

Daniels, Harvey, and Nancy Steineke. *Mini-Lessons for Literature Circles*. Portsmouth, NH: Boynton/Cook, 2004.

Dreikurs, Rudolf. *Children: The Challenge*. New York: Plume, 1991.

Duffy, John. *The Available Parent: Radical Optimism for Raising Teens and Tweens*. Berkeley, CA: Viva Editions, 2011.

—. Interview. www.keenreaders.org/john-duffy.

Dunn, Rita, and Kenneth Dunn. *Teaching Secondary Students Through Their Individual Learning Styles*. Toronto: Allyn and

Bacon, 1993.

Egeler, Daniel. *Mentoring Millennials: Shaping the Next Genera-tion.* Colorado Springs, CO: NavPress, 2003.

El Nokali, Nermeen E., Heather J. Bachman, and Elizabeth Votruba-Drzal. "Parent Involvement and Children's Academic and Social Development in Elementary School." *Child Development* 81, no. 3 (2010): 1001.

Farrald, Robert, and Richard Schamber. *A Mainstream Approach to Identification Assessment and Amelioration of Learning Disabilities.* New York: Adapt Press, 1973.

Feigal, Tina. *The Pocket Coach for Parents: Your Two-Week Guide to a Dramatically Improved Life with Your Intense Child.* Edina, MN: Beaver's Pond Press, 2008.

Fleischer, Cathy. *Reading and Writing and Teens: A Parent's Guide to Adolescent Literacy.* Urbana, IL: National Council of Teachers of English, 2010.

Fletcher, Ralph. *Boy Writers: Reclaiming Their Voices.* Portland, ME: Stenhouse Publishers, 2006.

The Franklin Institute. "The Human Brain." www.fi.edu/learn/brain/head.html.

Friedland, Ellen S., and Kim S. Truesdell. "Kids Reading Together: Ensuring the Success of a Buddy Reading Program." *The Reading Teacher* 58, no. 1 (2004): 76–79.

Friesen, Eric. "A Spirited Voice." *Nuvo Magazine,* Spring 2011.

Frost, Shari. Interview. www.keenreaders.org/shari-frost-is-red-hot-on-reading.

Gadsden, Vivian, and Aisha Ray. "Fathers' Role in Children's Academic Achievement and Early Literacy." *Eric Digest,* 2003, ceep.crc.uiuc.edu/eecearchive/digests/2003/ray03.pdf.

Garrison, Michelle M., Kimberly Liekweg, and Dimitri A. Christakis. "Media Use and Child Sleep: The Impact of Content,

Timing, and Environment." *Pediatrics* 128, no. 1 (2011): 29–35. DOI: 10.1542/peds.2010-3304.

Gibson, Megan. "Children No Longer Reading Children's Books." *Time News Feed.* October 9, 2010. newsfeed.time.com/2010/10/09/children-no-longer-reading-childrens-books.

Glasser, William. *The Quality School: Managing Students Without Coercion.* New York: HarperCollins, 1990.

Globe and Mail. "Are Boys Merely Misunderstood?" October 20, 2010.

—. "Children Need Not be Predestined." September 6, 2011.

—. "Every Child a Reader." January 3, 2011.

—. "Failing Boys Part 2: The Endangered Male Teacher." October 18, 2010.

—. "Fatherless, Yes, but No Statistic." October 21, 2010.

—. "How to Build Your Child's Learning Brain." November 19, 2010.

—. "Literacy in Canada." March 26, 2012.

—. "Mind the Gap: No 'People Skills,' No Job." March 5, 2012.

—. "More Activity, Less Screen Time Urged for Young Kids." March 27, 2012.

—. "No Wonder They Turn Away from School." October 15, 2005.

—. "Probing the Problem: Why Are Boys Falling Behind in School?" October 16, 2010.

—. "The Sins of the Fathers Are Visited on Black Youth." December 2, 2005.

—. "To Sir, with Love: U.S. Schools Seek Role Models for Boys." October 18, 2010.

—. "We Need Tool-Savvy Teachers." October 20, 2010.

—. "What's Your Degree Worth?" September 26, 2011.

—. "Women Make the Grade, but Not the Money." September 8,

2010.

——. "Young Hockey Players Hit the Ice, Then the Books." March 12, 2011.

Gojak, Linda M. Interview. www.kcenreaders.org/linda-m-gojak-on-youth-and-math.

Gray-Schlegel, Mary Ann, and Thomas Gray-Schlegel. "The Investigation of Gender Stereotypes as Revealed Through Children's Creative Writing." *Reading Research and Instruction* 35, no. 2 (1995–1996): 160–70.

Gurian, Michael. *Boys and Girls Learn Differently! A Guide for Teachers and Parents.* Hoboken, NJ: Jossey-Bass, 2001.

——. *A Fine Young Man: What Parents, Mentors, and Educators Can Do to Shape Adolescent Boys into Exceptional Men.* New York: Tarcher, 1999.

——. *The Minds of Boys: Saving Our Sons from Falling Behind in School and Life.* Hoboken, NJ: Jossey-Bass, 2005.

——. *The Purpose of Boys: Helping Our Sons Find Meaning, Significance, and Direction in their Lives.* Hoboken, NJ: Jossey-Bass, 2009.

——. *What Could He Be Thinking? How a Man's Mind Really Works.* New York: St. Martin's Press, 2004.

——. *What Stories Does My Son Need? A Guide to Books and Movies That Build Character in Boys.* New York: Tarcher, 2000.

Guys Read. www.guysread.com.

Guys Read Pilot Program: Final Report. Fairbanks North Star Borough Library in Alaska (2007).

Haig, Brian R., and Jeffrey D. Haig. *Unlock Your Educational Potential: What Every Student Needs to Know to Succeed!* Irvine, CA: THF Publishing, 2008.

Hanivsky, Olena. "Cost Estimates of Dropping Out of High School in Canada." *Canadian Council of Learning* (2008): 28.

Harris Interactive. "Video Game Addiction: Is It Real?" Harris Interactive. April 2, 2007. June 12, 2012. www.harrisinteractive.com.

Hart, Betty, and Todd Risley. *Meaningful Differences in the Everyday Experience of Young American Children.* Baltimore, MD: Brookes Publishing, 1995.

Hart, Carolyn. "Engaged by History: Bringing History to Life for Young Readers." *Canadian Children's Book News* 14, no. 2 (2011): 10.

Hayward, Christianne. Interview. www.keenreaders.org/bookclub-maestro-christianne-hayward.

Healy, Jane M. "Early Television Exposure and Subsequent Attention Problems in Children." *Pediatrics* 113, no. 4 (April 2004): 917–18.

Hill Strategies Research. *Who Buys Books and Magazines in Canada?*, by Kelly Hill. 2011. www.hillstrategies.com/docs/Who_buys_books_magazines2008.pdf.

Ipsaro, Anthony J. *White Men, Women, and Minorities in the Changing Workforce.* Denver, CO: Meridian Associates, 1997.

Jackson, David, and Jonathan Salisbury. "Why Should Secondary Schools Take Working with Boys Seriously?" *Gender & Education* 8, no. 1 (1996): 105.

Jackson, Yvette, and Eric J. Cooper. "Building Academic Success with Underachieving Adolescents." In *Adolescent Literacy: Turning Promise into Practice*, edited by Kylene Beers, Robert E. Probst, and Linda Rief. Portsmouth, NH: Heinemann, 2007.

Jeffrey, Mark. Interview. www.keenreaders.org/mark-jeffrey.

Jobe, Ron, and Mary Dayton-Sakari, *Reluctant Readers:*

Connecting Students and Books for Successful Reading Experiences. Portland, ME: Stenhouse Publishers, 1999.

Kaiser Family Foundation. *Generation M²: Media in the Lives of 8- to 18-Year-Olds*. 2012. 16, 32. www.kff.org/entmedia/upload/8010.pdf.

Kindlon, Dan, and Michael Thompson. *Raising Cain: Protecting the Emotional Life of Boys*. New York: Ballantine, 1999.

"Kids and Family Reading Report." New York: Scholastic, 2006, www.scholastic.com/aboutscholastic/news/reading_survey_press_call_2.pdf.

KidsHealth.org. "Auditory Processing Disorder." kidshealth.org/parent/medical/ears/central_auditory.html#cat138.

Kipnis, Aaron. *Angry Young Men: How Parents, Teachers, and Counselors Can Help "Bad Boys" Become Good Men*. Hoboken, NJ: Jossey-Bass, 2002.

Kleinfield, Judith. "Five Powerful Strategies for Connecting Boys to Schools." Presentation. White House Conference on Helping America's Youth. Indianapolis, IN, June 6, 2006.

Kochman, Thomas, and Jean Mavrelis. *Corporate Tribalism: White Men/White Women and Cultural Diversity at Work*. Chicago: University of Chicago Press, 2009.

Koskinen, P. S., R. M. Wilson, L. B. Gambrell, and S. B. Neuman. "Captioned Video and Vocabulary Learning: An Innovative Practice in Literacy Instruction." *The Reading Teacher* 47, no. 1 (1993): 36–43.

Kropp, Paul. *How to Make Your Child a Reader for Life*. New York: Random House, 2000.

—. *I'll Be the Parent, You Be the Kid: The Hot Button Topics in Parenting*. New York: Random House, 1998.

—. Interview. www.keenreaders.org/hip-help-from-paul-kropp.

Learning Disabilities Association of America. "One in Seven."

www.ldanatl.org/new_to_ld/index.asp.

Lehman, Kevin. *Have a New Kid by Friday: How to Change Your Child's Attitude, Behavior & Character in Five Days*. Grand Rapids, MI: Revell, 2012.

Lingo, Sandra. "The All Guys Book Club: Where Boys Take the Risk to Read." *Library Media Connection*, April/May 2007.

Lippman, Laura, Astrid Atienza, Andrew Rivers, and Julie Keith. "A Developmental Perspective on College and Workplace Readiness." *Child Trends*. Bill and Melinda Gates Foundation, 2008. www.childtrends.org/Files/Child_Trends-2008_09_15_FR_ReadinessReport.pdf.

Literacy Awareness Resource Manual for Police. Literacy and Policing Project of the Canadian Association of Chiefs of Police, 2008.

Los Angeles Caregiver Resource Center. "Fact Sheet: Traumatic Brain Injury." 2003. lacrc.usc.edu/damcms/sitegroups/Site-Group1/files/fact-sheets/DMH%20Funded/Traumatic%20Brain%20Injury.pdf.

Love and Logic. www.loveandlogic.com.

Lyngstad, Torkild Hovde. "The Impact of Parents' and Spouses' Education on Divorce Rates in Norway." *Demographic Research* 10 (2004): 121–142. www.demographic-research.org/volumes/vol10/5/10-5.pdf.

MacDonald, Barry. *Boy Smarts: Mentoring Boys for Success*. Surrey, BC: Mentoring Press, 2005.

"Male Teachers Show That Real Men Read." *Education World*. www.educationworld.com/a_admin/admin/admin551.shtml.

Manaster, Guy, and Raymond Corsini. *Individual Psychology: Theory and Practice*. Chicago: Adler School of Professional Psychology, 1982.

Marcus, Sander. "Personality Styles of Chronic Academic Underachievers." SelfGrowth.com. August 9, 2007

Mavrelis, Jean. Interview.

McKellar, Danica. *Math Doesn't Suck: How to Survive Middle School Math without Losing Your Mind or Breaking a Nail.* New York: Hudson Street Press, 2007.

MenTeach.org. "Children Learn Best from Role Modeled Behavior and Approaches." www.menteach.org/news/menteach_interview_children_learn_best_from_role_modeled_behavior_and_approaches.

Mesko, Cindy. Interview. www.keenreaders.org/cindy-mesko-senior-vp-of-big-brothers-big-sisters-of-america-reading-together-at-school.

Miller, Donalyn. *The Book Whisperer: Awakening the Inner Reader in Every Child.* Hoboken, NJ: Jossey-Bass, 2009.

Minton, Leslie. *What if Your ABCs Were Your 123s?: Building Connections Between Literacy and Numeracy.* Thousand Oaks, CA: Corwin Press, 2007.

Murnane, Richard J., and Frank Levy. *Teaching the New Basic Skills: Principles for Educating Children to Thrive in a Changing Economy.* New York: Martin Kessler/Free Press, 1996.

Murray, Kirsty. "How Is Non-Fiction Different?" Education Web Forum, September 2, 1999. forum.education.tas.gov.au/webforum/education/cgi-bin/ultimatebb.cgi?ubb=print_topic;f=102;t=000003.

Myers, Walter Dean. "Letter to Readers." *Handbook for Boys: A Novel.* New York: Amistad, 2003.

National Center on Addiction and Substance Abuse. *The Importance of Family Dinners.* New York: Columbia University, 2003, 2005, 2011.

National Dropout Prevention Center/Network. "Early Literacy Development." www.dropoutprevention.org/effective-strategies/early-literacy-development.

National Early Literacy Panel. *Developing Early Literacy*. National Institute for Literacy, 2008. www.nichd.nih.gov/publications/pubs/upload/NELPReport09.pdf.

National Education Association. *Rankings & Estimates: Rankings of the States 2011 and Estimates of School Statistics 2012.* Washington, DC: National Education Association, 2011. www.nea.org/assets/docs/NEA_Rankings_And_Estimates_FINAL_20120209.pdf.

—. *Status of the American Public School Teacher, 2005–2006.* Washington, DC: National Education Association, 2010. www.nea.org/assets/docs/HE/2005-06StatusTextandAppendixA.pdf.

National Institute for Literacy. *Fast Facts on Literacy & Fact Sheet on Correctional Education*. National Institute for Literacy, 1998.

National Institute on Deafness and Other Communication Disorders. "Learning Disabilities in Children." www.helpguide.org/mental/learning_disabilities.htm.

The National Literacy Trust. www.literacytrust.org.uk.

Nelson, Bryan G. Interview. www.keenreaders.org/bryan-g-nelson.

Newkirk, Thomas. *Misreading Masculinity: Boys, Literacy, and Popular Culture*. Portsmouth, NH: Heinemann, 2002.

Nicholson, Nigel. "Organization as Nature Intended: Human Universals and the Employment Experience." In *Workforce Wake-Up Call: Your Workforce Is Changing, Are You?* edited by Robert Gandossy, Nidhi Verma, and Elissa Tucker. Hoboken, NJ: Wiley, 2006.

Oak Lawn Patch. "Real Boys Read." October 18, 2010. oaklawn.patch.com/articles/real-boys-read.

Panettieri, Gina, and Philip S. Hall. *The Single Mother's Guide to Raising Remarkable Boys*. Avon, MA: Adams Media, 2008.

Parsons, Rhey Boyd. "Men and Women Teachers in Tennessee." *Peabody Journal of Education* (1935): 89.

Patterson, James. "How to Get Your Kid to be a Fanatic Reader." CNN.com, September 28, 2011. www.cnn.com/2011/09/28/opinion/patterson-kids-reading/index.html.

Peck, Don. "How a New Jobless Era will Transform America." *The Atlantic*, March 2010.

People for Education, Ontario Trillium Foundation. *Parent Inclusion Manual*. Toronto: People for Education, 2009.

Periodical Marketers of Canada. www.thebpc.ca.

PEW Internet and American Life Project. www.pewinternet.org.

PEW Research Center. www.pewresearch.org.

Pink, Daniel H. *A Whole New Mind: Why Right-Brainers Will Rule the Future*. New York: Riverhead Books, 2006.

"Preface." In *Workforce Wake-Up Call: Your Workforce is Changing, Are You?* edited by Robert Gandossy, Nidhi Verma, and Elissa Tucker. Hoboken, NJ: Wiley, 2006.

Pryor, John, Linda DeAngelo, Laura Blake, Sylvia Hurtado, and Serge Tran. *The American Freshman: National Norms for Fall 2011*. Los Angeles: Higher Education Research Institute, UCLA, 2011.

Publishers Weekly. "What Do Children's Book Consumers Want?" January 31, 2011. www.publishersweekly.com/pw/by-topic/childrens/childrens-industry-news/article/45943-what-do-children-s-book-consumers-want-.html.

Purvis, Karyn, and David Cross. "Trust Based Relational Intervention." Institute of Child Development. www.child.tcu.edu.

Purvis, Karyn, David Cross, and Wendy Sunshine. *The Connected Child: Bring Hope and Healing to Your Adoptive Family*.

Toronto: McGraw-Hill, 2007.

Rasinski, Timothy V. *The Fluent Reader: Oral and Silent Reading Strategies for Building Fluency, Word Recognition, and Comprehension.* New York: Scholastic Teaching Resources, 2010.

Ray, Becky. In Langerman 2004, www.booklistonline.com/Caldecott-Medal/pid=5306371. Cited in thesis by Kathleen Hunter.

Reynolds, Marilyn. *I Won't Read and You Can't Make Me: Reaching Reluctant Teen Readers.* Portsmouth, NH: Boynton/ Cook, 2004.

Richards, Regina G. *Learn: Playful Strategies for All Students.* Riverside, CA: RET Center Press, 2001.

—. "The Writing Road." Colorín Colorado, 2008. www.colorincolorado.org/article/5608.

—. "Understanding Why Students Avoid Writing." LDOnline. 1999. www.ldonline.org/article/5892.

Rimm, Sylvia. *Why Bright Kids Get Poor Grades and What You Can Do About It: A Six-Step Program for Parents and Teachers.* New York: Crown Publishers, 1995.

Rogers, Mary F. *Novels, Novelists, and Readers: Toward a Phenomenological Sociology of Literature.* New York: SUNY Press, 1991.

Rothenberger, Aribert, and Tobias Banaschewski. "Informing the ADHD Debate." *Scientific American* 17 (Nov. 2004): 36–41.

Royer, James M., and Rachel E. Wing. "Making Sense of Sex Differences in Reading and Math Assessment: The Practice and Engagement Hypothesis." *Issues in Education* 8 (2002): 77.

Rutter, Michael, Avshalom Caspi, Robert Goodman, John L. Horwood, David Fergusson, Barbara Maughan, and Julia Carroll. "Sex Differences in Developmental Reading Disability— New Findings from Four Epidemiological Studies." *Journal of the American Medical Association* 291, no. 16 (2004): 2007.

Salio, Fabio. "Laughing All the Way to the Bank." *Harvard Business Review*. September 2003, 16–17. Print.

Sax, Leonard. *Why Gender Matters: What Parents and Teachers Need to Know About the Emerging Science of Sex Differences.* New York: Three Rivers Press, 2006.

Schultz, Philip. *My Dyslexia.* New York: W.W. Norton, 2011.

Slocumb, Paul D. *Hear Our Cry: Boys in Crisis.* Highlands, TX: Aha! Process, 2004.

Small, Gary. *iBrain: Surviving the Technological Alteration of the Modern Mind.* New York: Collins Living, 2008.

Smith, Michael W., and Jeffrey D. Wilhelm. *Reading Don't Fix No Chevys: Literacy in the Lives of Young Men.* Portsmouth, NH: Heinemann, 2002.

Snow, Caroline. *Unfulfilled Expectations: Home and School Influences on Literacy.* Cambridge, MA: Harvard University Press, 1990.

Snow, Eric. Interview. www.keenreaders.org/parents/interviews.

Society of Children's Book Writers and Illustrators. www.scbwi. org.

Sommers, Christina Hoff. *The War Against Boys: How Misguided Feminism is Harming Our Young Men.* New York: Simon & Schuster, 2001.

Stanovich, Keith E. "Matthew Effects in Reading: Some Consequences of Individual Differences in the Acquisition of Literacy." *Reading Research Quarterly* 21 (1986): 360–407. web.mac. com/kstanovich/Site/Research_on_Reading_files/RRQ86A. pdf.

Statistics Canada. *Public Postsecondary Graduates by Institution Type, Sex, and Field of Study.* www.statcan.gc.ca/tables-tableaux/sum-som/l01/cst01/educ70b-eng.htm.

Steyer, James P. *The Other Parent: The Inside Story of the Media's Effect on Our Children.* New York: Atria, 2002.

Sullivan, Michael. *Connecting Boys with Books 2.* Chicago: ALA Editions, 2009.

Sutton, Roger, and Martha V. Parravano. *A Family of Readers: The Book Lover's Guide to Children's and Young Adult Literature.* Somerville, MA: Candlewick, 2010.

Thompson, Clive. "How Khan Academy Is Changing the Rules of Education." *Wired Magazine.* August 2011. Print.

Twenge, Jean M. *Generation Me: Why Today's Young Americans Are More Confident, Assertive, Entitled—and More Miserable than Ever Before.* New York: Free Press, 2007.

Twenge, Jean M., and W. Keith Campbell. *The Narcissism Epidemic: Living in the Age of Entitlement.* New York: Free Press, 2009.

Tyre, Peg. *The Trouble with Boys: A Surprising Report Card on Our Sons, Their Problems at School, and What Parents and Educators Must Do.* New York: Three Rivers Press, 2009.

U.S. Census Bureau. www.census.gov/newsroom/releases/archives/facts_for_features_special_editions/cb06-ffse07.html.

—. *Living Arrangements of Children: 2009.* By Rose M. Kreider and Renee Ellis. P70–126. Washington, DC: United States Government Printing Office, 2011.

U.S. Department of Education, National Center for Education Statistics. *Science 2011: National Assessment of Educational Progress at Grade 8.* NCES 2012-465. Washington, DC: United States Government Printing Office, 2011.

— *Strong Families, Strong Schools.* 1994. www.eric.ed.gov/PDFS/ED371909.pdf.

—. *The Condition of Education 2011.* By Susan Aud, William Hussar, Grace Kena, Kevin Bianco, Lauren Frohlich, Jana

Kemp, and Kim Tahan. NCES 2011–033. Washington, DC: United States Government Printing Office, 2011.

—. *Digest of Education Statistics, 2010.* NCES 2011–015. nces. ed.gov/programs/digest/d10/tables/dt10_199.asp.

—. *Highlights From PISA (Program for International Student Assessment) 2006.* By Stephane Baldi, Ying Jin, Melanie Skemer, Patricia J. Green, and Deborah Herget. NCES 2008–016. Washington, DC: United States Government Printing Office, 2007.

—. *The Nation's Report Card: Reading 2007.* By Jihyun Lee, Wendy S. Grigg, and Patricia L. Donahue. NCES 2007–496. Washington, DC: United States Government Printing Office, 2007.

—. *Trends in Educational Equity of Girls and Women.* By Yupin Bae, Susan Choy, Claire Geddes, Jennifer Sable, and Thomas Snyder. NCES 2000–030. Washington, DC: United States Government Printing Office, 2000.

U.S. Department of Education, Planning and Evaluation Service. *Everybody Wins!* 1998–1999. www.teachervision.fen.com/skill-builder/group-work/48775.html.

Upton, Bruce. "World's Greatest Tutor." Forbes.com. March 12, 2012.

U.S.News. "Average High School GPAs Increased Since 1990." April 19, 2011, www.usnews.com/opinion/articles/2011/04/19/average-high-school-gpas-increased-since-1990.

VARK: A Guide to Learning Styles. www.vark-learn.com/english/index.asp.

Varvil-Weld, Douglas. "Your Child's Underachievement and What to Do About It." Pauquette Center. www.pauquette.com/archive9.html.

Walsh, David. www.parentfurther.com. (Dr. Walsh provides

insights, valuable articles, and very helpful research for parents facing the many challenges in the twenty-first century.)

Ward, David. Interview. www.keenreaders.org/literacy-expert-david-ward-what-is-a-reluctant-reader.

Weiner, Eric. "Why Women Read More Than Men." NPR. org, September 5, 2007. www.npr.org/templates/story/story. php?storyId=14175229.

Weis, Robert, and Brittany Cerankosky. "Effects of Video-Game Ownership on Young Boys' Academic and Behavioral Functioning." *Psychological Science* 21, No. 4 (2010).

Wheeler, Gerald. Interview. www.keenreaders.org/dr-gerald-wheeler-on-youth-and-science.

Whitley, Michael. *Bright Minds, Poor Grades: Understanding and Motivating Your Underachieving Child*. New York: Berkley Publishing, 2001.

Zambo, Debby, and William Brozo. *Bright Beginnings for Boys: Engaging Young Boys in Active Literacy*. Newark, DE: International Reading Association, 2008.

ADDITIONAL RECOMMENDED BOOKS
FOR PARENTS

Ammon, Bette D., and Gale W. Sherman. *Rip-Roaring Reads for Reluctant Teen Readers*. New York: Libraries Unlimited, 1993.

Ansbacher, Heinz, and Rowena Ansbacher. *The Individual Psychology of Alfred Adler: A Systematic Presentation in Selections from His Writings*. New York: Basic Books, 1956.

Beers, Kylene, Robert Probst, and Linda Rief. *Adolescent Literacy: Turning Promise into Practice*. Portsmouth, NH: Heinemann, 2007.

Bettner, Betty Lou, and Amy Lew. *Raising Kids Who Can*. Newton Centre, MA: Connexions Press, 2005.

Bluestein, Jane. *Parents, Teens and Boundaries: How to Draw the Line*. Deerfield Beach, FL: Health Communications, Inc., 1993.

Clarke, Jean. *Self-Esteem: A Family Affair*. Center City, MN: Hazelden, 1998.

Elkind, David. *The Hurried Child: Growing Up Too Fast Too Soon*. Cambridge, MA: Da Capo Press, 2001.

Fay, Jim and Foster Cline. *Parenting with Love and Logic: Teaching Children Responsibility*. Colorado Springs, CO: NavPress, 2006.

Feigal, Tina. *The Pocket Coach for Parents: Your Two-Week Guide to a Dramatically Improved Life with Your Intense Child*. Edina, MN: Beaver's Pond Press, 2008.

Gardner, Howard. *Frames of Mind: The Theory of Multiple Intelligences*. New York: Basic Books, 1983.

Goleman, Daniel. *Emotional Intelligence: Why It Can Matter More Than IQ*. New York: Bantam Books, 1995.

Hartley-Brewer, Elizabeth. *Raising Confident Boys: 100 Tips for Parents and Teachers*. Cambridge, MA: Da Capo Press, 2000.

Huebner, Dawn. *What to Do When You Dread Your Bed: A Kid's Guide to Overcoming Problems with Sleep*. Washington, D.C.: Magination Press, 2008.

—. *What to Do When Your Temper Flares: A Kid's Guide to Overcoming Problems with Anger*. Washington, D.C.: Magination Press, 2007.

—. *What to Do When You Worry Too Much: A Kid's Guide to Overcoming Anxiety*. Washington, D.C.: Magination Press, 2005.

—. *What to Do When Your Brain Gets Stuck: A Kid's Guide to Overcoming OCD*. Washington, D.C.: Magination Press, 2007.

James, Amy. *School Success for Children with Special Needs: Everything You Need to Know to Help Your Child Learn*. Hoboken, NJ: Jossey-Bass, 2008.

Kowalski, Robin, Susan Limber, and Patricia Agatston. *Cyber Bullying: Bullying in the Digital Age*. Malden, MA: Blackwell Publishing, 2008.

Kranowitz, Carol. *The Out-of-Sync Child Has Fun: Activities for Kids with Sensory Processing Disorder*. New York: Perigree, 2003.

—. *The Out-of-Sync Child: Recognizing and Coping with Sensory Processing Disorder*. New York: Perigree, 2006.

Lazear, David. *Pathways of Learning: Teaching Students and Parents About Multiple Intelligences*. Tucson, AZ: Zephyr Press, 2001.

Lehman, James, and Janet Lehman. www.thetotaltransformation.

com. (This is a parenting program that is highly effective, especially for dealing with defiance and challenging children.)

McKay, Gary, and Steven Maybell. *Calming the Family Storm: Anger Management for Moms, Dads, and All the Kids.* Atascadero, CA: Impact Publishers, 2004.

Nelsen, Jane, and Lynn Lott. *Positive Discipline A-Z: 1001 Solutions to Everyday Parenting Problems.* Roseville, CA: Prima Publishing, 2000.

Neuman, Gary, and Patricia Romanowski. *Helping Your Kids Cope with Divorce the Sandcastles Way.* New York: Random House, 1999.

Newkirk, Thomas. *Misreading Masculinity: Boys, Literacy, and Popular Culture.* Portsmouth, NH: Heinemann, 2002.

Phelan, Thomas. *1-2-3 Magic: Effective Discipline for Children 2-12,* Glen Ellyn, IL: ParentMagic, Inc. 2010.

Tovani, Cris. *I Read It, but I Don't Get It: Comprehension Strategies for Adolescent Readers.* Portland, ME: Stenhouse Publishers, 2000.

Wallerstein, Judith, Julia Lewis, and Sandra Blakeslee. *The Unexpected Legacy of Divorce: The 25 Year Landmark Study.* New York: Hyperion, 2000.

Whitehouse, Eliane, and Warwick Pudney. *A Volcano in My Tummy: Helping Children to Handle Anger.* Gabriola Island, BC: New Society Publishers, 1998.

Zeff, Ted. *The Strong Sensitive Boy: Help Your Son Become a Happy, Confident Man.* San Ramon, CA: Prana Publishing, 2010.

Adolescent Literacy: www.adlit.org
Resources for parents and educators of children in grades four through twelve. Includes booklists, author interviews, writing contests, and an ask-experts feature.

American Library Association: www.ala.org
ALA Selected booklists: www.ala.org/ala/mgrps/divs/yalsa/booklistsawards/booklistsbook.cfm#booklists
ALA Teen Top-Ten Books (teen-voted): www.ala.org/ala/mgrps/divs/yalsa/teenreading/teenstopten/teenstopten.cfm
For educators but of interest to parents. The American Library Association has a division called YALSA (Young Adult Library Services Association), with recommended booklists and teen-voted annual top-ten booklists that go back to 2003.

The Book Smugglers: www.thebooksmugglers.com
Book reviews for readers of romance and speculative fiction; has a young adult section.

Boys Project: www.drjonherzenberg.com/The-Boys-Project.html
Primarily for educators but of interest to parents. "Showcases colleges, schools, teachers, and organizations with projects that help young males develop their capabilities and reach the potential that their families and teachers know they have." Also develops initiatives and offers research information.

Children's Books: www.childrensbooks.about.com
For adults. Information on books for children ages 0–3, 4–8, and 9–12. Includes articles such as "Best books for boys" and "Resources for reluctant readers." Also author profiles, useful links, and a discussion group.

Children's Literature for Children: www.childrensliterature.org
Supports volunteers who initiate, implement, and maintain book donation and reading buddy programs in libraries, commu nities, and hospitals that need them. A nonprofit educational organization.

Christianne's Lyceum of Literature and Art: www.christiannehay-ward.com

Book clubs and more.

Colorín Colorado: www.colorincolorado.org
A bilingual English/Spanish site for educators and families of Hispanic children learning English. The goal is to help children "read and succeed." Includes book reviews under "kids" and "teens," video interviews with authors, webcasts and podcasts of experts who study English language learners, and articles such as "What you can do at home" and "Helping your child succeed at school."

Common Sense Media: www.commonsensemedia.org
Founded by James P. Steyer (author of *The Other Parent* and *Talking Back to Facebook*), this site is dedicated to improving the lives of kids and families by providing the trustworthy information, education, and independent voice they need to thrive in a world of media and technology.

Dads of Great Students (WATCH D.O.G.S.):
www.fathers.com/content/index.php?option=com_content&task=view&id=21&Itemid=60
Engage men, inspire children, reduce bullying, and enhance the educational environment at your school.

Drop Everything and Read: www.dropeverythingandread.com
National Drop Everything and Read Day (April 12) encourages families to read together daily, to make reading together a priority. Includes resources, book suggestions, and other information.

Family Education: www.familyeducation.com
Launched in 1996, claims to be the first and most-visited parenting site on the web; offers "strategies for getting involved with your children's learning," email newsletters, and entertaining family activities.

Fatherhood Task Force of South Florida: www.fatherhoodtaskforceofsouthflorida.org
Includes an initiative called the Fatherhood Reading Squad, which actively encourages fathers to recognize their importance in reading or telling stories to children regularly.

First Book: www.firstbook.org
First Book is an organization that provides access to new books for children in need. The site provides a history of the program, resources on literacy and illiteracy, and information on how to participate in the program.

Good Reads: www.goodreads.com
Mostly for adults but has some young adult groups. "The

largest social network for readers in the world." Members recommend books, compare what they are reading, keep track of what they've read and would like to read, form book clubs, and more. Members also create trivia about books, offer booklists, post their own writing, and form groups and book clubs.

Graphic Novel Reporter: www.graphicnovelreporter.com

Reviews of graphic novels (including teen and kids categories), author/illustrator interviews, features, blog, book clubs, poll, resources, etc.

Guys Read: www.guysread.com

"Our idea is to help guys become readers by helping them find texts they want to read. These are books that guys have told us they like." Book recommendations (including by genre), reading lists, how to start your own reading group, blog.

K12 Reader: www.k12reader.com/boys-and-reading

Reading instruction and resources for teachers and parents, to help motivate young male readers.

Kids Read: www.kidsreads.com

Primarily for small kids but has sections for teachers, librarians, and parents. Information about books, series, and authors. Book reviews, author interviews, and special features on books. Also, trivia games, word scrambles, and contests.

Learning Disabilities Association of America: www.ldanatl.org

Information, resources, and support for parents of children with learning disabilities.

Literacy Collaborative: www.literacycollaborative.org
A comprehensive school improvement project designed to improve the reading and writing achievement of students in pre-K through 8th grade.

Literacy Connections: www.literacyconnections.com
Information on reading, teaching, and tutoring techniques, ESL literacy, and adult literacy.

National Literacy Trust: www.literacytrust.org.uk
The National Literacy Trust is an independent U.K. charity that "transforms lives through literacy." The following link is a goldmine of material on reluctant readers: www.literacytrust.org. uk/search?q=reluctant+readers.

The National Parenting Center: www.tnpc.com
"Dedicated to providing parents with responsible guidance from the world's most renowned child-rearing authorities."

Ontario Education
www.edu.gov.on.ca/eng/curriculum/meRead_andHow.pdf
www.edu.gov.on.ca/eng/document/brochure/meread/meread. pdf
www.edu.gov.on.ca/abc123/eng/tips/readboys.html

How to improve boys' literacy skills.

PBS Parents: www.pbs.org/parents
Information on child development and early learning. It also serves as a parent's window to the world of PBS KIDS, offering

access to educational games and activities inspired by PBS KIDS programs.

Parent Teacher Association: www.pta.org

The National Parent Teacher Association (PTA) provides U.S. parents and families with "a voice to speak on behalf of every child and the best tools to help their children be safe, healthy, and successful—in school and in life." Includes information on how to start a P.T.A.

Parents' Choice: www.parents-choice.org

Issues children's media and toy reviews for parents of middle-grade children and younger. Includes booklists and articles like "Tips for teaching kids to enjoy reading" and "Homework help."

Parents Connect: www.parentsconnect.com

Provides parents of children of all ages with daily tips, recipes, activities, product recommendations, and expert parenting information. Under "Your kids," there's a "Teen & tween Q&A" with some articles of interest, such as "Best teen books that you were obsessed with too" and "Dealing with bad grades in middle school."

People for Education: www.peopleforeducation.com

A parent-led organization to support public education in Ontario, Canada, but good tips and inspiration here for parents anywhere interested in using their influence to improve their children's reading and education. Includes news, research, and an online community.

Read Write Think: www.readwritethink.org

For educators but also of interest to parents. On teaching literacy, supports excellent teaching, offers classroom resources. By the International Reading Association (Newark, Delaware) and National Council of Teachers of English (Urbana, Illinois).

Reader to Reader: www.readertoreader.org

A charity dedicated to bringing books, free of charge, to needy school libraries and public libraries across the United States.

Reading Rockets: www.readingrockets.org

For parents and educators. Offers information and resources on how children learn to read, why so many struggle, and how caring adults can help.

Real Men Read with Kids: realmenreadwithkids.wordpress.com

A site advocating for men to read with kids, to promote literacy and provide role models to young readers.

Rick Lavoie: www.ricklavoie.com

Information and inspiration for parents and teachers of children with learning disabilities.

Smart Kids with Learning Disabilities: www.smartkidswithLD.org

Dedicated to helping parents of children with learning disabilities see the potential for success and development.

The Student Center: www.shortstories.student.com

For high school and college students: information on health, life, and resources (especially how to get into college). Includes a section where one can write short stories and read fellow viewers' writing.

Students First: www.studentsfirst.org

A national movement to "defend the interests of children in public education and pursue transformative reform, so that the U.S. has the best education system in the world."

Teaching Books: www.teachingbooks.net

For educators but of interest to parents. Its online database is developed and maintained to include thousands of resources about fiction and nonfiction books used K-12. Includes author interviews, book readings, author websites, booklists, information on book awards, and links.

Teen Lit: www.teenlit.com

"Our goal is to promote teen literacy locally and globally by building small libraries in schools and in a free medical clinic, and by sending newly released teen literature worldwide to be reviewed by teens."

Teenagers Today: www.teenagerstoday.com

Includes parenting stories, expert Q&A, and preteen/teen articles such as "Ten signs your child may need a tutor."

U.K. Children's Books: www.ukchildrensbooks.co.uk

A U.K. website that aims "to increase the profile of U.K. children's books on the Internet." Includes lists of authors, illustrators, and publishers. Also has "help for young writers" links and U.K. events and literacy organizations.

USA Writes: usawrites4kids.drury.edu

For adults and youth. Introduces viewers to the work of "real, live" children's authors.

CYNTHIA'S RECOMMENDED PARENTING BOOKS
FOR CHRISTIAN PARENTS

Arterburn, Stephen and Jim Burns. *Drug-Proof Your Kids: The Complete Guide to Education, Prevention, Intervention.* Ventura, CA: Regal Books, 1995.

Campbell, Ross. *How To Really Love Your Teenager.* Wheaton, IL: Victor Books, 1993.

Coleman, William. *What Children Need to Know When Parents Get Divorced.* Minneapolis, MN: Bethany House Publishers, 1998.

—. *What Makes Your Teen Tick?* Minneapolis, MN: Bethany House Publishers, 1993.

Dobson, James. *Bringing Up Boys.* Carol Stream, IL: Tyndale House Publishers, 2001.

—. *The New Strong-Willed Child.* Carol Stream, IL: Tyndale House Publishers, 2007.

Egeler, Daniel. *Mentoring Millennials: Shaping the Next Generation.* Colorado Springs, CO: NavPress, 2003.

Eldredge, John. *Wild at Heart: Discovering the Secret of a Man's Soul.* Nashville, TN: Thomas Nelson, 2001.

Harris, Alex & Brett Harris. *Do Hard Things: A Teenage Rebellion Against Low Expectations.* Colorado Springs, CO: Multnomah, 2008.

Kimmel, Tim. *Basic Training for a Few Good Men.* Nashville, TN: Thomas Nelson, 1997.

—. *Grace Based Parenting.* Nashville TN: Thomas Nelson, 2004.

—. *Little House on the Freeway: Help for the Hurried Home.*

Colorado Springs, CO: Multnomah, 1994.

—. *Raising Kids for True Greatness*. Nashville, TN: Thomas Nelson, 2006.

—. *Why Christian Kids Rebel*. Nashville, TN: Thomas Nelson, 2004.

Leman, Kevin. *The Birth Order Book: Why You Are the Way You Are*. Grand Rapids, MI: Revell, 1998.

—. *Making Children Mind Without Losing Yours*. Grand Rapids, MI: Revell, 2005.

Sanford, Tim. *Losing Control and Liking It: How to Set Your Teen and Yourself Free*. Carol Stream, IL: Tyndale House Publishers, 2009.

Smith, Timothy. *Connecting with Your Kids: How Fast Families Can Move from Chaos to Closeness*. Minneapolis, MN: Bethany House Publishers, 2005.

—. *The Danger of Raising Nice Kids: Preparing Our Children to Change Their World*. Downers Grove, IL: InterVarsity Press, 2006.

Townsend, John. *Boundaries with Teens: When to Say Yes, How to Say No*. Grand Rapids, MI: Zondervan, 2006.

VanVonderen, Jeff. *Families Where Grace Is in Place*. Minneapolis, MN: Bethany House Publishers, 1992.

CYNTHIA'S RECOMMENDED WEBSITES
FOR CHRISTIAN PARENTS

Calm Christian Parenting: www.calmchristianparenting.com
As the name describes, this site provides many resources for Christians seeking to raise their children successfully.

Connected Families: www.connectedfamilies.org
Jim and Lynne Jackson have authored several outstanding books and speak regularly on grace-based parenting. Their material is an excellent blend of Biblical theology and sound psychological principles. It is suitable for individual families or as curricula for parenting classes and groups.

Family Matters: www.familymatters.net
Dr. Tim Kimmel provides education and encouragement to equip parents in their quest to raise well-adjusted children.

Focus on the Family: www.focusonthefamily.com
Source of much helpful information. Recommended is *Thriving Family* magazine, which can be ordered from this website.

Northland Counseling: www.northlandcounseling.us
Dr. Hal Baumchen has written quite a few brochures on parenting and other issues of interest to families, available free of charge on the website.

The Rebelution: www.therebelution.com

Young people blog and address the question, "Why do hard things?" Challenging and encouraging each other to "dare greatly," these youth network and stimulate each other to action, creating a counterculture that refuses to follow the expected norm of low expectations for adolescents.

154 Best Books for Reluctant Readers
www.goodreads.com/list/show/488.Best_Books_for_Reluctant_Readers
A list of 154 books geared to reluctant readers in different age groups.

Literacy Trust (U.K.) Booklist Recommendations for 13-plus
www.literacytrust.org.uk/assets/0000/1669/Book_list_2010_13_yrs.pdf

Literacy Trust (U.K.) Booklist Recommendations for ages 9–12
www.literacytrust.org.uk/assets/0000/1676/Booklist_2010_9_-_12_yrs.pdf

Literacy Trust (U.K.) Booklist Recommendations for nonfiction for ages 8–11
www.literacytrust.org.uk/assets/0000/5607/Non-fiction_booklist_8-11.pdf

PUBLISHERS OF BOOKS
FOR RELUCTANT READERS

ABDO Publishing Company: www.abdopub.com
Badger Publishing: www.badger-publishing.co.uk
Bearport Publishing: www.bearportpublishing.com
Black Rabbit Publishing: www.blackrabbitbooks.com
Capstone Press/Stone Arch Books: www.capstonepub.com
Gareth Stevens Publishing: www.garethstevens.com
Heinemann-Raintree nonfiction books: www.heinemannraintree.
   com
H-I-P Books: www.hip-books.com
Orca Book Publishers (Currents, Soundings, Orca Sports): www.
   orcabook.com
Rosen Publishing: www.rosenpublishing.com
Saddleback Educational Publishing: www.sdlback.com
Scholastic Books' Bluford Series: www.scholastic.com/ups/
   booklists/51121b2ee4b0177ede630f29#booklists/cleanup
Sundance Publishing: www.sundancepub.com
Tea Leaf Press: www.tealeafpress.com

WEBSITES FOR PRETEENS AND TEENS

America Writes for Kids: usawrites4kids.drury.edu
Promotes literacy and creativity by introducing young readers, parents, teachers, and librarians to the work of children's authors.

The Book Smugglers: www.thebooksmugglers.com
Book reviews for readers of romance and speculative fiction; has a young adult section.

Good Reads: www.goodreads.com
Mostly for adults but has some young adult groups. "The largest social network for readers in the world." Members recommend books, compare what they are reading, keep track of what they've read and would like to read, form book clubs, and more. Members also create trivia about books, offer booklists, post their own writing, and form groups and book clubs.

Graphic Novel Reporter: www.graphicnovelreporter.com
Reviews of graphic novels (including teen and kids categories), author/illustrator interviews, features, blog, book clubs, poll, resources, etc.

Guys Read: www.guysread.com
"Our idea is to help guys become readers by helping them find texts they want to read. These are books that guys have told us they like." Book recommendations (including by genre), reading lists, how to start your own reading group, blog.

Kids Read: www.kidsreads.com
Primarily for small kids but has sections for teachers, librarians, and parents. Information about books, series, and authors. Book reviews, author interviews, and special features on books. Also, trivia games, word scrambles, and contests.

Motivating Boy Writers: motivatingboywriters.blogspot.ca
A blog aimed at helping motivate boys to write. Contains tips, books, ideas, and resources for parents and boys.

Read Kiddo Read: www.readkiddoread.com
A site dedicated to making kids readers for life, with book suggestions and resources for varying age groups and demographics.

The Reading Zone: www.thereadingzone.wordpress.com
A book-review blog by a sixth-grade language arts teacher who "strives to instill a love of reading and writing in her students."

SJ Boys Read: www.sjboysread.org/Founders_XBAV.html
An organization in New Jersey that encourages young guys to read. It is run by ninth graders Kyle Thumar and Cameron Pendino, who organize events and encourage reading among peers.

The Student Center: www.shortstories.student.com
For high school and college students: information on health, life, and resources (especially how to get into college). Includes a section where one can write short stories and read fellow viewers' writing.

Teen Link: www.teenink.com
A teen literary magazine and website written by and for teens since 1989. Includes contests and book reviews.

Teen Lit: www.teenlit.com

"Our goal is to promote teen literacy locally and globally by building small libraries in schools and in a free medical clinic, and by sending newly released teen literature worldwide to be reviewed by teens."

Text Messages Codes: www.textmessagecodes.net/resource-guide-young-readers-writers.html

Resource guide for young readers and writers.

U.K. Children's Books: www.ukchildrensbooks.co.uk

A U.K. website that aims "to increase the profile of U.K. children's books on the Internet." Includes lists of authors, illustrators and publishers. Also has "help for young writers" links and U.K. events and literacy organizations.

Writing with Writers: teacher.scholastic.com/writewit/poetry/index.htm

Well-known authors/poets provide tips and tricks to encourage children to write poetry and creative fiction.

YA Books Central: www.yabookscentral.com

A large site that targets tween and teen readers. Book reviews, author interviews and bios, industry news, and more.

YA Reads: www.yareads.com

Good young adult reads, especially for girls. Includes author interviews, book reviews by category (including "steampunk" and "dystopia"), young adult fiction news, and a forum.

TEACHING, MENTORING, AND READING BUDDY WEBSITES

Big Brothers Big Sisters: www.bbbsalumnimembers.com
Canada:www.bigbrothersbigsisters.ca/en/home/mentoringprograms/default.aspx
USA: www.bbbs.org/site/c.9iILI3NGKhK6F/b.5962349/k.A334/So_many_ways_to_get_started.htm

Boys to Men: Mentoring Today's Youth: www.boystomen.org
Educator, clinical counselor, and author Barry MacDonald's site on helping mentor boys to become "caring, courageous, and ethical men."

Braum's Book Buddy Program: www.braums.com/BookBuddy.asp
Provides information on starting a book buddies program if you live in Texas, Kansas, Arkansas, or Missouri.

Huntington Learning Centers: huntingtonhelps.com
Dubbed "your tutoring solution," Huntington's mission is to "give every student the best education possible."

Kids Hope USA: www.kidshopeusa.org
Develops one-on-one relationships through the creation of church-school partnerships that pair church members with at-risk kids in supportive, mentoring relationships.

Kids Now Canada: www.kidsnowcanada.org

"National youth charity that provides free afterschool in-school group mentoring programs to students in grades seven and eight. We empower youth to believe in themselves to make positive choices that help them reach their full potential."

Learning Rx: www.learningrx.com

"LearningRx has developed the nation's most powerful and effective brain training program. Our network of cognitive skills training providers—a team of concerned parents, educators, and business and medical professionals—are devoted to the idea that students simply do not need to be pigeonholed by labels or held back by learning or reading disabilities."

Mathnasium: www.mathnasium.com

"Our goal is to significantly increase your child's math skills, understanding of math concepts and overall school performance, while building confidence and forging a positive attitude toward the subject."

Mentor Kids USA: www.mentorkidsusa.org

Provides males with mentoring resources, especially related to childhood abuse and sexual abuse.

Mentoring Boys: www.mentoringboys.com

A resource on boys, literacy, mentoring, and being a positive male role model.

Mentoring USA: www.mentoringusa.org

Become a mentor.

Open Books Buddies: www.open-books.org/programs/programs_
buddiesfull.php
Provides information on joining a book buddies program in
Chicago.

Sylvan Learning Centers: tutoring.sylvanlearning.com
This tutoring system is dubbed "assess, plan, teach, apply." "It
pinpoints your child's academic strengths (skills they already have)
and 'skill gaps' (those they need to learn)."

Teacher Vision: www.teachervision.fen.com/skill-builder/group-
work/18775.html
An article about reading buddy programs written for teachers
but of interest to parents.

ACKNOWLEDGMENTS

Above all, Cynthia and I would like to thank our two researchers, Rob and Dorothy.

Rob Bittner is a Ph.D. student at Simon Fraser University, Vancouver, Canada, studying gender and sexuality in young people's literature and culture. A voracious reader, Rob thanks his parents for encouraging him to go to the library as a child, instead of getting him a Nintendo.

Dorothy Distefano of Rochester, New York, is not only a successful writer, editor, and researcher (www.wotverge.com), she is an activist when it comes to getting boys to read. Her research skills got us out of the starting gate on our book and we're proud she has been part of it.

Cynthia and I truly appreciate the efforts and patience of our agent Lynn Bennett, as well as Brenda Knight and all the team at Viva Editions, who encouraged us from the start.

I would also like to acknowledge all the schoolteachers, school librarians, and schoolchildren who have inspired me over the years. Only gradually as I began doing school presentations many years ago, did I become aware of the issue of reluctant readers in general, and boys as underachievers in particular. When Cynthia and I discovered we had a mutual passion for addressing that, it launched this project. Cynthia, you have been inspiring to work with, and I've gained much respect for all you do and who you are. And thanks, Jerry, for hosting our "write-athon" in your home and supporting us in every way.

Thanks to Chris Patrick, my speaking tours agent. And finally, special thanks as always to my husband Steve and son Jeremy, who always support me right to the finish line.

—Pam Withers, www.pamwithers.com

Special thanks to my husband Jerry, my greatest encourager and best friend, and to my sons Jon, Matt, and Jay, whose enthusiasm cheered me on as they shared their hearts with me about their own reading experiences. I also wish to acknowledge several mentors, whose help has been invaluable in my journey from teacher to therapist: Dr. Jan Norman, Psy.D., LP; Dan Munson, D.Min., LMFT; Jim Peasley, MA, LMFT; and "Dr. Hal" Baumchen, Psy.D., LP. Also, thank you to my students and clients who have been my best teachers; whenever they are referred to in this book, stories have been disguised and blended to protect their privacy.

Finally, Pam, you have been awesome to work with, your thoroughness and perseverance are exemplary. Thanks for taking me along on this exciting ride! And most of all, I would feel that this were incomplete without thanking Jesus Christ, for He has given me hope and love.

—Cynthia M. Gill, MA, LMFT, www.cynthiagill.info

TO OUR READERS

Viva Editions publishes books that inform, enlighten, and entertain. We do our best to bring you, the reader, quality books that celebrate life, inspire the mind, revive the spirit, and enhance lives all around. Our authors are practical visionaries: people who offer deep wisdom in a hopeful and helpful manner. Viva was launched with an attitude of growth and we want to spread our joy and offer our support and advice where we can to help you live the Viva way: vivaciously!

We're grateful for all our readers and want to keep bringing you books for inspired living. We invite you to write to us with your comments and suggestions, and what you'd like to see more of. You can also sign up for our online newsletter to learn about new titles, author events, and special offers.

Viva Editions
2246 Sixth St.
Berkeley, CA 94710
www.vivaeditions.com
(800) 780-2279
Follow us on Twitter @vivaeditions
Friend/fan us on Facebook